Vietnam from the Back Seat

Việt Nam từ ghế sau

My year as a worker bee at the Marble Mountain Air Facility

Năm của tôi như một con ong lao động tại cơ sở không khí núi đá cẩm thạch

LCpl Stephen T. Madden

COPYRIGHT

Vietnam from the Back Seat

My Year as a worker bee at the Marble Mountain Air Facility

Most of the photographs in this book have been provided by the USMC/Combat Helicopter & Tiltrotor Association. To examine their entire collection of stories and photos or for additional information about this excellent organization contact them at www.popasmoke.com.

Stephen T. Madden
Cover design by Andy Crossfield
Technical direction by Andy Crossfield

First edition published in August, 2016
First printing in August, 2016

—

We trained hard . . . but it seemed that every time we were beginning to form up into teams we would be reorganized.

I was to learn later in life that we tend to meet any new situation by reorganizing; and a wonderful method it can be for creating the illusion of progress while producing confusion, inefficiency, and demoralization.

Gaius Petronius AD 66

Men have never fought for a cause, a flag or even a great leader. The truth is they have always fought because their friends and brothers in arms were standing next to them on the battle line. They stood and fought because they respected the person next to them on that line and would rather die themselves than let that man down.

3

CONTENTS

This book is dedicated to the memory of
PFC Raymond M. Clausen, Jr.
Medal of Honor recipient

PFC Clausen was the only Marine enlisted crewman to receive the Medal of Honor during the Vietnam War. Not only did PFC Mike Clausen uphold the finest traditions of the United States Marine Corps, he also reminded people of the skill and dedication that resided in each of the men who wore the silver wings of a Marine Corps Crew Chief.

INTRODUCTION

We were inconsequential cogs in the vast military machine supporting the Marine Corps helicopter air war in Vietnam. Unseen and unrecognized, hordes of enlisted men kept the wheels greased, the engines turning and the windshields polished so that the pilots could accomplish their daily flying assignments.

Every day the crew chief arrived early to inspect and prepare his machine for flight. Later he hopped in back and participated in every combat mission. When the flying was finished, the enlisted men then stayed behind to refuel and repair the bird so that it would be ready for the next day's adventure.

This is the personal story of one enlisted man's journey from the drudgery of staging battalion in California to the almost lawless Wild West that was the Marble Mountain Air Facility in 1970.

For the most part no names are used because to the vast majority of the officers, we were just faceless drones in service to the hive. At Marble Mountain, it was understood that enlisted men always came with a high level of expendability.

—

Chapter 1
Staging Battalion
Total U.S. killed as of May 1970 in the Vietnam War: 52,031

It was May of 1970 in a land we called America. In advance of our scheduled deployment to Vietnam we were each given thirty days of leave from our designated occupations in the United States Marine Corps.

We eagerly accepted this month of freedom and prepared ourselves to seamlessly jump back into the old life we had left behind when we joined the Corps. We arrived home and found an unfamiliar landscape. During our absence the world we had known before was gone. We each slowly realized that it had moved on without us. Not knowing anything else to do, we tried to fit back into the niche that we had voluntarily left some time before. Each of us put on the clothes of our past lives and pretended that this temporary illusion would never end.

We had thirty days to enjoy our old life while unsuccessfully attempting to avoid the television and its increasingly depressing broadcasts about this war. As our time for departure drew ever closer daily events seemed to fly by.

The illusion of freedom too quickly impacted the harsh reality of the calendar with its impending departure date. Freedom in the beginning seemed like it would last forever but now it had become just a matter of hours. Without warning there were things that could not be done and places that could not be visited. It was time to return.

We each put on a brave face but deep inside no one wanted to leave. We had been given thirty days to reflect on an entire lifetime of memories, to renew old friendships and make new ones that we hoped would survive the year to

—

come. We also knew that for some of us, this would be the last vision of home we would ever have.

Each of us said farewell to friends and family in our own way. Some of us slipped out of our childhood homes quietly at night and took a cab ride, alone to the airport. Others were walked all the way to the airline boarding gate so that the family might have one last moment together, one last photo and one last smile.

But no matter how we got there we all waved freedom goodbye, turned our backs on the world that we knew and squeezed ourselves into a large silver airliner full of strangers. Most of us had five hours or so alone, in quiet thought about our future and what fate had in store for us during this return flight back to the Marine Corps.

Upon landing the first surprise we got was that a lot of our friends had arrived at the same time and for the same reason. We all sat around the terminal talking and waiting for the transportation that would take us to our new adventure. Everyone told lies about the good times they had during their leave and some of us even believed them. We were like a closed fraternity in an immense university with our shared values, short haircuts and green austere uniforms.

The people at the airport swirled around our group like we were a solitary rock in a fast flowing river and together we paid them no mind. We knew that we were better than they were because we had a mission, we had a place to go and a job to do that none of them could ever understand.

It was never stated out loud, but to a man we knew one fact for sure. At this time in 1970 the war in Vietnam had already been lost. Every news report pounded the drum

—

beat of death and defeat. The peace demonstrations were becoming larger by the week and ironically they turned more violent.

The North Vietnamese Tet Offensive of 1968 had been a complete U. S. military victory but it soon morphed into a total psychological defeat for the Johnson Administration. The news of Tet broke open the floodgates and exposed years of lies about the progress of the war. This revelation then allowed the anti-war movement to claim both a moral and psychological victory.

We knew we were like those warriors of history who went before us. Men sent to guard a lonely Roman outpost on Hadrian's Wall in Britannia or the fresh German troops sent in by Hitler for the final assault in the battle of Stalingrad. We knew the war was over and we knew we had lost but we went anyway. We went because it was both our job and our duty. We also went because at one point in our lives we had promised that we would be there when our country called. Today was that day.

Our transportation finally arrived and we all proceeded to the rear seats of a well-cared for silver Greyhound bus that would drive us most of the way to Staging Battalion in Camp Pendleton, California. A bottle of Johnnie Walker Red had been someone's going away present and now it was being slowly passed around within our group. We hoped its contents would make the journey a little more palatable. Everyone else in the front of the bus knew what we were doing back there but they also knew where we were going so they kept quiet and let us enjoy the ride.

That long ride ended in the unkempt and dusty Oceanside, California bus terminal. Here we left the comforts of Greyhound and Johnnie Walker behind. Within a short time

—

squeaking brakes announced the arrival of the last vehicle in our passage back to military life. With personal property in hand we climbed aboard a dull green Marine Corps bus that looked and sounded neglected. The final leg of our journey from freedom to Staging Battalion was to be done with transportation better suited to a 1965 rural Nebraska school district than for members of the most elite fighting force in the world.

Well, that's what they told us we were.

In 1970 the Military Police at the main Camp Pendleton gate stopped every car, truck and bus to check ID cards and look over everyone's written orders involving change of duty station. The June mid-day Southern California sun beat down on the dark roof of our transportation and when the bus stopped moving the un-air conditioned interior began to heat up immediately. What had originally started out as a mildly hot and dusty ride quickly went downhill.

The sun and lack of movement turned our transportation into a stationary green steel oven. Lines of sweat were running in little rivulets down our faces and dripped onto the top sheet of a multitude of papers being held tightly in our hands.

Our Class A uniforms were too tight, the seats were too small and the windows would not open all the way to let even a little dusty air in. There was no way to cool off or even to stand up until these document processing robots completed their assigned mission. Did they really think anyone had ever tried to sneak onto this place so they could play Marine?

I think I remember an inscription in the stone at the top of the gate, it read something like, "Abandon all hope, ye who enter here".

—

When all of these future Transportation Security Administration supervisors felt we had been held up long enough, the bus, with its entire cargo of overheated passengers was allowed to continue. After driving through the brown parched hills for another half hour we came to a building and told to disembark.

We had to wait for the front of the bus to clear out, then we slowly moved ourselves and our gear through the narrow aisle between the seats and down the bus steps. Our group congregated in the thin shadow of the bus as we stood on the hot asphalt of the administration parking lot waiting for orders.

It was late afternoon and we were all tired, very thirsty and starting to feel the first effects from an excess of alcohol consumed during our drive from the Los Angeles airport. Everyone carried all of their uniforms and issued gear in a green canvas container known as a sea bag which was slung over our right shoulder.

By this time in the day this bag felt as if it weighed two hundred pounds and the single two-inch nylon carrying strap was cutting off the normal blood flow into our right arms. Finally, some junior corporal walked out onto the porch and ordered us to toss our sea bags next to the parking lot in a straight line and then come inside. Like little green robots we walked up the well-worn wooden stairs and into the dark grey poorly lit hallway of the Staging Battalion headquarters building to start processing for deployment.

No air condition unit had ever been incorporated into this thirty-year-old building because it had been placed on the list for demolition in 1962 and the glorious Marine Corps did not wish to waste money. The temperature inside the hallway is about the same as outside but at least the sun

—

wasn't beating down on your body. Once inside, everyone made a beeline for the closest water fountain. A marginal performer on a normal day, this twenty-year-old appliance was now only capable of producing a weak stream of lukewarm alkali tasting water. Thirty seconds trying to lap water from this unresponsive tease of a fountain and then we were off to deal with the Marine Corps bureaucracy.

Behind each dark wooden door in the processing center we found lines for this form and then lines for that form. Each line had two or three clerks whose only job was to find fault with your paperwork and insist on a hand written revision so they could produce a correctly filled out form.

Complete one form, then take that document along with this additional form and go wait in the next line. We were told to go here then go there; sit here, wait then stand over there and wait. After completing a process that made getting your driver's license seem enjoyable, we were sent back outside. There on the sun baked asphalt of the parking lot we stood and waited for additional information about our future.

We were Marines and we were good at this standing around and waiting business.

Darkness was becoming noticeable and while the air remained hot, at least the sun had mercifully set behind the hills to the west. The parking lot street lights started to come on which brought out dozens of little buzz bugs which came over to welcome us to our new home. When all the troops had received their corrected paperwork our new master arrived on the porch and everyone was directed to fall in at attention. Then with as much fanfare as anyone could muster in this nasty little parking lot we were told about our next military adventure.

–

It seems this time we had been twice blessed by our glorious Corps. Not only were we on the fast track to Vietnam, but before we were to go, our unit had been designated as the next service company for Staging Battalion. What that meant was that for the next month or so we would be working in the mess halls of Staging Battalion or walking guard duty instead of preparing for deployment to the Far East.

Now the first thought that came through everyone's mind was, what a good deal, I don't have to go to Vietnam for another month. Then the real truth hit them, this was not going to be leisure time or some kind of vacation in California. Everyone still had to go to Vietnam, but now they got to work for an extra month in this place before training even started. Our immediate future consisted of working seven days a week in a nasty mess hall or walking a guard post all night long in the rain around an empty building.

Tired, dirty and hung over, we adjusted our overstuffed sea bags for minimum discomfort. Then with little ceremony our unit schlepped about a half a mile to our new living quarters. As luck would have it, our group had been assigned the squad bay on the second floor. With sea bags wearing a groove into our shoulder blades we dragged ourselves and our increasingly bad attitudes up the gray wooden stairs.

With little concern about location each of us picked out an inviting steel spring rack and then a thin lumpy mattress, preferably with a minimum of stains on it. Because this would be our new home for the next month, we needed to make the best of it.

Soon the lights went out and so did we.

—

Early the next morning, at about five thirty, our new head overseer arrived. He came complete with assorted minions who then proceeded to turn on the squad bay lights. They then attempted to get us up so we could be assigned to our individual mess halls and take over our new duties. The overseer loudly proclaimed that we needed to get up, get dressed and get to work. We were told that the men working there now needed to be replaced by us so they could start their own training.

Some individuals were truly lacking in motivation

Not one Marine moved from his rack and no one spoke. One person did lean over the side of his brown mattress and puke on the floor but he was an exception. Our new head overseer was quite unhappy with our lack of motivation and began to threaten us with this and threaten us with that. With a total disregard for their authority they were ignored, because to us, they were irrelevant.

The Marine Corps problem was this: we knew that they could hold no threat over us worse than what was already spelled out in that ream of papers we carried from base to base. We figured correctly that they needed us much more than we ever needed them. So if we failed to rise and obey their orders what were they going to do? Threaten to throw us out of this new duty and give it to some other lucky unit? Cut our hair and send us to Vietnam right now with a letter in our personnel jacket stating that we had a bad attitude? That's what we were prepared for anyway, so it didn't really work very well as a threat.

Next they threatened to call in the MP's and send us all to the brig for insubordination. Tell us, fearless leader, do you have room in your brig for fifty and was that better or worse than coming home from Vietnam inside an aluminum box?

Got anything else in your bag of threats? Physical violence wasn't much of a threat because, if they started that crap, we would have thrown them out one of the second story windows. Then they would have ended up with a stupid look on their face while lying on the grass and we still wouldn't go to work.

I mean really, what's the worst punishment they could give us?

It took a while but finally we just got tired of listening to their incessant babbling and besides we were starting to get hungry, so we got up and pretended to get ready. I figure we were at least two hours late by the time we were marched over to our new employer.

They told us that they were very unhappy with our displayed lack of motivation, but we still didn't care.

About forty of us were assigned to work at one of the main mess halls in Staging Battalion. This building was just another ugly gray wooden holdover from World War II that should have been torn down in 1950. The building was barely functioning in 1970 which was common to most of the other structures in that part of Camp Pendleton.

Our existing world consisted of row upon row of two story gray firetraps housing two hundred men in each one. On the other side of the street there were single story administration and service buildings as far as the eye could see. The atmosphere surrounding these shabby gray boxes could easily be described as either utilitarian or depressing, depending on how much sun light got through the southern California smog during the day.

Immediately upon arrival we were given the official designation of "mess men". You could be an aircraft radar technician or a recon scout in the regular Marine Corps but here in Staging Battalion you were the very bottom of the pecking order, a mess man. Directly above the lowly mess man was the Marine Corps cook.

These were people who lacked the skills and common sense to be a Marine Corps rifleman and had to be assigned somewhere where they would do the least amount of damage to themselves and the reputation of the US Military. Above the common cook was the head cook, usually a Staff Sergeant complete with attached underlings and assorted weasels to do his dirty work.

We were lucky that all of the meals prepared at every mess hall came directly from a Marine Corps manual that gave each meal a number and then described each step in its preparation using large pictures and small words. Independent thought or creativity was expressly forbidden in any mess hall due to the real danger of incapacitating an entire company of Marines by accident.

History has shown that these cooks could disable more of their own troops than an entire Division of French soldiers who had been allowed to use live ammunition.

In every mess hall, food entered into the rear of the building by the truckload. When a truck pulled up and the bell rang, (Pavlov's Dogs) almost everyone was required to stop what they were doing and go unload the food truck. This was a time before pallet jacks, forklifts and box conveyers so we had to do all of the work of unloading every box in each truck by hand.

Some of us were assigned to form a long line from the inside of the truck box, down the hall and into one of the many empty store rooms. Unloading the truck involved picking up all of the cardboard boxes, one at a time and handing it to the next person in line and on and on. Some mess men went into these store rooms and were assigned to stack this incoming river of cans, boxes and bags where directed by the cooks.

We soon learned that the cooks would quickly lose interest in our truck unloading and box stacking activities inside the storerooms. They would all congregate out on the loading dock to smoke, laugh and get out of the stifling heat and cardboard dust which was always inside the storeroom.

Because we were not allowed to take any break while unloading, we took this opportunity to mix up the cases inside the different storerooms. We then turned the boxes around so the cooks wouldn't see what we had done when they returned. After we had completed our vehicle unloading exercise, the cooks yelled at us to quit standing around in the cool air and get back inside and finish our uncompleted regularly assigned duties.

—

These people were true jerks and it was our mission to make their lives as miserable as possible.

Before the truck could leave, the cooks, not the mess men, had to verify the driver's bill of lading and that was when they found out about the discrepancy in the count. The excellent quality of our work inside the storerooms could be determined by the volume and quality of profanity coming from the head cook when the count was found to be wrong by one of his weasels. The next truck couldn't unload until the first truck's delivery was verified and so it sat in the sun out on the roadway for all to see.

It seems that our crew got a well-deserved break while waiting for the cooks to straighten out the mess we had just made.

The dedicated mess men of staging battalion

It soon became apparent to the mess hall management that my talents were being poorly used in such an unsupervised setting. They decided that I, along with five other Marines, were misfits and troublemakers. Our group was assigned to the dishwashing room for the remainder of our assignment at the mess hall.

Ironically there were no dishes to wash in the dishwashing room.

Long ago the glorious Corps had found that the basic Marine did not have the social skills or dexterity necessary to balance a loaded plate on a plastic tray and then walk to a table before dropping his entire serving of swill onto the concrete deck.

All low ranking enlisted men were required to eat their portion controlled, partially cooked Marine Corps chow from a multi-section heavy stainless steel tray. It is also a tradition that proper tray handling etiquette was always taught to each Marine private during basic training from his life coach and drill instructor.

In this land of the great dishwasher there were stainless steel eating trays, heavy stainless steel eating utensils, ceramic cups and even glasses but again no plates. My new room was a windowless box with nothing inside but a giant stainless steel tray washing machine that took up half of the floor space just by itself.

This appliance was the culmination of years of collusion inside the Military-Industrial complex that President Eisenhower had warned us about. Its usefulness was limited to military bases and prisons. Large prisons where they treated the prisoners badly and didn't care if their food trays were properly cleaned and sanitized.

This machine was nothing but a chain drive stainless steel conveyor belt with exposed copper pipes and mechanical gauges used to display different water temperatures for

—

different cycles. To save money the temperatures and pressures required for proper food and bacteria removal never reached minimum acceptable standards except on inspection day. What a surprise! This oversized cleaning machine pumped heat and humidity into the air and many gallons of soapy water and assorted food particles onto the red tile floor of this room. It made horrid noises like it had dry rusty bearings and the conveyer belt acted as if a broken section was catching on a sprayer head but the thing never stopped washing.

The steam it spewed was always special because it became flavored by the meal of the hour. Breakfast smelled like pancake syrup and eggs that had been sitting in the sun too long. Lunch always smelled like wet meat patties and catsup with a hint of chlorine. Dinner always smelled the same; week old road kill.

Dirty steel food trays and buckets of silverware went into the front of our magic cleaning machine and somewhat clean trays and silverware came out the other end. We carried these hot trays by hand to the beginning of the food serving line for refilling.

On our trip back we picked up a stack of food encrusted used trays and carried them to the front of the wash cycle. Here they were rapidly banged on the inside of a heavy steel garbage can until the glue like substance, passing as food attached to the tray was knocked off. This cycle was repeated for fourteen hours a day, seven days a week.

This was a closed, miserable little room in the rear of the mess hall with no redeeming value except one. The unwritten rule was, as long as clean silverware and trays came out of our private cave, no one wielding any authority stuck their head in there for any reason.

—

—

20

This was our little steamy kingdom. We soon began to realize our power and dominance over the system as we started to plot revenge on the man.

Shut the dishwashing machine down for any reason and the stream of clean food trays and silverware instantly stopped. When the trays stopped, the food line stopped. When the food line stopped, the troops could not be fed and the training schedule was delayed.

When this happened the mess hall went absolutely insane.

First the troops waiting to eat would become restless and start bitching at the cooks behind the serving line. The cooks would start yelling at the mess men and when no trays came out they would stick their heads inside our room and demand action. Usually they were ignored but on special occasions they became the recipient of some especially nasty food item that was thrown in their general direction. This item was always something special that we had been saving for the proper occasion.

They would then go running to contact our master, the head cook, who would then make his grand entrance and demand that production recommence. It was at this point that we would work out a bargain between both sides and after we felt our point had been made, the flow of stainless steel chow containers would resume.

This battle between us went back and forth for the full month. We grew stronger because we had nothing to lose and the powers that be survived as they always did with no lasting damage. Over time our battle against our masters in the mess hall let us believe that it is difficult to damage a large wet sponge. Attempts at insurrection and control had

21

no effect, for good or evil, other than for our own personal entertainment value.

Our support company consisted of about two hundred Marines who were both bored out of their minds by their daily activities and yet still inwardly nervous because of what they knew their imminent future held.

Then one day without warning our little steamy bad smelling world changed. The indignation of mess duty became history and faded from our collective memories as we all marched off in formation to the land of Staging Battalion.

So far the Marine Corps had been pretty smart in how they treated us. They were about to make a couple of big mistakes.

The Marine Corps, as with most other branches of the military at that time, did not rotate entire units in and out of Vietnam. Originally the Marines had sent intact units into Vietnam and left them there while their personnel were rotated in for a thirteen-month tour and then out again. In and out for one tour and never again would your feet touch the sandy shores of Da Nang unless you extended your combat tour while in-country or you re-enlisted. This was something that not many people did.

This process worked like a champ for the paper pushers and high generals of logistics. It was a whole lot easier to ship one man or even one thousand individual men than it was to pack up an entire helicopter squadron or infantry battalion and send them as a unit over to Vietnam or back to the states. The unseen problem with this process was that it destroyed individual moral and unit effectiveness.

—

Men have never fought for a cause, a flag or even a great leader. The truth is they have always fought because their friends and brothers in arms were standing next to them on the battle line. They stood and fought only because they respected the person next to them on that line and would rather die themselves than let that man down.

In all wars up until Vietnam men trained together, formed their units stateside and then went to the front to fight as a single cohesive unit. In Vietnam men were picked like grapes from a vine and used to fill in blank number spaces on a Pentagon spread sheet. You were sent off alone to join an unknown unit populated with people you didn't know in a foreign county where everyone hated you just for the mere fact of being there.

No matter who you were or what your accomplishments were up to that point, you meant nothing to the new unit you were joining and you cared nothing about them. This was a fact of life in Vietnam.

You knew it and they knew it.

Staging Battalion in those days was made up of between three to five companies of Marines going through pre-deployment training at one time. Each company of about two hundred men was in a different phase of training and things moved along swiftly till each company was shipped out and then the process started all over again.

Because of the short time in actual training and the fact that most members of each company started out as total strangers, the different companies never bonded as a unit. When our company was released from our month long detail together we had become brothers in the fight.

—

Our collective hatred for being dropped into mess duty and the shameful way we had been treated caused our company to have without exception a very bad attitude towards the Corps in general and Staging Battalion in particular. With no thought whatsoever except for filling out the proper forms, our masters shipped us directly from mess duty over to our pre-deployment training as an intact unit. This turned out to be a bad move on their part.

The instructors at Staging Battalion were, to a man, returned Vietnam veterans who were just marking off the days until they were released from the glorious Corps. These were the men who dug bunkers in the red clay of Khe Sanh in 1968 and defied three North Vietnamese divisions to try and take their base. They were the same men who ran across the bridge under constant fire to recapture the Citadel at Hue during the Tet offensive.

Now, they were stuck in a Camp Pendleton wasteland dreaming of the freedom of home and not the drudgery of instructing two hundred less than eager new faces every day.

That being said these instructors had developed a few bad habits of their own. Instructing groups of people who were still shell shocked from the transition back into the Corps after their thirty days of leave made them very lax in their attitudes towards the individuals they were attempting to train.

Our unit integrity came as a complete shock to most of them. As a unit we refused to put up with their bad attitudes and incompetent instruction. Unlike other companies we became quite vocal with our displeasure in the way we were sometimes treated. Our company soon obtained a well-earned reputation of being both belligerent and unmotivated.

Our classroom education first involved learning the tricks of the wily Cong and how to beat them at their own game. We were given handbooks that showed all of the enemy's weapons, real and improvised and a collection of our latest equipment. These classes told us that we had all the good stuff and the bad guys had nothing but sticks and rocks. We asked questions that our instructors did not care to answer truthfully.

We wanted to know, if they had all the junk and we were killing them like fish in a barrel then why were they winning? No one really had any good answers for that one. We sat in classrooms and learned that there were additional forms to fill out.

As an added bonus from our brothers in arms, the Navy corpsmen, we received the finest in inoculations to save us from all sorts of exotic Asian diseases. Our medical records were properly stamped and we were pronounced to be disease free and ready for deployment to the meat grinder.

After classroom time ended we were transferred into the bush of Southern California so that we could play with lots of the real toys. Our first stop along the road was to our old favorite, the standard Marine Corps rife range. The range consisted of fifty targets that were set up on movable supports that could be raised or lowered to check the score of each shooter. Embankments with target numbers at two, three and five hundred meters made up the qualifying course of fire.

We shot the course twice and then we were marched down to spend time in the "butts". Here, our job consisted of pulling those targets up and then down while keeping score for the person doing the actual shooting. Rule number one; never stick your head above the embankment to see who is shooting.

If you forget rule number one there was no rule number two.

When you are behind the embankment pulling targets you are normally standing with your head about three feet below where the bullets were passing. A rifle bullet travels many times the speed of sound and makes a very distinctive noise when it passes that close to your ear. During the course of a normal day pulling targets you might have as many as five hundred bullets pass within ten feet of your head. You learn the sound that they make and you never, ever forget it.

After each of us qualified on the standard rife range with the M-16 we were then sent out to a number of other ranges so that we could add to our firearms knowledge. These additional ranges allowed us to shoot up many hundreds of rounds of ammunition through our M-16's in less than optimal conditions. We each also fired off another thousand rounds through the M-60 machine gun.

There was one positive thing we could say about the training we received. They were never hesitant to bring out a full truck load of ammunition and let us shoot it all up in one day. If we wanted to shoot, they brought out all the guns plus lots of ammunition and it was free.

The most useful experience we ever had was in learning how to clear jams and malfunctions caused by the design of that piece of crap M-16 rifle. Who could have foreseen that a combat rifle designed for use in the swamps and jungles of Vietnam would ever get dirty.

—

It was rumored that this rifle was designed and manufactured by the Mattel Toy Company because of its light weight plastic construction and complete lack of reliability. It took years of field trials by the Department of Defense along with testing, additional redesigns and the lives of a large number of front line troops before this abomination was ever brought up to acceptable standards.

May the people who got rich off of this national disgrace never get another peaceful night sleep thinking of all of the names on the Vietnam Memorial Wall that they were personally responsible for!

Included in our training was learning about the weapon of our enemy, the AK-47. This rifle was not as well made as ours and the rounds were heavier and not nearly as accurate at long range. The stock looked like it was made with a band saw and the frame and internal parts were thin and still had rough tool marks on them.

That being said, the AK magazines held thirty rounds vs. twenty for our M-16 and they usually had two of them taped together for faster reloading. The AK could be buried in the mud for a week, washed off in a stream and it would still function without any jams. It was ugly and poorly made but totally reliable in any combat situation. The general consensus of the day was that most of our troops would have carried it in a heartbeat if they had been given their choice.

After we had completed our education about small arms, we went onto bigger and better toys. Some days we went out and played find the land mine. Next we got to play defuse the land mine. To make our lives more enjoyable the instructors used to booby trap a couple of them with a secondary charge. We also learned how to set ambushes, prevent ourselves from walking into one and how to act if you did.

27

Then there were days we practiced 100 useful things you can do with detonation cord. During these classes most of our time was spent living in the bush. Life for us was getting to be stinky and very unpleasant. Canned food cooked over a smoky fire, bugs and little restful sleep did not make for a happy group of campers.

We were more than ready to get out of Dodge and make the trip across the big pond by the time we finally completed this course. No more mess duty, classes, standing in formation or long lines for us. We returned back to our two story grey wooden paradise awaiting our final paperwork and deployment across the Pacific Ocean.

The day finally came and we were given our marching orders, or in this case, our flying orders. As fate would have it, all of us were kept together as a unit and even assigned to fly away on the same aircraft. Very early one morning we stacked our sea bags in the parking lot and waited for our wheels to arrive. This time a fleet of higher quality green Marine Corps buses arrived and soon all of us along with all of our baggage were loaded up and ready to go.

The gate guards just waved our convoy through without as much as a check of our papers or ID cards. We were so hoping to have one last shot at those clowns. We kissed Camp Pendleton goodbye and headed north through the central part of California. The buses rolled on for hours through the hills and deserts until we arrived at an Air Force base for our transport to Vietnam.

Our air mobility service for this new adventure was being provided by a fleet of aircraft used only for the purpose of military troop movements and never for hauling real paying passengers. These charter flights operated under military

—

contract which meant they were the low bidder and it showed.

Most of the planes were the old stretch DC-8s that had kind of a droopy nose which also gave them a droopy tail. It was hoped the airstream would straighten things out when we got going and that none of the important aircraft parts would fall off. Those of us who had experience in the aviation industry knew that a loss of small parts was inevitable with an aircraft of this age.

As we walked out to the movable steps, cleverly placed by the front door for our self-loading pleasure, we noticed that there was a noticeable puddle of oil under engine #1. I figured that someone on the crew would at least walk around the plane before engine start and perhaps slip in the oil which would be an important clue about the engine's condition.

There was the slight possibility that the puddle might have been there from some piston aircraft that had been parked at that exact location right before our DC-8 got there. Piston engines do leak a lot of oil as a normal function of their existence and that spot may be their favorite place to park.

I didn't mind the esthetics of faded paint or worn out interior but these were a telltale sign that this plane had not had the finest in preventive maintenance during its lifetime. The only redeeming value in this entire adventure was that this model of aircraft had a long history of very reliable service.

It was well known that if a DC-8 crashed it was usually due to weather or a drunken pilot and not to a mechanical failure. Even so I had a really bad feeling about this aircraft

—

as we slowly made our way up the stairs and settled down into our seats for the long trip ahead.

The truth was that there was not one thing I could do about it at this point in time.

Chapter 2
One Final Adventure
Total U.S. killed as of June 1970 in the Vietnam wars: 52,590

Our lives, as we had known them, were over. We were told to fill up the interior of the aircraft from rear to front without even the faux dignity of assigned seats. We belted ourselves into our nylon covered posture modifiers and waited for the obligatory roll call from the all-knowing clipboard.

The count never is correct the first time so someone ends up walking all the way down the aisle and counting each and every person. Tapping everyone on the top of the head is optional. This actual warm body count was then checked against the list of people who were supposed to be on the flight but it still didn't match.

Somehow we all knew what was going to be the end result. We came prepared because as any good Marine knows, this is the way it always goes. Newspapers and magazines were opened and pillows were adjusted and properly fluffed. Not one passenger was paying any attention to the frustrated people in the front of the aircraft as they checked one long list against another long list.

We figured they would either get it straightened out, change one of the lists to match the other list or they would send us on our way without any list at all. We didn't care one bit, list or no list, proper count or not, it didn't matter, we were going to go. By the look of the pilots who were sticking their heads out of the crew door we were going sooner than later. The list was not their problem, departure time was. As for all of us sitting in the back of the bus, it didn't matter because we had given up all hope.

—

Without any announcement the aircraft door was closed and locked with a thud that reverberated throughout the seating area. Then without notice a small mobile aircraft power plant outside my window started up. Soon the far left engine, the one that had lost all of its oil on the flight line, began to snort smoke and shake in its pylon, it gave a small tongue of flame and then it spun up and settled down to run at idle.

Maybe settled down isn't the proper description because I could still feel a slight vibration transmitted through my nylon seat cushion. Now engine number two did the same thing, except it was a lot closer to my window which made it sound much louder as it slowly came on line.

Our fearless crew soon had all four of their Pratt and Whitney engines spinning at idle. The mobile starting unit was disconnected and then the plane began to sluggishly roll forward. We taxied out to the edge of the runway where we sat for five minutes or so as the pilots got their final clearance from departure control and completed the standard flight control checks before takeoff.

As we lined up on the runway centerline the pilot pushed the throttles all the way forward and the old DC-8 started its takeoff roll. Finally, after lots of strange noises, unusual vibrations and billowing clouds of black kerosene smoke we roared off into the west.

The aircraft's acceleration felt good and I could feel the flaps coming up along with a change in climb angle that this brought to our well-worn aluminum tube. Next the landing gear made its way into place inside the aircraft and the gear doors slammed shut with a reassuring series of mechanical thunks. So far everything seemed ok but then the aircraft quickly leveled off and stopped accelerating.

—

It was like we were slowly coasting through the sky at 250 knots over the barren brown hills of California instead of climbing for flight level 390. I quickly figured that something was wrong. The problem could have been as simple as another aircraft that was slow to clear the airspace we were assigned to up ahead or it could be something else.

Then without warning I knew it was something else. I heard the gear doors open and felt the drag as the landing gear dropped back down into the airstream. Next the flaps came back down and as the airspeed decreased the nose went back up. Everyone knew we weren't going to make it very far driving along like this and even the non- aviation types, on board knew something was very, very wrong.

The plane's intercom clicked on but at first there was no sound other than the wind whistling through the lowered landing gear. Now all of the passengers had stopped reading, talking or even looking out the window.

Everyone including the cabin crew was looking forward, directly down the aisle as if they could look through the closed cabin door and see the problem that the plane was having with their own eyes. After an eternity of holding our collective breath the captain's voice came over the loudspeaker and told us what we already knew, "There appears to be something wrong with the aircraft". Then more silence.

What he said next was going to change our entire day.

He apologized for not getting right back to us. We were informed that he and the co-pilot had been canceling the flight plan and this aircraft was now on a direct approach for landing at Los Angeles International Airport also known as LAX. The pilot told us that the aircraft had an issue that

—

needed to be taken care of and LAX was the closest facility where he could receive the needed repairs. He went on to say that he had no idea how long the repairs were going to take, but he would let us know as soon as he was given that information. He never did say what the problem was but I bet it had something to do with an oil leak from the #1 engine.

Fine aircraft crew we have on this flight. Nice preflight boys, did you learn that at the Moe, Larry and Curley school of airplane driving?

We looked at each other and slowly realized our secret wishes had been answered. We had been given one last chance to have a good time. We individually swore that we would not let this opportunity go to waste. This was an unprecedented event and was an open slate for us to express our creativity. We had standards to uphold and stories we needed to tell to our grandchildren.

Thank you Lord for the gifts which we are about to receive and for the civilian airport that has been delivered to us.

We landed without incident and a "follow me" truck popped out of nowhere and led us through the maze of terminals to our new home. Our large aluminum goose taxied to the gate under its own power with no LAX Fire Department crash trucks surrounding it.

For those of you unfamiliar with aircraft protocol, this is considered a good thing. This meant that it wasn't a fire on board or even the possibility of a fire that had brought us back to the earth. These are known as bad things. A single generator failure or losing anything we have four of, except perhaps an engine, is not usually considered a bad thing on an aircraft of this size.

—

We were directed to an assigned a parking location and we stopped at the proper spot without hitting anything immovable. All four of the engines wound down and the lighting switched back over to ground power. Everyone put down their reading material along with their recently fluffed pillows and waited for the big announcement. We sat there and smiled because we all knew what was going to happen next.

Every military transport flight has an officer in charge of that particular adventure. His name goes down in the official military log book as being the officer responsible for the conduct of the flight and the safe arrival of all of the military people to their intended destination.

The military log book always stays on the ground at the point of departure in case the plane goes down or someone on board tries to erase the assigned officer's name. There is not much thought given to this choice because on a normal flight all the officer has to do is count bodies and make sure the numbers match up with the printout he was given. His next official job is to close the doors.

There may be a fight on board or someone might die of a heart attack but there is not much he can do to control either of those things. I mean really, what could happen other than the plane falling out of the sky, in which case it doesn't matter who is in charge. Yes, yes, what could possibly happen?

What were the chances that this DC-8 would have a mechanical failure so severe that it would have to stop at Los Angeles International Airport for repairs immediately after takeoff? What were the chances that the only open spot to park was at the main terminal? Add to those calculations the chances that this plane would also be full to the brim

—

with a group of the worst malcontents and subversives ever to be thrown out of Staging Battalion on the same day.

Finish the equation with the understanding that everyone was heading to Vietnam so there was no way to provide any meaningful punishment for common or even uncommon unacceptable behavior. This unforeseen alignment of the stars had happened, and now you have a truly interesting situation ready to unfold.

All eyes were riveted to the front of the plane and there he stood, 1st Lieutenant Whoever ready to make his first big announcement to the troops. He knew he was in big trouble and there was not one thing he could do about it.

He looked down at his notes and just as he was about to flap his lips and make his big pronouncement, along with all of the required threats, the pilot of the aircraft overrode him on the intercom. He stated that all passengers needed to be removed from the aircraft immediately so that they could start with their repairs. There was also something about an FAA requirement and we needed to unload *now!*

The pilot's final statement to us was that everyone would have to remain in the terminal and we could not re-board his aluminum bus until the work was completed. We still just sat there in our faded nylon seats not moving, but each of us smiled a little more.

1st Lieutenant Whoever had a quick animated conference with his underlings at the front of the aircraft. There was much pointing at the door, arm waving and muted voices in discussion trying to find any way out of this ever deepening hole they had found themselves in. There was no way out; so from the lips of 1st Lieutenant Whoever there came forth a series of rules that he demanded we follow during the time that we were inside the terminal.

We listened intently and each of us now had a very serious look on our faces because we knew freedom was very near. We did this without laughing out loud because poor 1st Lieutenant Whoever looked incredibly pale, even from the back of the bus. He then forcefully made his pronouncements:

1. We were not allowed to drink any alcohol.
2. We could not enter into any bar even if we did not drink alcohol while inside the terminal.
3. We would conduct ourselves in a manner befitting the reputation of the United States Marine Corps.
4. We would stay in the general area of the gate and not go into the main terminal because we had to be prepared to depart at a moment's notice.

We all said, "yes sir", hopped up, and marched out the front door of that airliner. We went down the jet way and found ourselves in the middle of the boarding area for a major airline with passengers who had actually paid lots of money to be there. Here we were, all dressed up for war in our recently issued Marine green jungle camouflage uniforms without nametags. Our jungle boots looked funny with their green fabric sides plus they squeaked when we walked on the tile floor.

We poured out of that jet way like our asses were on fire and became instantly intermingled with all of the well-dressed civilians that were restlessly waiting to board their own airliner. Behind us in the gathering crowd we heard the loud squeaking voice of 1st Lieutenant Whoever reminding

—

us of what we had just been told. We were insolent and disrespectful, not stupid.

We heard every word that he had said and understood him completely but to a man we planned to totally ignore him.

It was at this point in time that we proceeded to give the employees and passengers at LAX a performance they had not seen in quite a while and probably never would see again. There are some events that are recorded for prosperity and those that are recorded for future instructional purposes. Time will determine how history will remember us.

Most of us left the boarding area as soon as we were turned loose. Our noses were in the air and we were searching for a sign with only three letters on it. BAR. Our search proceeded down the escalator, through the pedestrian tunnel and straight out into the main part of the airport.

This didn't require walking because LAX had installed what was known back then as a people mover. This was nothing more than an escalator that was flat and ran straight for almost two hundred yards but we were having a good time on it anyway.

For some of our crew it didn't move fast enough. They went into the area between the inbound and outbound people movers and started running. Don't ever run in an airport while in uniform because some people might think there is a serious problem and they will get quite upset. Well, too late for that now.

Remember this was 1970 in California and the rules then were quite different than they are now. Wear a military uniform, especially the camouflage Vietnam battle uniform

—

that all of us had on, and you could drink at any bar no matter what your age. Instantly forgetting the especially moving speech given to us by 1st Lieutenant Whoever inside the aircraft we started looking for a good time.

Well what do you know, we found one.

About 20 of us marched into the first empty establishment we came across, sat down and started ordering drinks. Actually doubles to tell the truth. Within seconds of our arrival the second wave hit and the place was packed.

The owner must have thought he had died and gone to retail heaven. One minute the place is almost empty and the next there is a sea of strange uniforms taking up every chair and table while he is praying that his inventory holds out. Green men were throwing cash in all directions and to the owner it seemed as if they were spending money like there was no tomorrow. A couple of businessmen types in dark suits were quickly shown the door and their seats were taken over by individuals wearing green.

In time, some of the men got up to find other sources of entertainment while others stayed firmly planted in their seats and continued to drink with much enthusiasm. As they got up and left, their places were quickly filled by willing replacements and the drinks kept flowing.

We sat in the air conditioned darkness, sipping away with smiles on our faces for over an hour when we saw 1st Lieutenant Whoever running down the corridor toward the airport main offices. He didn't even stop when he looked over to his right and saw his green uniformed charges filling up the entrance to an off limits drinking establishment.

—

Now we were always looking for sources of additional entertainment so our group picked up our bar glasses and left to follow our fearless leader down the hallway. Also motivating our decision to relocate was we felt the existing service and female companionship were totally below acceptable standards. We needed to find another watering hole. Our group went down the hallway searching for both our fearless leader and any overlooked yet inexpensive drinking locations that were more suitable to our immediate needs.

The problem was that by the time we had gotten up and out the door through the milling crowd of new Marine faces 1st Lieutenant Whoever had disappeared. We got moving in the general direction we had seen him going, but our leader was nowhere to be found. We didn't know where he was going but we came to the unanimous conclusion that we should be there to help him. I bet he would have liked that. Now that's the sign of true leadership when men will follow without even being asked.

We knew it had to have been something important for him to be running like a fool down the middle of the terminal. We were soon led to believe, by a reliable source, that some of the more intoxicated members of our group had tried to steal a car and take it for a joyride around the airfield.

Everyone assumed that it was an automobile but I didn't think so. I bet they had tried to drive away in one of those unlocked clunky baggage train tugs that you see all over the place. There is no doubt they were too drunk to realize they could only escape at about ten miles an hour.

It's hard to outrun even the airport police in a baggage tug.

—

Whatever they did we collectively owed them a boatload of gratitude because they cleared out every L.A. county sheriff, city police officer and LAX security guard in the entire building. The rest of us had a free run at complete mayhem with no one to annoy us with silly rules and regulations because they were out chasing wayward Marines playing wrinkle fender with a stolen baggage tug. Like most of the events of that day we never did find out the whole truth about what damage they really did.

We were soon to learn, to our great pleasure, that our unusual uniforms and tales of great adventure worked wonders with a lot of the young ladies who were sitting around the terminal. They were bored and had nothing interesting to do while they were waiting for their flights. We were desperate and so this worked out to be a great combination.

These young Marines had been around enough veterans for a long enough time to have learned a thousand war stories. Some of these stories would just break your heart and these guys could certainly sling the crapola. I was even starting to believe some of them myself when we had to leave; I was starting to get all teary eyed. If 1st Lieutenant Whoever had caught any of that action, he would have really gotten upset.

Not as upset as some the young ladies' boyfriends or their parents got, but still quite upset.

The truth is that even by this time in the day the Lieutenant's group of military misfits had already reset the bar quite high for outrageous conduct in a public location and as they say, the evening was still young.

While we were wondering what to do next to bring a little excitement into our decreasing segment of free time one of

—

41

our team members spotted his former supervisor. This was a sergeant who had a bad reputation with a lot of people. He was a perfect example of a person who likes to abuse his authority when dealing with the little people.

He also reminded us of those cooks we had to deal with back in mess duty. We really hated those cooks from Staging Battalion so we figured it was payback time at the old airport.

At this time in United States history airport security was not something that was taken too seriously. This was a simpler time before aircraft hijackings, bombings and the TSA. There were no metal detectors or baggage searches and a lot of the airport equipment was just left lying around because no one ever fooled with it. Most passengers just cared about getting on their transportation and flying away.

From our co-conspirator we knew the sergeant's name and we could see the location where he was sitting, just waiting for his flight. We knew we needed more than just that to make this work.

About thirty seconds later our prayers were answered when this egotistical, lard ass, blue blazer wearing member of the LAX management team came strutting into sight. He was followed by two of his lackeys and he was publicly giving them hell about something. We could almost be sure that it had something to do with someone in our group.

Two of our team got up and headed in his direction. One approached the front and obtained Mr. Leonard's full name from his white name tag which had a gold border and a tiny red ribbon attached to it. The second member, who was good with voices, turned around behind him and learned

—

the nuances of old blue blazer's speech pattern when he was upset.

By the time Mr. Leonard had passed by and our team was back together we had finalized the plan. We found an unlocked office with an internal airport phone and an official LAX phone directory. Using this internal airport directory, we located this person and found out what his job title was. Then we worked on a script for our voice over man and we went quickly to work.

This was going to be fun.

We placed a call to the security office of LAX from this airport internal phone. The person who answered the phone sounded highly stressed when he was told by Mr. Leonard that he demanded to speak to his supervisor. Mr. Leonard was told that due to a large amount of unusual activity going on in the airport, at this time, there were no security supervisors available. Mr. Leonard, as was his nature, went off on the little security officer which did not make his day go any better.

When Mr. Leonard got done being obnoxious, the security officer was told that he, Mr. Leonard, Director of Airport Operations, demanded that a certain Marine Sergeant be taken into custody and returned to the airport security office. In the security office the sergeant was to be questioned about his recent activities in one of the airport's rest rooms.

The security officer was provided with the sergeant's name and where he was sitting, which was at gate number 4 in A concourse. The security officer was then told to hold the sergeant in their office until he, Mr. Leonard arrived to personally take charge.

—

Mr. Leonard slammed the phone down to emphasize his point and to illustrate his importance.

After slamming down the phone we laughed till the tears ran down our faces. We wiped off all of the finger prints from the desk, phone, phone book, door knob and then departed. Looking very innocent and walking as quickly as possible we exited the area.

It would have been nice to have seen the upcoming confrontation but we realized that everything was going to go as planned when we started to hear coded announcements coming out of the public address speakers and then observed security officers walking in the direction of gate 4 in A concourse.

By this time, we had logged almost three hours of unexpected freedom and we were in need of more alcohol. But as luck would have it, none of us had the foresight to carry a large amount of US currency on this trip. We had enough for snacks and things to read but not enough to pay for any more quality bar room drinking.

Not one of us had the foresight to realize that we might need serious drinking money where we were going. After everything we had been put through, who would have thought that fate would be so kind to us?

But we were nothing, if not resourceful.

Our wanderings took us into the airport passenger arrival area where our small squad stood around for a while looking stupid. Our group was very good at this also, but we were out of money and quickly running out of time. We needed to think of a way to get back into the bar and start drinking again without actually robbing someone or knocking out the bartender.

44

Well at least without getting caught.

There were about eight of us standing around loudly complaining to each other and to anyone else who would listen when we came upon a sure fire way to get more cash for drinks.

The actual setup worked out to be very simple. We commandeered an official airport wheelchair that was unoccupied and plopped our smallest Marine into the seat. We had him fold one of his legs up so he was sitting on it and it was out of sight. We then placed a blanket in his lap and tucked it in nicely so that all that was showing was his one good leg and the protruding stump of his missing leg under the blanket.

We wheeled this poor handicapped veteran through the arrival area and then down to the location in the terminal where the passengers had to get out of their cars and walk to the ticket counter in preparation for their flight. We were now in a position of advantage over our enemy because they were distracted, on foot and in a hurry.

We had our targets in sight and were ready to fire for effect.

Oh the humanity! A wounded Marine with only one leg sitting in a wheel chair holding his Marine cover in one hand and a look of guarded anticipation on his face. Hope of a better life was in his eyes.

When you are small in the Marines you have to be a really good actor to survive and this guy was first class. He would look the victim right in the eye while stretching out his cover to receive a donation. At the same time, he would scratch his stump in case the victim had not noticed his physical condition.

—

—

The rest of us stood in a semi-circle behind him blocking the victim's progress toward the ticket counter while we asked for donations from the mark and his family to help this disabled veteran in his hour of need. Actually we did a little more than just ask, but it wasn't strong armed robbery so who cares.

We would always pick a business man who was well dressed but moving quickly with a family and lots of luggage tagging along behind him. We blocked their way with scowls on our faces and crossed arms. We looked them in the eye and talked about all of the sacrifices we had made for their personal freedom while stump boy held out his cover. Time was on our side.

We babbled on until they donated some folding money into the upturned cover of the wounded marine. They knew they were being scammed. To them the price they paid was a small fraction of what it would cost if they missed their flight but it was just enough to get us to move. It took two or three times to get the system into place but once we got it working it was money magic.

We were kind of like the skycaps at curbside, except we didn't do any actual work.

All Los Angeles people's hearts were hardened in these years due to never ending requests for donations from the local street people. Remember we were going up against the best that California had to offer at that time. In the 1970's they had Hare Krishna's and real hippies out begging for money on the streets and they had to be good or they didn't eat that night.

Our advantage was that we hit them at the airport arrival gate where they didn't expect to be molested by people in

—

uniform and we were not afraid to stand our ground. We even bumped a couple of them with the wheel chair until they donated. If we could have figured out a way to get stump boy to drool and bite one or two of them, we would have made even more money.

Almost everyone we solicited donated but some people are just too cheap for their own good. A couple of them almost got hurt falling down. It didn't hurt our collection efforts at all that most of airport security was busy fighting with some Marine sergeant in concourse A.

To say the least, we were quite successful in our little enterprise. I remember we got a little over $70.00 in a short period of time and this was exceptional cash for 1970. We were Mission Accomplished so we wheeled our wounded Marine back into the main terminal where we found a new and more appropriate bar. This bar had stewardesses, female passengers and lower priced drinks for servicemen in uniform. We went back to doing what we did best until we blew through most of our recently acquired funds.

By this time old 1st Lieutenant Whoever must have been catching hell from all directions. An announcement went out over the loudspeaker that all Marines were required to immediately return to their boarding area for loading. We knew the announcement was bogus, but we were tired and all of the stewardesses had left to catch their flights.

This airport was starting to lose its appeal. In addition, we had run out of money so we said goodbye to our new friends at the bar, went down the corridor and up the escalator to our boarding area.

As we suspected the aircraft was still not repaired, but we didn't care.

—

One of the other groups had found a unique and equally enjoyable way to spend the afternoon after they had run out of money at the bar. They would move as a large pack into a crowd of unsuspecting people and steal hats off of their heads.

They would take the hat and then pass it around through the group as they became part of a larger crowd getting on or off of an aircraft. They had acquired a number of hats during their time of freedom and they were proud to show them off. These consisted of one Navy chief's hat, an Army hat or two of different styles along with an assortment of civilian hats in different colors.

1st Lieutenant Whoever had been on the edge of losing control before he saw the hats and now he quickly came apart at the seams. He started screaming about theft and then asked everybody, "Where did you get those hats from?", as if he actually expected an answer.

Finally, someone looked at him with a straight face while wearing an Army hat with little silver buttons and said, "We found them somewhere". Funny as it sounds, 1st Lieutenant Whoever accepted this answer and went off on a rant about some other alleged criminal activity.

This officer is going to have no combat effectiveness if he doesn't learn to get control of himself. He must have just graduated from the Naval Academy because he took everything so seriously. He started mumbling to himself and was last seen talking to his underlings about all of the complaints he had received; as if any of them even cared.

As you can imagine with two hundred semi-intoxicated enlisted marines hanging around a major international airport there were a lot of things happening at once. Finally,

—

there were so many reports coming in about our adventures that 1st Lieutenant Whoever had taken control of an airport internal phone because he was now being contacted directly by airport security almost every five minutes about some new outrage.

It got so bad he couldn't keep track of everything that was going on. He now designated one of his underlings to take notes and answer the phone for him while he tried to put out an ever increasing number of fires.

About 50 of the men who had not been drinking to excess and could still stand had taken up positions around a Plexiglas wall surrounding the concourse escalators leading up to the boarding area. This group found mission fulfillment in providing live color commentary plus loud appreciation to all of the young ladies who were in view from our downward perspective during their slow trip up or down these escalators.

The female portion of a number of the commercial air crews were real players and gave back comments as good as they got. A couple of the other ladies were so appreciative of all the attention they received that they found an excuse to make a second escalator trip and were well rewarded by our men for their efforts.

At some time during our rampage through LAX the overwhelmed airport security must have called the military police and requested assistance in controlling an unruly mob of drunken individuals dressed in green uniforms. Well here they came.

Two smartly dressed US Navy shore patrol officers in their finest white sailor uniforms. They came complete with little white sailor hats and official black Shore Patrol armbands.

—

These weren't the brightest bulbs on the tree because it wasn't until they got on the escalator and started their trip upward to our gate area that they decided to look around to see what was happening.

As they started the trip upward the fifty Marines surrounding the top of the escalator started saying very unpleasant things about them personally and the branch of service that they represented in general. This increase in vocal activity and volume woke up some of the drunks who then came over to the railings and proceeded to assist our men on the front line with appropriate verbal abuse toward the squids.

The two shore patrol officers did not look left, they did not look right and they definitely did not say a word. They rode the escalator all the way to the top, made a left U turn and rode the other escalator all the way to the bottom and then they just walked away to the sound of laughter. It was as though we were invisible and they were just there to check out the functioning of the escalator and to inspect the tops of their shiny black shoes.

1st Lieutenant Whoever watched this performance with his mouth open. His last hope of regaining any semblance of order was marching away just as fast as their little sailor legs could take them.

With the Shore Patrol show now officially over, most of us drifted away from the railing and started to wander around. There was a limited space to wander at the gate and the show out the windows was pretty boring. If you have seen one aircraft pushed back from the jet way, you have seen them all. Soon most of us found comfy plastic chairs or a nice spot on the carpeted floor and went to sleep. One of the more drunk individuals went to sleep in the dirt

—

50

surrounding a large potted palm tree and seemed to be quite comfortable there.

The evening was done and so were we.

Later that night convict airlines obtained a resupply of duct tape and repaired their flying aluminum tube. They told our fearless leader that it was now time to gather up his charges and load everyone up for the trip across the pond. Some of our team was still awake and made it to their seats under their own power. Others were in a deep alcohol fueled snoring contest and never did make it all the way back to consciousness.

But in the end we all made it back on board. Some walked and some were carried but we slowly filled up the plane. The aircraft seats were a little bit better than the plastic ones we had left in the waiting room, but not by much.

After all of the walking wounded had re-boarded the airliner, we observed the criminals who had taken the airport baggage tug for an unauthorized ride being marched into the plane by LAX security. These Marines were placed in a special section in the front for the entire flight. We were never allowed to talk to them directly and those who actually knew the truth never would say anything about the event to us.

"Inquiring minds want to know."

The bodies were counted and 1st Lieutenant Whoever was pleasantly surprised to find out that no one had hauled ass and turned back into a civilian during our stopover. This was probably the best thing that was going to happen to him for the entire trip. I wasn't pleasantly surprised like the Lieutenant that everyone made it back on board, but I was somewhat amused.

A golden opportunity like that for freedom does not happen every day.

With everything that had happened and the noticeable foul mood of 1ˢᵗ Lieutenant Whoever I never did get a chance to ask what had been wrong with the aircraft and the pilot never volunteered that information to his captives.

The engines were started and the aircraft was pushed back from the gate. The DC-8 taxied to the active runway and we tried it again. This time there were no problems and our aluminum bus climbed westward into the darkness and high above the smog.

The California sunshine was long gone by the time we got airborne and launched the next phase of our new adventure.

It would be over a year before I looked upon the dry dusty hills of California again, but then again I was one of the lucky ones.

—

Chapter 3
We Should Have Taken the Boat
Total U.S. killed as of July 1970 in the Vietnam War: 53,084

Our newly repaired and refueled metal sled lumbered off into the nighttime darkness. We quickly climbed above the dense brown smog that was quite normal for California in the summer. We soon figured out that there would be no more swings at the freedom piñata for our group because this mighty DC-8 was not returning to Los Angeles International Airport any time soon.

The bird reached cruising altitude with no more equipment failures, parts falling off or scary warning lights coming on. As we tracked westward through the late night blackness more and more fluffed pillows, newspapers and magazines were reluctantly removed from their hiding spaces. The background talking quieted down while we turned back inside of ourselves and prepared for the long movement restricted flying bus ride to Hawaii.

As befitting an aircraft of this age all of the passenger seats were both well-worn and uncomfortable. The air conditioning and air exchange system was probably below acceptable standards while the overhead lighting fixtures that worked, bordered on dim. There was one category where we did have to give this airline an A+ rating.

This corporation may not have had the newest equipment, the best repair people or even the most skillful flight crews but there was one place where they outshined their competition. Their underrated skill was in interior design and seat placement.

It is very possible that their aircraft interior designers had recently been employed in the aviation cattle transport

—

industry. A careful eye could see the work of engineers who have incorporated into this airliner some of the newest design features for confining restless bovine during long international trips.

Looking around I didn't think it was possible to fit one more living creature into the interior of this plane given the amount of floor space that was available. The food preparation area was next to nothing. The cabin crew provided all inmates with stacks of sandwiches wrapped tightly in plastic film, steel cans of off brand soda or semi-warm coffee in a Styrofoam cup, for their dining pleasure.

Some of the soda cans still had carbonation when they were opened, which was an unexpected plus. The coffee flavor was weak enough that you could detect a slight hint of chlorine in its fragrant aroma. No cooking was required and none was attempted.

Remember what was said earlier about this airline being the winner of a military contract, which meant they were the "low bidder". There was nothing in their contract that said the food served had to be fresh, hot or even tasty. As long as it was an actual food item and it didn't kill a significant number of troops being transported, it was acceptable to the people responsible for approving the services of this airline.

Remember Marines: We never promised you a rose garden.

Additional aircraft seating was obtained by reducing the number of restrooms available for use by their military cargo. Some of the more hung over members of our group solved their urgent sanitation issues by going into the rear quarters and throwing up in an unlocked flight crew closet.

Soon the individual overhead seat lights started going out and it was time to try to sleep. A window seat was best because you could wedge your head between the aircraft bulkhead and the side of the seat, using your fluffy pillow to stop any excess movements. This was ok as far as placement went but after a short period of time this position caused a real #8 headache. Well the headache was either from that or the excess alcohol that was consumed at the airport coming back to bite the traveler.

Most of the seats reclined only a limited number of degrees before they hit the knees of the person sitting behind them in the next row. There were a few seats that did not recline at all and because the plane was packed like a sealed sausage container there were no other locations available.

Luck of the draw I guess.

Sleep came and went. You could close your eyes and try to shut down all of the systems inside your mind, but you always stayed in that nasty little gray area between sleep, and telling yourself to go to sleep.

The entire trip was like this. Towards the end we had lost count of how many times we had tried to sleep or even how long we had been in the air. The ride just went on and on.

The speed, the altitude and the darkness outside stayed the same as did the long lines waiting for the few restrooms. At least restroom standing gave you something to do besides sitting still and growing blood clots. Everyone was starting to take bets as to whether or not the pilots had fallen asleep and Hawaii was actually two hours behind us.

Finally came the beginning of the end. The pilots reduced power to our faithful but leaky engines and we started our

—

long slow descent down to the big island of Hawaii. Some of the cattle started getting restless in anticipation of our arrival to the island paradise but most of the herd stayed asleep and were unaware of either time or place.

Open the shade and it was still dark. What happened to the sun? Off in the far distance you could just make out little lights on the ground but there was no sun creeping up over the horizon to greet us and help us with waking up.

It had to be time for the sun because we felt like they had kept us in this box for at least ten hours. We were sleep deprived, confused and sore from our forced sitting positions. All of us were in the process of learning a big lesson from old Mr. Jetlag.

The truth was our flight time was only a little bit over six hours with about an additional half an hour of ground time but it didn't feel that way to us. The aircraft stopped its slow descent toward the water, turned onto final and landed without incident. Our flying tube pulled up to the terminal area but there was no LAX style Jetway for us.

A Marine green pickup truck with mobile stairs pulled into position while the aircraft door opened wide. Look outside and there is nothing but midnight darkness, bright vehicle headlights and groups of people milling around. It appears to us as if a whole bunch of people have arrived to greet us on our arrival in paradise, isn't that nice.

A new voice came over the little speakers above everyone's head. Not an apathetic voice like one of the cabin crew and not a hesitant and apprehensive voice like 1st Lieutenant Whoever. Nope. This voice was clear and direct. It said, "Everyone get out of the aircraft and go to the large building at the end of the walkway.

—

After our forced upright sleeping position getting up onto our feet was difficult. Standing upright was painful enough but then came the first fifty steps of our trip down the long aisle to the open door. Halfway down the aisle we could finally walk without limping or falling down.

The massive blood clots that had formed in our legs were pumped through the heart and finally lodged in our brains. Walk and stop, then walk some more as the front of our narrow bodied cattle car emptied and allowed those of us in the back to make a less than graceful exit.

A warm strong breeze that actually contained moisture hit us in the face as we stepped outside. Moving along we slowly hobbled down the steel boarding steps and onto the pavement where we were forced to take a break.

We had to move slowly because we had no desire to trip and roll around on the flight line, not that anyone would have noticed. All of us were like extras in a science fiction horror movie where the people in town had their brains sucked out but they are still walking around with dazed looks on their faces.

Jet lag and forced sobriety has turned all of us into mumbling morons.

We didn't know where we going or what we were going to do when we got there. We followed the men ahead of us and tried not to throw up in the well-tended flower gardens on either side of the concrete pathway. Everyone came to a general consensus that this place looked very well maintained and spiffy, as opposed to your basic military base.

—

For some unknown reason we observed a large number of Marine and Navy security officers standing around different areas of the walkway watching us as we made our way into the gray metal building at the end of the path. Due to our physical condition we did not fully understand why they were standing there nor did we particularly care. The general agreement of everyone walking along was that this was a normal reception for every late night arrival.

Our destination turned out to be a small auditorium near the airfield operations building. There were no chairs available so we were directed to stand together near the raised stage at the front. It seemed like two or three high ranking officers were already on the stage and they were waiting impatiently for all of us to enter. Some of the cattle were actually wondering why the brass had gotten up so early in the morning to greet us, but most of us really didn't care.

Soon rumors started to fly that there was a real first class blow up about what happened at the LAX airport. Not knowing the total extent of criminal activities conducted by all of the different groups, we couldn't understand what the big deal was.

From what we were told in an unofficial statement, it appears that there were five or six groups who individually produced unprecedented mayhem inside LAX during the time the aircraft was being repaired. Such activities had been reported, with much embellishment we assume, to the proper military authorities. The net result of those reports was the basis for tonight's meeting.

Who would have thought that we had been so creative?

There was no doubt between us, that persons of low moral character had called ahead of our arrival and spread

—

malicious rumors about our personal conduct while we were at LAX. Mr. Leonard comes to mind first or perhaps those two Navy shore patrol officers. We all said that we would like to pay Mr. Leonard a personal visit on our return trip in a year and express to him, our appreciation for all of his hard work and dedication in being a fat squealing rat.

Along with other members of our company I would have been more than willing to defend the reputation and the honor of our unit if we hadn't felt so sick. This feeling was obviously the result of not being able to sleep on the flight along with the jetlag and the alcohol we had illegally consumed earlier at LAX.

Luckily we did not have to defend our actions because none of the officers standing before us had the name of a single individual Marine who allegedly participated in any unmilitary behavior while at the airport.

With the exception of course of those dumbasses that were too drunk to run away from the airport rent-a-cops and were caught red handed allegedly bumping into very expensive things with the allegedly stolen baggage tug. We considered that to be an isolated incident which of course, was not representative of our unit as a whole.

These brothers became known as prisoners of war from the battle at LAX. Now other than that single event, we didn't do anything wrong, that they could prove. We believed that their rush to judgement was based on nothing but wild hearsay and innuendo which was floating in the wind that dark Hawaiian morning.

After listening to the accusations coming from the men at the podium, we stood in total shock and complete disbelief at the charges. To think that anyone in the military, much

—

less a respectable member of our unit, would do any of the things that our group had been accused of doing during our last stopover was outrageous. "No sir!!!" we replied, with a loud voice and much indignation, when we were accused. "Absolutely not us!!!" we volunteered when questioned.

This was not the first time we recognized the value of wearing interchangeable uniforms with no military insignia or name tags. We were like yellow corn in a silo, if you've seen one kernel, you've seen them all.

There was no security camera coverage back in those days. No pictures, no names, no fingerprints on any door handles, phone handsets or wheelchairs had left us home free. We were just little green angels who were flying off to war when asked to fight for our Nation.

Without any individuals to blame, the powers to be were at a loss as to what to do with us. They knew that some of us were guilty as sin. But knowing and proving are two different animals.

They couldn't hold up our entire group's progress to the war zone with just alleged individual criminal charges because we were considered valuable replacements. Also without an impressively good reason, these Majors and Lieutenant Colonels couldn't take a military transport aircraft out of service or send it on its way half empty.

The Vietnam War clock had stuck midnight and it was time for us and our jet powered pumpkin to move on. This newly formed inquisition was left with no time to complete a proper investigation about something that may or may not have happened five time zones away in someone else's jurisdiction.

—

The other thing in our favor was that the accusations involved only inappropriate conduct and minor offenses involving the consumption of alcohol, not murder or armed robbery. We were all hoping that the wheelchair thing didn't rise to the level of strong armed robbery but it was looking mighty good for us so far.

Whispered conferences complete with finger pointing, book referencing and desk pounding consumed the time of all the assorted majors and captains on the front stage. You could tell they wanted to do something to us, they really did, but the question was, "what?"

In that morning and in that place the answer was, they couldn't do anything.

We never got a complete reading of the stories that were being sent out in regards to our activities at LAX. It is important that we state for the record that there was probably a great deal of embellishment done by the upper management of that airport in an attempt to cover up their own gross incompetence.

At the end of another hushed conference, the highest of the high was called upon to make a decision. A full bird Colonel looked out over the swaying hung-over multitude and realized that he couldn't make a case that would hold up in any legitimate or even military court.

After all was said and done it was like we figured, Vietnam would be punishment enough for everybody involved. We knew that deep in his cold dark military heart he wished he had caught us on the homeward leg of our journey. There was an unspoken understanding that he would have loved to have kept us on his base until the Hawaiian mountains had turned into sand and flowed into the sea.

—

Even though he was unable to provide our group with a formal judicial hearing regarding our alleged transgressions, nothing required him to make our lives on this island paradise any more than minimally acceptable. His exact words were, "Eat quickly, get back in your plane and get the hell off of my base."

We all felt like such criminals.

We were driven a short distance to a military mess hall and fed an improvised but adequate breakfast considering the early hour of our arrival. As soon as everyone was done eating our company was herded back into a fleet of buses which were idling outside, just for us. We were driven directly back to our refueled and re-oiled flying bus.

Upon arrival we were not even allowed to leave the buses and walk the short distance to the ramp. No time for a Hawaiian souvenir, local newspaper or even an assortment of candy bars. Under direct orders from the base commander, each bus would pull up to the aircraft stairs; the door would open and directly up into the aircraft we went. All this was done under the watchful eye of an overabundance of base security.

Each member had been briefed about what terrible people we were and the trouble they would be in if even one of us escaped to spread havoc on this base. Having to get up and play security at that time of the morning didn't help with their obvious foul moods.

After the first bus was emptied the next bus in line would follow and take its place allowing the process to continue. All of us were soon back in our seats and ready to go on the next leg of our journey except for 1st Lieutenant Whoever. He never returned to our flight and like the story of the

—

broken aircraft landing at LAX, we never found out exactly what happened to him either.

He probably needed a deserved rest after his adventure at the last airport. We assumed that he stayed in Hawaii to talk to all the Majors and Colonels who got up nice and early to greet us because they were really interested about what happened back in California.

We bet he had some great stories to tell those guys.

The flight crew had been replaced, the aircraft had been fueled up and our seats had been sprayed with a sweet smelling insecticide. We imagined that this was used to kill any fleas or any other insects that we might have been carrying over from Camp Pendleton.

You could tell that we were not the first rodeo that had come through this town.

Quick as a bunny the aircraft started up and with fits and starts it rolled over to the runway. The tower cleared our DC-8 for immediate departure and so with four trails of jet black smoke and noise from our leaky engines we left our Hawaiian paradise behind. Next stop Midway Island. We occupied the same seats with the same old newspapers and magazines as before but thanks to our less than gracious host in Hawaii, we had no snacks.

Airtime to Midway was only about three hours but it felt like forever. We were about an hour out when it finally started getting light outside. We couldn't see the sun rise because we were facing westward but the ocean started to lighten up and we could now see little white top waves. The daylight also allowed us to see dark stains on the silver aluminum wings of our aircraft where engine oil had been

---

63

venting, either on purpose or as a result of leaks or excess consumption.

We didn't care at this point because this product of the Douglas Aircraft factory had proven itself to be reliable enough and our engines just kept humming along. Soon we had sunlight, glorious sunlight, flooding into the aircraft through the cracked and glazed over Plexiglas circles they called windows. Everyone stared outside and the mood turned joyful once again.

Final approach during daytime into Midway Island is something that everyone should experience at least once in their lifetime. It starts with a straight in approach over the water. The gear comes down, the flaps come down, and the aircraft slows to landing speed with some minor wing fluttering. We begin to lose altitude and start what appears to be a controlled descent into the water. You get closer to the water and you still can't see anything but wet.

Just when you figure that you should have paid more attention to the ditching in the ocean lecture, the landing gear slams into something concrete and the brakes and reverse thrusters come on hard. The aircraft safely slows down and at the end of the runway turns toward a group of buildings. Our machine rumbles along on uneven tires that should have been replaced five landings ago as it is directed into its parking space next to the tower.

Talk about tiny. A single runway running down the longest section of the island pretty much sums up the entire architecture with the exception of some homes and standard airport hangars left over from the 1930's.

We walked in the sunlight, rolled around on the grass and did little stretching exercises while waiting for the aircraft to be refueled. For some reason everyone was much more pleasant to us on Midway Island. We were able to buy magazines and lots of candy bars to sustain ourselves during the next leg of our trip.

We were tired of flying in this tube with seats and ready to spend a night in a real bed, even if it was just a nasty old Marine Corps rack. But beds were the things that dreams were made of, not the reality that was before us in the shape of our trusty DC-8. All of us were finding that the old girl was not much to look at but at least she got us across the big pond safely.

We had one final trip to make that day and that was another six hours of aviating to reach Okinawa. We loaded up, took off and flew into the pending sunset, again. We finally landed at our new home and were transported by an aging fleet of ratty green buses to another Marine staging base for final preparation and transportation to Vietnam.

Okinawa turned out to be the final inglorious end for the united mess men of Staging Battalion.

The military gave us a day off when we first arrived to recover but they should have given us a week. It took me a full two days to get over the jet lag which was summarized by location and time confusion along with an inability to sleep during night time hours. Upon arrival we were all sent to live in a Quonset hut city that was aligned around a central mess hall and office complex Ahead of us were days of more forms, more lines and more shots.

All transients were allowed unrestricted travel inside the base perimeter but we were forbidden to cross through the gate and into Japan for sightseeing and "recreational"

—

purposes. We promised everyone that we would be good and they still said no.

We ended up spending our days picking up reading material and eatable goodies at the PX along with making up for lost meals at the 24 hour a day mess hall. Everyone acknowledged that it was our duty to eat as many snacks as possible while idling away our time awaiting our move to our final destination.

Time passed slowly at Camp Smedley Butler. Each tick of the clock produced a sense of fearful anticipation growing inside of us. Kind of like what you get when you are sitting in pre-op waiting for an operation that you know you really need. During this time of waiting we would run into lots of Marines who were returning from Vietnam after completing their standard thirteen-month tour.

You could always tell the ones who had been stationed on a remote firebase or some other small outpost. To a man they all had brand new uniforms because the ones they wore in country had already rotted off and were left behind in a stinking pile. Anytime that they went anywhere as a group they walked in a straight line and always looked down to see what they were stepping on.

A year of landmines, booby traps and trip wires hooked to claymores will do that to a person.

At first these little ten man groups were a closed society even to us because to them, we were outsiders. To a man they had almost nothing to say about where they had been or what they had done.

After a little while, when they trusted us enough, we were told a little about what life in "The Nam" was like. After

—

listening to some of the things that they had gone through I was glad my time was going to be spent around expensive aircraft on a real base, instead of out in the bush playing find the sniper or setup the ambush.

This was a simpler time in the world before we knew about Post Traumatic Stress Disorder, (PTSD), and the effects it would have on so many of these men. Even back then in 1970, when you spoke to them you knew these people were damaged goods.

This stinky little political war had changed every one of these individuals all the way down to their core. Every Marine dreamed about returning back to the life they had left behind but their homecomings were not going to be pleasant. Most families would not recognize the person who returned home to them in the body of a son who had left only a year or so before.

While the living shell had returned home from the war, the mind never would.

Time moved on and so did our group. In Okinawa we were broken up and fed into the war machine from a dozen different directions. Almost every one of us had a different military occupational specialty or MOS, (that's Pentagon speak for your job number), so we were processed at different speeds.

The ground pounders were processed first and sent on their way because you can never have too many bodies with rifles walking around in the bushes. The rest of us sat on our butts, drank multiple beers at night and waited for the great green machine to spit out our name and tell us it was time to move on down the road.

—

Our final call to war came with the feeling of resignation a Roman gladiator must have felt when his Coliseum cell door opened up and he heard the deafening roar of the crowd. Like us, he was as well prepared as possible but he never really knew what his immediate future held.

He could walk out into the arena and if he was only part of a side show he would face a three legged Bambi, take care of business and be back in his dormitory before rush hour. If he was the main attraction, then there could be three really large Germanic warriors with bad attitudes and sharp swords anxiously waiting for him. Like those of us in Okinawa, that gladiator in Rome had no control over what future he faced or when he would face it.

One day our names just appeared as a line on a multi-sheet document pinned to the area's outdoor bulletin board. It detailed our departure time, location for muster and what was to be expected of us before we could leave. The day we had all been thinking about since joining the Marines, had finally arrived.

This time our flying chariot turned out to be a smaller member of the Boeing family of commercial jet liners. This model was a 727 which had three small engines in the back and a unique boarding stairway that hinged down from the rear under the tail. This plane was probably half the size of our old friend the DC-8 and it had been designed to be profitable on shorter runs. We climbed up the tiny boarding ladder and sat down for the short and final leg of our journey westward.

As we were flying along, I could never figure out why the North Vietnamese never attacked one of our military transport planes while it was in the air. On occasion they would damage a parked aircraft by accident with steel

—

shrapnel when they fired a dozen or so 140mm (about 5 ¾ inch) diameter rockets into the Da Nang or Saigon airports. But never anything direct.

Now it wouldn't be as simple as bombing a restaurant in Saigon or blowing up a motorcycle inside a crowd of pedestrians but it was physically possible to accomplish at this time. Everyone in the world knew the route and the exact flight times, because all flights went over southern Taiwan and a couple of other little municipalities as a regular registered airline flight.

Next we flew over the ocean along the coast of China within eighty miles of the island of Hainan. This is within easy range of a North Vietnamese single seat fighter using ground based Chinese radar for guidance. It didn't even need to be a one-way mission for glory. Talk about a real blow to our already shaky morale if they were able to take out one of the freedom birds on its way back to the states.

Lucky for us, we weren't on the way home so we didn't have to concern ourselves with suicidal North Vietnamese pilots flying from Chinese islands. Our immediate issues involved the local weather which had turned ugly along our flight path. Normally at thirty-five thousand feet things like thunder storms don't bother you.

Then again you normally don't have towering cumulus clouds in the South China Sea pushing upward past fifty thousand feet on both sides of your insignificant aircraft. Our pilots were working overtime using their outdated monochrome weather radar to keep themselves and our high mileage flying dumpster in the sunlight and out of the turbulence which was all around us. Despite their skills, we were driven into one or two of the smaller storms which

—

69

provided real time testing of the approved structural limits for this child of Mr. Boeing's aircraft factory.

Later in the day most of the large pieces of our 727 safely landed at the Da-Nang Marine / Air Force airfield to the sounds of nothing. There were no banners celebrating our arrival or even young ladies throwing flowers at our feet. Not even a pre-recorded patriotic marching song to make us feel appreciated.

Well really, what did you expect; someone to actually care?

On the date that we arrived, there had been over two million people wearing green uniforms who had come before us. We were now all just numbers. It was time to accept our new status in the military ant colony and try real hard not to become a future unpleasant statistic.

Our only greeting came from the obligatory group of derelicts in mixed green uniforms slouching around the arrival area. Their only job in military life was too loudly make fun of the new fish as we stumbled off the plane and stood around looking like lost souls, which we were. At least they brought a sense of normalcy to the ending of our journey.

It seems that the military always provides an appropriately sized group of malingerers at every air field or sea port as soon as the concrete is hard enough to assist in their slouching. There were enough of them to make you wonder if they were assigned this duty every morning or if there was some kind of a warning system in place to let them know when it was time to get into position and malinger?

In time all of us were led into another Quonset hut and additional processing was started. I don't know if we could

—

70

ever participate in any future war without filling out reams of paper per fighting man which then required an entire platoon of multi speed typewriter operators.

In our time these office people were known as, "Remington Raiders". Remington Rand was the name of a manual typewriter that our military always purchased by the case load and it was required to be in place and functioning in every war zone before the bombs or bullets arrived.

We soon left the semi-dark interior of the initial processing hut and following the written directions we had just received, loaded ourselves into waiting open military trucks for transportation to our new neighborhoods. There were about six of us, along with all of our gear riding in the open back of the truck going south. We sat under the Vietnam sun as we drove through the streets of the base and then suddenly across the threshold of the gate we went.

We had arrived in the war zone.

Visions of Vietcong hiding behind every tree took over our collective imaginations as we looked left and then right. It was one thing to read about this place in a book or even see it on TV, but to be here in person was something else altogether. The crowds, the confusion and the smells were overwhelming.

No more were we under the false illusion of protection inside the perimeter of the base, this was the real deal. Our driver and the truck's armed guard had done this trip already twice today and didn't think of it as any kind of deal.

The driver was less than impressed with the local culture as he bleated his weak truck horn at all the bicycles and little

—

90cc motorcycles zooming around us from every direction. The locals would ride with two or three tiny people on a Honda motorcycle, turning and stopping without any signals or warnings. It appeared that they had little concern for oncoming traffic or the laws of physics that a large unnoticed green military vehicle would teach them.

Our first observation inside the city of Da Nang was this was a land of nasty old buildings, dirty sidewalks and uncontrolled traffic flow. In this place motorists honked their way about and slow pedestrians were considered second class citizens who were unworthy of a change of either velocity or direction from most of the motorized vehicles.

The daily lives of these people involved the buying and selling of goods in hundreds of little gray colorless stalls along the road's shoulder. They would have boxes and bottles stacked up on little tables or on little colored cloths sitting on the dirt by the side of the road. Almost all of the stalls were made of local materials which usually consisted of only a palm frond roof held up with untrimmed sticks.

This would be their office, sales room and at night even their sleeping quarters. These people with their pointed straw hats and loose clothing would stand right at the edge of the pavement playing let's make a deal with some of the other locals with absolutely no concern for the motorized traffic only feet away.

We were to learn later that if a Vietnamese civilian was struck by a US military vehicle their family could make more money from that accident than from an entire year of selling stolen stuff. It was not unusual for parents to push their children into the sides of moving vehicles so they could attempt to collect lots of money from Uncle Sam. It was

—

important that the trucks didn't kill the child because that would render them useless for rice planting or for making another attempt for an additional payout next year. It was a balancing act to get it right but a broken bone or two was worth quite a bit more to the family than just a cut or simple bruise.

By observing the markings on the boxes, most of the goods the locals were selling appeared to be all sorts of stolen military property. Nobody, including the military police, who we observed wandering around, did anything about this because it was as common in this country as the sun rising.

If the military ever attempted to take back our stolen property, there would be a total civil uprising that would overshadow even the violence of Tet. We figured that the US Government decided that it would be better in the long run to allow them to sell what they stole rather than make them even more vocal about their displeasure with our presence in their nation.

We were less than shocked.

Our truck turned onto the main road heading south toward the Marble Mountain Marine Air Facility and picked up speed. We were lucky that the local Viet-Cong militia did not pick this time to attack our truck because our single security guard had gone to sleep on a pile of boxes stacked on the floor of the truck. He was snoring loudly and we were on our own.

As we traveled along with our heads in the breeze we all came to the same conclusion. Da Nang smelled like wet cardboard and the Vietnam countryside smelled like an open sewer. Actually I believed that it was a combination of

—

human waste, animal manure, rotting vegetation and the lack of basic sanitation that gave Vietnam a unique odor. It looked like all the pictures we had seen with the bright green rice paddies, people with funny hats and black water buffalos grazing in the fields but there had been no smell-o-meter on any of those pictures.

We were all hoping that this was an oddity of nature and that the rest of Vietnam smelled at least neutral. We later learned that this was the way the entire county smelled. After a couple of weeks, you begin to think it is normal when the truth was you had just lost one of your senses.

We made it to our new duty station's main gate with no one attacking our convoy of one. As we made our turn off of the highway the guard was given a sharp kick in the flak jacket to wake him up. It was important that we should at least look presentable as we entered through the gates of the Marble Mountain Air Facility, also known to all as MMAF.

—

Our truck drove through the main gate on the Army side of the base, then around the north end of the runway till we reached Marine land on the beach side of the base.

My journey ended where it had begun, standing in front of some interchangeable person sitting behind a grey metal desk complete with a manual typewriter filling out all of the required forms. Our individual paperwork was again taken, stamped and recorded in a big book, then handed back to us. We were told that transportation from our assigned units would arrive soon to bring us down the line to our new home.

The jeep for Marine Light Helicopter Squadron 167 was not in sight so my time in the office was spent reading some of the in-country literature that they had lying around for our education and enjoyment.

According to the Da Nang area military newspaper, we were winning the war. They also remarked that all of the Vietnamese citizens they had spoken with thought that we were the best foreign devils to invade since the Chinese came through here in 1241. After absorbing three interesting pages, my jeep arrived.

I quickly loaded my sea bag into the backseat and then trailing a blue cloud of un-burnt hydrocarbons, we went down the road. We motored through a small cluster of tin hooches where all of the enlisted men lived, and then down the flight line till we got to my new squadron's hangar.

Crystal white beach sand, green sand bags piled into bunkers and a sun faded galvanized steel building in the shape of an aircraft hangar greeted my eyeballs. My workplace was about one hundred yards west of the South China Sea with a road, a fence and some buildings between

—

the blue-green salt water and us. The main hangar door and all of the aircraft parking revetments were west of the hangar and so was the runway.

Finally, my entire collection of sweat stained paperwork was turned into the assigned squadron paper pusher. As a reward I was provided with additional useless documents that I would throw away later. After the paperwork was properly filed away I was given the official new guy grand tour which was a ten-minute walk through the hangar. Having been assigned two separate military occupation specialties I was put into the avionics section for starters and then taken to one of the avionics hooches to rest from my travels.

Home Sweet Hooch, I had arrived.

—

Chapter 4
A New World with New Rules
Total U.S. killed as of August 1970 in the Vietnam War: 53,536

Your first night in a new home is always stressful. Did you lock the front door, is the toilet running in the downstairs bathroom and where is that cat? It is more so if your new house is made of plywood sheets covered with a galvanized steel roof and has a double row of green sandbags stacked four feet high along the outside walls to stop the intrusion of steel shrapnel from incoming rocket blasts.

Each new guy naturally assumed that these protective walls of sand filled plastic bags were designed to stop warhead fragmentation from entering into his green plywood shack and becoming one with his anatomy. New guys always visualized the bad guys' 144mm rockets landing outside of

77

his hooch, exploding with a big bang and producing lots of stinky gray smoke. In the mind of all FNG's, the sandbag wall would provide complete blast protection for all of the huddled masses inside the hooch.

Soon after arrival everyone learned the big secret. The sandbag wall's primary design was to keep the blast contained inside the hooch which would then funnel the explosion and shrapnel upward. Any individual protection provided by these walls was just a secondary function.

My new home / hooch came complete with six other members of the HML-167 aviation electronics shop whose exclusive interest at this time of the day was in starting the evening's recreational activities. As a group, they barely acknowledged my intrusion into their dimly lit plywood world before they returned to their recreational activities.

With very little enthusiasm on my part, the gray, multi-spring official Marine Corps rack that I had been assigned was made up and ready for the first of many nights we would spend together. All of my jungle green uniforms were put away and I was ready to go exploring. I was told by everyone inside our slum that there was nowhere to explore because I had seen it all during my first day's ten-minute tour.

This was my first night in a foreign land. There was no doubt in my mind that nearby there were lots of dangerous places crawling with leaches, large bugs and communist fighters. But tonight I was sitting on my thin mattress inside my tin shack and I was bored already.

Winning the war would just have to wait until tomorrow.

—

At the end of my first day in country, I looked around and observed my well-worn and minimalist surroundings. Later I would realize that this provided me with my first realistic glimpse of "the war". As usual, reality is much bleaker than the glossy hype and propaganda that had been provided to us by both sides back in the States.

The dayshift avionics crew, which I was now a part of, was officially "off duty" so they commenced to emotionally turn their backs on the war.

Every evening this quality time consisted of drinking and testing their skills with a card game which was long on rule variations and short on cash. Recorded musical accompaniment from a tape deck in the corner tried to overpower the constant chatter of players and spectators.

In addition, there was also the constant shuffling in and out of assorted friends, alcoholics and co-workers. These people would always come in with their own unauthorized beverages firmly in hand and if requested, we would

—

79

provide them with a supply of ice and cans of coke from our little Panasonic refrigerator.

The only requirement of each guest was to find his own comfy place to sit so that he could commence to babble on, in an authoritative manner, about any and all official rumors of the day. Some of these wandering individuals were mildly disturbed to find that I had been assigned to sleep in their normal seating location and I had the audacity to have already turned it into my bed.

Unannounced change was a normal thing in hooch land, so they grumbled a little bit but always ended up wandering around to find another location where they could rest their tired anatomy. There was no way to tell how many of this endless parade of people were actually looking for someone in particular or happened to be just another person wandering about in an intoxicated haze.

Being the New Guy in the hooch, it was impossible to tell one from the other.

Our entire base, from the mess hall to the runway, had been built on nothing but white quartz beach sand which had the same color and granularity as that of the most expensive private Florida beach. It didn't take more than a couple of nights before you realized you were not an actor in a Hollywood movie and there were lots of unexpected problems when you lived on a white sand beach.

First there was the wind. A gentle breeze worked fine for cooling everyone off and keeping the vicious Vietnamese bugs in motion but when the wind reached a certain velocity it started to move the sand. At first the wind could only push the sand close to the ground which would cause it to sting the bare skin on your feet. The faster the wind blew,

—

the more of the dry sand became airborne and the higher it went into the sky. Soon white beach sand was an unfocused cloud covering the base.

Airborne sand at almost any velocity would immediately enter into your hooch and embed itself in your Marine Corps rack, clean clothing and any open drink that you had foolishly left on the table.

Because alcohol was difficult to obtain and eating sand with a meal was not that uncommon an act, a certain quantity of white beach sand was always tolerated at the bottom of your nighttime beverage glass. No matter how accustomed you were to sand in your drink, the best rule was to never do the old, "bottoms up", with your beverage glass at the end of the evening.

The next problem was that, over time, the sand around the hooches would turn brown and then black from a constant rain of unseen particles that fell onto it from the inhabitants of our little town. Enlisted men brought home droplets of turbine engine oil, chopped tobacco leaves from the discarded end of a cigarette, crumbs from an almost finished

—

sandwich and red dust from a forward fire base medivac site.

This constant supply of nutrients fed an unseen army of microorganisms that laid dormant on the beach until we showed up and started to nourish them. As a result of this feeding, the little sand bugs grew fat and multiplied causing the color of the sand around them to turn slowly from white to brown and then to black.

When the sand turned black it had the adhesive quality of industrial glue which bound the grains together. They never moved again when the wind blew through hooch land. Thanks to the constant ocean breezes, thin layers of fresh white sand drifted in and around our town all year long.

This fresh white sand covered over the adhesive black dirt and produced the next layer for our little growing colonies of bacteria to move into. Whenever you walked off the sandbag pathways that were constructed between the dwellings, your boots would pick up two or three layers of this nastiness which would then be deposited on the floor of the next hooch you entered.

Growing in the nearby tidal swamps were unknown tropical diseases, sand fleas, mosquitoes and little tiny biting flies, also known as no-see-ums. Because of the bugs and the assorted disgusting diseases that they carried, the military sprayed the waterline all around the base almost every day with super bug poison in an attempt to kill off most of these miniature pests.

Once or twice a week they even came on the base and drove around with their official green ten wheeled fogging truck. This five-ton truck had an oversized red hot burner in the bed which emitted a diesel fuel based chemical smoke that consisted primarily of DDT as its active ingredient.

The truck would drive slowly down each road with a driver who was wearing a regulation gas mask, hazmat suit and gloves. A dark gray killer fog would boil out of the back of the bug truck after striking its red hot mobile burner. A motor driven blower would then blast the cloud twenty feet upward into the air.

Oily DDT smoke would slowly settle onto the ground, drifting with the wind into all of the living and working areas. Even during the workday this death fog was so dense that other vehicles on the road had to come to a complete stop and wait until it dissipated.

The vapors would enter into every hooch and building on the base leaving a light oily residue on every surface it touched. I have to admit, it did its job exceedingly well because the next day you could go into all the shops and find dead little insect carcasses all over the workbenches and desks. What did all of us actually know about the lingering effects of this diesel fuel and DDT bug killer back in 1970? The only thing we knew for sure was that it worked great and the bugs stayed away.

For us, at that time and in that place, dead bugs were all that mattered.

Each of the hundred or so multi-person living quarters was made using the same cookie cutter dimensions and materials. Row upon row of little plywood boxes, each sitting alone on concrete pillars about two feet off the ground with their exterior walls painted using official Marine Corps green paint. Each hooch was framed out with 2 x 4s and then the floor and walls were covered with

—

plywood while the roof was made up of corrugated galvanized steel sheets also on a wooden frame.

No insulation had been included in the official design to deaden the sound of the tropical rainstorms or minimize the inward radiated heat from the building's sun baked galvanized steel roof. Each roof was given a nice slope and a healthy overhang so the rains of the monsoon season would run off quickly and channel the water away from the building.

Screens in place of glass for the windows and more steel roofing material that was hinged on the top gave us a combination of sun awning and adjustable device to keep out a portion of the monsoon wetness.

Power was limited to one single power cable coming into the slum which had the capacity to handle exactly thirty amps, for our safety, of course. Thirty amps was all the energy we were supposed to have for lighting, refrigeration, radios and running our tape decks. Somehow we didn't believe that this was ever going to be adequate for our needs.

The first assignment in upgrading our slum was to bribe the enlisted power distribution person so that he installed oversized wires running from the main transformer pole into our little tin box. We checked the gage and length of the wires and figured they were good for one hundred amps, at least.

Next we went into our slum's electrical distribution box and replaced the official thirty-amp fuse with a nice group of aircraft circuit breakers that we got from an Air Force C-130 squadron over in Da Nang. Given our new found electrical freedom and our access into an unlimited supply of multi strand aircraft wire the only limits in electrical hooch life was our creativity.

We were the avionics shop for the squadron so we were required to have the best lighting in the neighborhood. Somehow a competition had developed between the different squadrons involving hooch lighting and power usage.

Hooch dwellers never had any concerns about moderation because we were at the unregulated consumption end of a line of goodies stretching all the way back to the Pentagon in Washington D.C.

About once a year this unbridled consumption of electricity would come to the attention of the base commander after he started getting increasingly urgent letters from the MMAF power company. It seems base usage was going up to the point where they were going to have to start instituting rolling blackouts or request additional generators.

The next day official letters would go out to all of the squadrons about this rule or that rule and before long, out would come the wire cutters. To satisfy our bosses and to keep them from having to enter into hooch land for an inspection, we agreed to return our home built power distribution systems back to Marine Corps standards and hide the extra wires, for a little while anyway.

When they were designing our little hooch city they found that on occasion the South China Sea would come inland to the location where our homes were projected to be built and turn everything wet and unsatisfactory for living, even for the Marines.

—

The answer to this problem consisted of dredging enough sand from somewhere to raise the entire hooch land building site an additional two feet above the standard high tide elevation. The designers cut the tops off of hundreds of fifty-five-gallon steel drums, filled them with sand and buried them two feet down in a line that formed the eastern wall of our community.

This wall protected our sand island from erosion and gave us something else to fall off of when retuning home after a long night of fighting and alcohol consumption at the enlisted man's club.

From the rear of our hooch we placed a single piece of temporary steel runway matting, anchored on one end to prevent movement and extended the other end a little more than two feet into space past the drum wall. This had the appearance of your basic steel pirate's plank and on occasions actually served that purpose.

The truth was that we had become incredibly lazy and didn't want to walk an additional twenty-five yards to the provided official restroom facility. The pirate's plank became our nighttime urinal which was always rinsed sparkly clean every time there was an unusually high tide.

We were so becoming one with nature.

As there was one mess hall on base for the enlisted servants, there was also one shower, but it was a big shower. It had features that displayed an understanding of what its basic function was and others where the designers must have been on drugs when they planned this thing.

It was constructed in a well thought out location in the middle of enlisted hooch land and it had more shower heads than were ever needed at one time. No waiting in the blowing sand to take a shower at this place. Step right up, if you dared. The primary problem, which was never corrected during all the time we were there, was with the 220-volt hot water heaters.

It wasn't that we didn't have enough hot water because we always did. The issue was that the water heaters were always covered in water spray from leaking pipes and rusted fittings.

After a while this wetness got inside the shell of the water heaters becoming one with their exposed electrical wires, switches and thermostats. This constant spray caused both the entire bank of water heaters and the galvanized steel pipes that were connected to them to become electrified.

These electrified steel pipes went all the way back inside the shower room where they took on the appearance of common ordinary chrome plated brass shower handles. While they looked common, they were in fact, electrified chrome plated brass shower handles. I mean they were, knock you on your naked ass, electrified chrome plated brass shower handles.

Sometimes you could grab a knob and nothing happened, other times you felt like the target dummy at a Taser electroshock weapon range. We tried rubber gloves that we stole from the Navy Corpsmen, but the water went inside the glove and zap, you were on your ass again. Sometimes we would bring sticks to move the knobs but it was impossible to adjust the temperature with a wet stick.

Wearing flip flops didn't help because of another fine design mistake they made. The six inch cast iron drain pipes, (think large electrical grounding pipes), went from the floor of the shower room directly into the salt water of the South China

—

Sea. They worked fine when the tide was out but when it was high tide city, we stood in salt water up to our ankles and still got shocked every time we touched the handles.

We eventually found a workable solution that solved our problems with the electrified chrome plated brass handles. We learned to never shut the showers off. Just let them go all day long. Everyone got their shower and no one got shocked anymore. Problem solved for us, but it's a good thing we didn't have to pay the water bill at that place.

One of the first things we had to do when we got to MMAF was to attend a mandatory lecture from the Navy Corpsmen who took care of our medical and emotional needs. They provided us with true horrid tales about the local women who lurked outside the base just waiting to have their way with any unsuspecting Marine who passed by one of their stinky mud huts.

These ladies were referred to by the medical establishment as bad girls with interesting diseases. We were told by the corpsman, using graphic and colorful terms, how, upon a single contact, we would be closely associated with these diseases for life.

Our Navy friend said these evil things would happen to us if we ever stopped at the home of one of these ladies for an unsanctioned afternoon delight. Instead of deterring us, these tales of great sexual adventure produced a subject of conversation and interest that lasted for a good two days.

It is said that curiosity killed the air crewman.

The other medical horror story about life in our new home had to do with malaria. The local mosquitoes who escaped the swamp patrols and the spray trucks were carriers of the

—

most common form of malaria. Quite accurately we were told that if we didn't take our weekly anti-malaria horse tablet, our bodies would become infected with the disease.

The big problem with malaria was that it could be prevented but if you ever caught it, you could never be cured. The Corpsman was correct about living with malaria but the pills were horrible both because of their size and taste.

To us these tablets looked like fat slices taken from the center of a pale yellow golf ball but the reality was, they didn't taste nearly as good as they looked.

What we didn't know about at the time, involved the long lasting effects of this medication which had the official name of Chloroquine. It seems that when you take this drug and are exposed to either Agent Orange or Malathion, which we were, then you have greatly increased the possibility of contracting Parkinson's disease later in life. To our leaders this was a small price for us to pay in this war to win the hearts and minds of the local citizens of Vietnam.

One good deal after another, as we always used to say.

There were many ways to get into serious trouble while living at MMAF. The first and most popular way was by the over consumption of alcoholic beverages which caused you to do things that you sometimes later regretted, if you remembered.

Number one on my list of things not to do involved a serious drinker who was also a member of our squadron. It was his belief late one night that he was being "bad mouthed" by a member of another helicopter squadron who was living close to our plywood hovel.

—

89

On this night, our boy finishes off the remnants of his liquor bottle and announces in a loud voice that he is going to kick someone's ass.

Not believing for a minute that we could stop him and also not wanting to miss this evening's entertainment, we encouraged his virtuous desire for revenge. He staggered out the door and actually made it down to the other hooch where he started calling everyone in that squadron very bad names.

This activity resulted in him getting his ass beat in a thoroughly convincing manner by assorted members of that squadron who had nothing better to do for entertainment that evening.

When he was done being a punching bag, he slowly made his way back to our hooch. Not being one to lick his wounds, which he couldn't feel at this point, and suffer in silence, he decided he was going to teach that entire squadron a lesson.

He stood before us, somewhat upright while wearing his ripped uniform shirt which was covered with white beach sand and tinted red from his own blood. He proceeded to tell us what horrible people lived down the path from our beach house and exactly what he intended to do to them this time.

This all sounded more than reasonable to us. With additional words of encouragement from our group we pointed him in the right direction and watched him go slowly go off into the darkness to meet his destiny.

On his way to tonight's second battle, he stopped at another hooch where he grabbed a CS gas grenade, (CS gas is used as a military riot control form of tear gas). With grenade firmly in hand he continued on to the scene of his original humiliation.

Upon arrival he yelled the appropriate derogatory comments at his opponents which cause them to abandon their drinking and rush for the door. When their screen door slammed open our boy releases the spoon on the CS grenade which ignites its two second fuse.

This is the first step in tossing it inside. Being incredibly drunk, he forgot he needed to do two things. Be rude to your opponent first and throw the grenade second.

He only managed the lip flapping thing but forgot about the grenade throwing thing.

After about two seconds it ignited and began to burn with a chemical fire that bubbled the paint on the outside of its steel shell. Still standing there our boy stopped talking and looked at his hand which is now smoking badly. He realizes what has happened, drops the grenade at his feet and takes a deep breath so he can scream in pain.

—

All he sucks in is a cloud of CS gas in a concentrated form which does not improve his situation in life one little bit. He can't see because of the burning gas, his hand is on fire and there is a river of snot coming out of his nose. Time to leave but when he turns to run away he trips and falls face down in the sand.

His opponents along with the rest of that squadron have all come out to watch the entertainment. They are all laughing at the funniest thing they have seen so far this year. Some members of our squadron put on gas masks and ran down to this disaster area.

They searched through the clouds of stinky teargas and recovered our fallen warrior. Half carrying and half dragging, they return this drunken disaster to the avionics hooch for examination. Damages include possible broken ribs and maybe one finger along with lots of burns and interesting blisters on the palm and fingers of his right hand.

Snot was still running down his face and had covered the front of his shirt, a result of the CS gas after he got a snoot full. We all concluded that this was not a bad night's work; it was just a shame he wouldn't remember it the next day.

Later he was in so much pain as the alcohol wore off we couldn't get any sleep with all the noise he was making moaning and thrashing around. We stopped a jeep that was driving by hooch land and loaded him up in the back. He was then driven to sick bay where we left him there by the front door. I know it was a juvenile thing to do, but we rang the doorbell and then hauled ass into the night. The medical staff took him in and ended up keeping him for three days.

The morning after the great CS gas adventure the doctor from sick bay called our squadron duty officer. He told him

—

that the hospital was keeping one of his people for observation. Later in the day he also provided our Commanding Officer with a complete list of hooch warrior's injuries. The officer in charge of his shop wanted to know what happened to "gas man" that night and who was to blame for his extensive injuries?

We didn't have the heart to tell him that old Dumbo, the drunken elephant, did it to himself. As usual, we didn't see anything and we didn't know anything.

Marine Light Helicopter Squadron 167 had been formed a couple of years earlier in Vietnam from discarded aircraft and unneeded technicians from other squadrons. It is said that all of the pilots for this new squadron came from a list of those who were either too sick to complain or away on leave when this historic event took place.

At this time in 1970 our entire aircraft fleet consisted of about twenty Bell UH-1Es, generally known as Hueys. The E model had a shorter airframe along with a less powerful Lycoming engine than most of the common Army Hueys in Vietnam at that time. We quickly found out that most of our common helicopter parts were interchangeable with the Army UH-1C model and Army parts were always available just across the runway by theft or for the right price.

At our base, the war in Vietnam was kind of like a day job in one of those old factory towns in the 1800s. You had the factory owned housing where all the peasants had to live and the company store where you got to spend your company issued money. Instead of the get up and go to work steam whistle we had an eager clerk from the office section that had not moved up the corporate ladder to full time paper pusher. He was assigned the official duty of whistle boy.

–

This little clerk would have a list of all of the aircraft that were needed for the day's early activities along with the names of all the people needed to make these aircraft zoom into the sky. At about 0400 hours this troll like creature would go from hooch to hooch waking everyone up by falling over something or someone left in the aisle.

At this point he would give up trying to be stealthy and just turn on all the hooch lights. This was enough of a disturbance that all of the required people were out the door on time and walking in the right direction.

This early wakeup gave you time to detour to the mess hall and eat breakfast, if you felt up to it. After chow you were required to navigate the roads to the squadron hangar in total darkness. The prevailing theory being that operational streetlights gave the bad guys something to aim at and flashlights were for sissies or new guys. It was better in the long run to get lost and walk into a gray metal building or roadside ditch than to fire up the flashlight and be called a sissy by your co-workers.

There was one additional surprise that awaited every new guy on his quiet early morning foot commute through the blackness that was Vietnam. Our base had perimeter security that was provided for us through the courtesy of the grunts. This security consisted of real riflemen manning the gates, the fence lines at night and a heavy weapons platoon.

The heavy weapons platoon consisted of four 81mm (3.2 inch) mortar tubes that were set up in a cluster in the center of the base, across the road from the first hangar that we went by on our morning slog to work. They had these mortars set up where they could defend the base in any direction with high explosive rounds if we were being attacked.

—

At night they also provided illumination rounds at random intervals or when requested by the perimeter guards to light up the fence line. Essentially they could drop a flare round down the tube anytime they wanted to.

As you walked in the darkness on your way to work the mortar men would silently wait in anticipation until there was an appropriate group of people talking like FNG's on the road across from their position. They would then take an 81mm illumination round and leave all four bags of nitrocellulose powder propellant attached to it for maximum explosive effect during launch.

When the new guys were at their closest point they would drop the round down the tube and the new guys' world would explode. From total darkness their entire world would instantly turn bright white from the flash and the explosion would make their ears hurt for hours. It was quite impressive and incredibly startling when you are not expecting it and the new guys were never expecting anything on that scale.

Complaints directed toward the mortar crews were always responded to with roars of laughter from inside their concertina wire fenced compound.

Worker bees who had been around the block and knew the tricks of the wily mortar men would listen for the telltale sound of a mortar round being dropped into the tube before it hit the firing pin and blasted upward and out on its way.

It made a very distinctive sound usually preceded by muffled giggling from inside the grunt's heavy weapons compound. This would give the experienced person time to close their eyes and cover their ears.

—

If you didn't get lost in the sand or attacked by the mortar crew, you would finally arrive at the office and were now ready to start your twelve-hour day fighting the war. The first requirement for your workday is the ever present coffee pot for your mandatory cup of lifer juice. After that liquid refreshment, your next stop is the avionics assignment desk where your first official task for the day sits before you in black and white.

Oh, hold me back
.

Bad UHF radios and navigation gear were the primary problems that were on the fix-it-list almost every morning. Most of the time these problems could be resolved by just replacing the radio's black box and then, as if by magic, the aircraft radio worked.

Everyone involved would pat themselves on the back, write up a long and detailed narrative report about the skills and man hours required to complete this task. They would then go and visit friends in other shops, far away from their own. Because black box failure was so common, we never checked anything else first. Change black box, check radio, get more coffee.

On the rare occasion when that didn't bring the system back to life, we were required to open little doors and crawl around inside the bird and actually find out what the problem was. Bad connectors, bad control modules or broken transmitter switches usually came in second place as to why the radio was dead. If that didn't fix the problem, then it was time to send the junior technician inside the hangar for additional coffee and the UH-1E aircraft wiring and systems diagrams manual.

—

About this time one of us would remember where we were and the places where these aircraft had been flying during the day. When the junior technician returned with the book we would then have him crawl into the ever-present oil puddle under the aircraft and look upward with a flashlight for AK-47 holes in the skin of the helicopter. Most of the time he would find that a bullet had gone in through the bottom and cut one of the radio's wire bundles, causing the radio failure.

Good thing they spent so much time sending us to school to learn all that wire and radio repair stuff.

A cut wire bundle was designated to be beyond our level of repair competence so the aircraft was then shipped off to the base headquarters and maintenance squadron, (H&MS-16), where the grand wizards of repair were located.

Almost all of the bullets that hit our planes always came up from the bottom. If you had some of the machine guns or rocket pods in operation at the time the aircraft was struck you wouldn't even know it, unless the bullet hit a crew member.

Little AK-47 bullet holes were not uncommon and usually produced an immediate secondary problem so even our newest pilots knew it was time to go back to the shop for repairs. Multiple bullet holes created multiple problems which caused even the most obtuse squadron pilot to return back to base, quick like a bunny.

The Huey was actually large enough that the occasional round could enter into the bottom of the ship, not hit anything vital and go unnoticed for days. A bullet strike in one of the rotor blades was a different matter altogether.

When you got hit in the blade with an AK round, the change in airflow would cause a noticeable whistle. No need to worry about that. Even multiple AK rounds could be fixed with some blade tape and a little squirt of magic blade goop inside the hole. Main rotor blades could always be repaired unless the round hit one of the main spars in the blade. When that happened the blade was removed from the aircraft, stuck in a box and sent off to Japan for a rebuild.

When one of the birds had been hit in the rotor blade and it was doing the AK-47 whistle, there was an established protocol to follow. The pilots would very slowly fly their wounded machine down the main taxiway towards the front of the hangar so that everyone would have time to gather, observe and comment.

This observation allowed the gathering crowd to place bets as to the number of holes in the blades based upon the sounds they were hearing. At some point one of the majors, who had been designated as squadron maintenance officer, would emerge from the rear of his cave. With a look of

—

perpetual exasperation on his face, he would tell the pilots to shut down. The blades would stop rotating and everyone would give them a close inspection whereupon a general consensus would be reached regarding the total number of bullet holes that were observed.

Winners and losers would be determined and military play money would be exchanged between all players.

At the conclusion of this break from routine, everyone would trudge back to their jobs and babble on about how lucky the aircrew was. The next step in this progression would be when the old timers started telling everyone, tales of past helicopter crashes while all the new guys stood around listening with focused attention.

Story telling is a proud tradition in the Marine Corps and it is important to learn each and every detail, true or not, for later enhancement and retelling. This went on until the maintenance officer came by again, scowled and sent everyone retreating back into their own shops. The troops would hide in there and pretend to do something useful until he went off to bother someone else.

Wars, like every other major business, had always been fought during the daytime hours and Vietnam was no exception. Now there were always some people who had to get up extra early to make breakfast and a few who stayed at the hangar overnight, cleaning the offices or fixing machines that were damaged on the job during the day.

The command staff that was running the war in the Pentagon must have figured out that they needed to be extra tricky in their planning to defeat the North Vietnamese Army, (NVA). They came up with a plan that called for airborne attacks at the break of dawn. I guess they figured

—

that the NVA would still be asleep in their little hammocks out in the open and we would catch them before breakfast, or some such nonsense.

This day our squadron got up in the early morning darkness so that we could be ready to strike our communist enemies at first light. Now just because we had been using this same tactic from day one didn't mean that the North Vietnamese Army wouldn't be totally surprised this time.

The NVA are out in the field carrying on their backs, all their weapons, ammunition and rice to last each one of them a month. They have walked or ridden bicycles along hundreds of miles of jungle trails all the way down from Hanoi and we are going to surprise them with helicopters that you can hear from ten miles away, by attacking at dawn?

This example of strategic planning is why we have had so much success up to this point and why the war was already lost.

It's the middle of the jungle and you can't even see the ground much less little people wearing green uniforms with leaves and branches attached. But our squadron does its duty and attacks the designated target with everything we had.

We kill lots of trees, vines and small jungle creatures that were too stupid to run away when the first white phosphorus marker rocket hit the ground. We shoot, climb and turn, then come back and shoot some more. Bullets and rockets are flying everywhere and the ground shakes with the force of our attack.

It is very impressive.

—

All ammunition is expended so our squadron's aircraft fly home at the end of another successful mission. Our leaders are pleased because all ordinance was delivered on target without the loss of a single aircraft. The grunts riding around in the transport helicopters are also pleased. With the jungle being too dense no one was able to find a landing site large enough for the transport helicopters to set down so the troops could get out and stretch their legs a little bit. The men were all looking forward to a stroll in the bush where they could be bitten by spiders or have a leach or two attach itself to their legs.

Even the NVA was happy with this display. None of their people were injured and it allowed them to take a break from their journey southward during the time when we were flying around. For most of them, this is the first time they have seen an actual American close air support mission and it gave their officers another opportunity to drive home some of the lessons they were taught up north in NVA school. Even though their unit is a long way from this aerial display they wouldn't take the chance of discovery by continuing their march until they can no longer hear the sound of our helicopters.

They are mighty tricky, these NVA guys.

For wars to be won military equipment has to be tested, cleaned and then inspected. It makes perfect sense for mechanical equipment but not so much for hangars. Every couple of months someone high in the chain of command would send down a letter saying that on such and such a day they would be in the area conducting a squadron inspection.

Oh how those words brought joy to the hearts of every squadron commander and his underlings. Now in addition

—

to the regular requirements of keeping his aircraft in the air and launching for all assigned missions, there is an inspection of the squadron on the horizon.

The question of what to do and who can I dump this on goes through his military mind.

Upon being informed of the upcoming event, each of the different division commanders is now required to update all his manuals and records for this inspection. Next they are told to clean their shops along with the hangar deck. Lastly make sure those men who rarely take showers or wash their uniforms are gone for this one day. Nothing will screw up a well-executed inspection faster than the 1st Marine Air Wing Colonel waking into one of the shops and meeting face to face with lance corporal pig pen.

When they say cleaning what they are really saying is, the FNGs will clean the shops and the hangar deck while real people continue to do actual work. It is understood that new guys have no other value. First step is to have all the peasants gather together and receive precise instructions about tomorrow's day of cleaning from the least valuable sergeant they can find. "We will start here first thing tomorrow morning; we will go here and go there then finish the day with a complete scrub down of the hangar floor". All for the glory of the Corps, we are told.

To a man we just cannot wait for the joy that tomorrow will bring us.

The cleaning started on schedule, first thing in the morning and by lunch time the "rent a sergeant", announces that the offices and the heads, (bathrooms), look better than when we started. An earthshaking accomplishment if I have ever heard one. This guy must have gotten promoted because his father was a general or something. We are told that the hangar floor will be done after lunch so come back at exactly thirteen hundred hours.

The fluids that we use on the aircraft for parts cleaning came to us in either fifty-five gallon drums or five gallon containers both of which were painted green with the chemical name and manufacturer stenciled on the outside. Most of us had never heard of any of this stuff before we went into the military and at the time we used it, none of us understood how it would affect us.

Like the men who worked with Agent Orange and loaded it onto the aircraft, we were given five gallon cans of this stuff and never told how to safely use it. No one had masks or protective gear of any kind, not even gloves. The most common stuff that we used every day for cleaning aircraft parts and weapons was Methyl Ethyl Ketone or MEK along with Carbon Tetrachloride.

Carbon Tetrachloride was originally used as a fire extinguisher agent until it was found that when it was squirted on a fire, the heat caused phosgene gas to form. Phosgene is the same chemical that was used in WW I inside poison nerve gas shells to kill lots of the enemy. This was very nasty stuff but it is safe enough for us to use for cleaning with our bare hands and a rag.

With a joy in our hearts for the upcoming cleaning event we arrive a little after 1300 hours and shuffle into the hangar. All of the aircraft that could be moved outside have been relocated. There was one UH-1E, designated as official hangar queen. This machine was in such a state of disrepair, no one wanted to take the chance of structural failure by moving it, so there in a lonely corner of the hangar it sat. It was in this case that paperwork magic was brought in to save the day.

HML-167 Aircraft Hangar

All required parts that were needed to make this shell airworthy again were shown to be on back order. On inspection day the Colonel was told, "Any day now these parts would arrive and this queen will fly again". We didn't believe that crap and neither did the Colonel who was not nearly as dumb as most of the staff officers we had met.

The truth was that the Marine supply system was in such disrepair that this machine would never move again, except with a tractor, until we went over to the Army parts supply people and said, "Let's make a deal".

To clean the hangar floor everyone, meaning all the peasants, got their push brooms and in a disciplined, military manner, swept all the sand, dead bugs, assorted nuts, bolts and small parts, out of the hangar and into a pile which was then made to disappear.

We returned to our starting positions and did the same thing except this time we wet the floor down with twenty or thirty gallons of Carbon Tetrachloride and used our brooms to scrub it into the floor. This instantly removed all of the grease and paint stains from the concrete. We scrubbed and moved the puddle of chemical slush around the floor until it was as clean as possible. Then we took air hoses and blasted the wet concrete floor with compressed air until the chemical vaporized and left the floor clean and dry.

Each one of us smelled like that stuff for days. It got into our clothes, our hair and soaked our boots like we had walked in a puddle of stinky rainwater. I was amazed that no one passed out and had to be carried away due to chemical fumes. The one good thing was that my hands were the cleanest they had been for a long time.

With the great inspection over, we could return to our normal every day existence in the avionics shop without anyone looking over our shoulder and making us take extra showers.

Chapter 5

Time for a Change
Total U.S. killed as of September 1970 in the Vietnam War: 53,889

Without ever saying a word, every aviation squadron in the world divides itself into two groups, squadron members who fly and squadron members who wish they could.

Being a non-flying member of any squadron causes you to be looked down upon as an earthbound second class citizen. The analogy is being assigned as a member of a Rifle Company and your job is such that you don't carry a rifle. You are, "In the rear, with the gear". This happens no matter what your rank or job title is and there is only one cure.

Flying means freedom from a world that tries its best to tie you down. Become a flightless worker bee in any of the squadron shops and they have you nailed down each and every day. You are told what time to arrive, what to do after you arrive and when you can leave.

The sergeant bee stands around grasping a clipboard complete with multiple forms and an official checklist so that it looks like he has something important to do. He makes sure all the boxes are checked in a precise military manner before you are allowed to buzz on to your next mind numbing job in the squadron hive.

A flying assignment means all those little jobs still have to get done but they have to find someone else to do them or the little clipboard holders can just wait until you return to earth and then try to find you.

Good luck with that one, sergeant bee.

—

One of the oddities of life in every aviation squadron is that first thing every morning, rain or shine, everyone, meaning all the worker bees, get to participate in a futile exercise known as FOD walk.

FOD stands for Foreign Object Damage because it seems in real aircraft squadrons little pieces of metal, cigarette butts or sea shells could get sucked into an aircraft's engine and do a lot of damage.

So as dictated to by the official rules, everyone, every morning gets to stand in a long line and walk slowly along, looking for anything that isn't part of the flight line. Pick the offending item up and take it to the bag being held by the head FOD bee. At the end of the walk all of our leaders can look at the collected trash and say what a wonderful job they had done today.

The truth is that plain old beach sand did more damage to the blades and engines of our aircraft than any FOD that was ever left on a flight line or put into a bag.

Aviation for most people has always meant fighting your way down a long carpeted isle inside a plastic paneled aluminum tube and franticly searching the overheads for your assigned seat number. Find your seat, stuff your junk into a tiny overhead bin and then buckle up. This isn't flying; this is riding in a 652 mile per hour, (.85 Mach) Boeing bus that will take you and two hundred other unhappy cattle to your destination.

Sit at the window seat if you are adventurous and watch the world go by at forty-one thousand feet inside your pressurized flying can. Flying today is a means to complete a journey that most people would rather not experience, but because of the constraints of time and distance, they have no other choices.

In our world of rotary flight, we didn't care where we were going or when we would get back. There were no scheduled meetings to attend or long commutes home after work. We lived just for the pleasure of the flight mixed with a little anticipation about our actual physical survival.

The view from my office window

Most of the time we felt like eight-year-old kids riding in the back of dad's pickup truck as it sped along a country road with no stop signs in sight. That was a time in life before stifling government rules. It was a time when we could move around anywhere inside the bed or stick our heads over the side and let the blast of wind push our faces into funny shapes.

Today our helicopter, like those pickup trucks of our childhood, allows us to live in that old fashion unsafe world. My world was restricted only by a well-founded fear of gravity and the boundaries of movement imposed by the limitations of the aircraft's aluminum cargo deck.

My flying pickup truck can follow the road if it likes or it can skim just above the surface of one of the many dark winding rivers in our area. One thousand horsepower allowed my machine to slowly climb high into the mountains just west of our base or skim across the tops of the ripening fields of green rice causing startled domesticated water buffalo to scatter in all directions. And like that truck of old we still get to sit in the back, open to the elements and by sticking our faces out into the wind stream we can still make the same funny faces at all of the unfortunate earthbound locals.

My transfer from California to MMAF got me into the action but I was not yet in a position where I could return to flying. In my last duty assignment, I had also started out in the avionics shop where I was just one of a hundred lost souls.

We were so overstaffed that three or four of us would go out on each service call just so we could keep up to speed with fixing aircraft radio problems. Whenever a call came in to the avionics shop, mamma duck would gather up all of her baby ducks and we would all go waddling along in a line out to the job. When the opportunity popped up in my old California squadron to transfer over to the flight line I took the big leap and never looked back.

My time away from the aviation side of the Marine Corps during pre-Vietnam leave and Staging Battalion had caused

—

me to forget all about the horrors of the avionics shop and being a fat baby duck. After a month of fixing radios, patching wires and adjusting antennas I remembered why I was sick of this electronics crap and figured now was the right time to take a step up the helicopter food chain.

Because of the thirteen-month rotation schedule there was always a daily parade of, "old timers", packing up their trash in anticipation of heading across the pond and back home to the land of the big PX. This caused all of the shops to always be in a state of transition and turmoil as their most skilled technicians left and everyone else moved up the ladder.

I figured that there were always openings for talented individuals who were willing to display a little initiative along with some personal horn tooting. One day, while doing something incredibly useless involving electronics, I noticed a going away party for one of the senior crew chiefs on the flight line.

Bright and early the very next day I was sitting at the desk of the lieutenant in charge of flight line. He got to listen to my tales of woe about working in a shop full of tweets and my longing to return to my rightful place in life which was riding around on a thin nylon seat in the back of a helicopter.

He dug up my personnel jacket and found that I already had a secondary MOS as a UH-1E mechanic and crew chief. The paperwork showed that I had met all of the qualifications needed to take the exams in this or any other Huey squadron. After our little conversation, he stated that he would chat with the head of the avionics shop and the major who was in charge of all the repair divisions about my transfer.

—

The next day I got transferred to the flight line. This was either do to the fact that I was so exceedingly qualified that the air operations officer realized that my superb talents were being wasted in the radio shop or the flight line just needed more warm bodies. Throw in the fact that the avionics shop was tired of all of my self-serving whining and I was gone.

Good bye radios with static and hello flight time.

My study guide for aviation freedom was the NATOPS (Naval Air Training and Operating Procedures Standardization) manual which surprisingly, was not an aircraft repair manual. It was a procedures document that covered almost every single event that might come up in the care and feeding of this machine.

The way NATOPS worked was like this. If something happened to your aircraft that was bad, the flight review board or the squadron commanding officer would break out the old NATOPS manual and see what it said. If the book said you were not allowed to do what you just did, then you can just hang your head in shame because the verdict is already in and you are dead meat.

If the book did not specifically prohibit your actions, you have now crossed your first hurdle toward aviation forgiveness. While the flight review board or the squadron commanding officer gets to hand out punishments for alleged transgressions, NATOPS writes the law.

The first step to flight time in Vietnam involved taking the aircraft NATOPS manual with me everywhere I went. With this big blue book in my hands I felt like a seminarian at his first day of class with a new bible. Ahead of me were open book tests, closed book tests, practical mechanical tests and

—

then flight tests. The end of the road was a final check ride which would then place me at the bottom of the crew chief pecking order.

That may have been the bottom of the barrel in some people's minds but for me; I was going to be on top of the world again.

After passing all of the written tests I was issued a couple of green flight suits, black leather steel toe boots and a nice new helmet for riding around in proper crew chief style.

The next phase involved spending my working days as a mechanic on the UH-1E flight line, getting my hands dirty and relearning all of my helicopter's specialized needs.

As you could imagine with our location and all of the flight hours, sand clogging up the particle separator (air filter) was a major issue. The book said to check it every twenty-five hours but here it was cleaned after every day of flight. Take the screen box apart, reach in with your hand and scoop out sand, twigs, assorted dead insects and bird feathers. Wipe it down with stinky cleaning compound, snap it all back together and now you are ready for the next day.

One of the more interesting functions that we had to perform was the monthly cleaning of the compressor blades on the helicopter's gas turbine engine. It seems that when we are flying in this area, a thin sticky film would build up on all of the rotating and stationary blades of the compressor section.

If we don't remove these layers of goop, then the engine will develop compressor stalls or hiccups while it is running. The word hiccup makes it sound nice and pleasant but the reality is kind of like a one thousand horsepower gas turbine engine that has issues with backfiring.

Hear it once, especially at night and you will never forget it.

As with most things, the cure for the problem is simple to explain but hard to accomplish. Put five gallons of good old Methyl Ethyl Ketone film killing solvent into an oversize garden sprayer then climb up and stand on the deck behind the transmission. Pump the MEK onto the engine

—

compressor blades with your sprayer nozzle while the electric starter turns the turbine blades. After that's done, quickly hand the sprayer can to someone on the ground to fill with water.

One of the pilots will start the engine while you are squeezed into the space between the engine intake, the rotor mast and the rotating blades of death directly above your head. The MEK solvent breaks the bond between the slime and the compressor blades but you need to remove it from the engine. For that you need to take the spray can that is now full of water, hose down the intake and flush out all the MEK / sludge. Next reach into a cloth bag containing five pounds of finely ground up walnut shells and slowly toss these chips into the intake, one handful at a time.

Here is the picture. Your head is between the engine intake and the two-foot-wide stainless steel rotating main rotor blades with the engine screaming so loud that you will have lost your ability to hear anything for the next four hours. Try to slowly toss the walnut shells into the engine intake without losing your footing on the oil covered deck or have the bag ripped from your hands by the volume of air being sucked into the engine.

Do everything correctly and you will still get about ten percent of the walnut shells kicked back into your face by the steel compressor blades rotating at 10,000 rpm inside their outer casing. The remaining ninety per cent go through the engine with a great poof of burning wood and exit out the exhaust of the engine with a shower of red sparks.

This cleaning is always scheduled for the end of the day because when you are done with that job you are more worthless than normal. The remainder of the evening will

—

be spent picking tiny walnut shell pieces out of your face while your hearing returns to normal.

Knowing what you are going through, your fellow worker bees will do whatever they can to torment you during your time of suffering.

All of the main rotor blade leading edges had stainless steel caps to protect them from sand abrasion. The caps helped to slow the rate of destruction but they couldn't stop it. At the conclusion of each day we would climb up on top of the helicopter and examine the stainless steel leading edges for tiny pin holes caused by the sand.

There was no repair at our location for that type of damage so if we found holes above a certain size then these blades would be removed from the rotor head, put in metal boxes and sent away to Japan to join their brothers that had too many AK-47 holes in them.

After a short period of time as junior mechanic and low peasant on the flight line, I was moved up the ladder to junior boy in the flight training program. Every morning I would go out in the darkness to do the pre-flight checks on the helicopter and then the regular crew chief would come out to inspect my work.

It didn't take long before my less than meticulous instructor stayed in the flight line drinking coffee and telling war stories while I went out to complete the pre-flight checks. Then without as little as even a thank you very much, he would just sign off my work and go on again with his tales of great aviation adventures.

The first part of any preflight involved checking the aircraft log book. This would give you information about past

—

problems and what, if anything was done to repair them. It would also give you the name of the pilot who reported the issue.

A few of the aircraft drivers actually knew what they were talking about when they were writing up helicopter mechanical issues. Others just pulled random complaints from a cheat sheet they kept in their flight suit so they wouldn't look like complete aviation incompetents. The most important thing to learn during your time in the ready room was the name of the pilots who were going to take the aircraft up for the day.

Finding out who was assigned as your aircraft driver for the day would dictate what type of preflight inspection you would perform. Every helicopter in the entire squadron had been beaten like a $5.00 rental car and was always legally unsafe for flight due to one reason or another. That was if you went strictly by the stateside NATOPS rule book.

Luckily this fine collection of rules also provided you with the legal flexibility to determine how your day was going to start. If we knew that the pilot sitting in the right seat was a good stick and put up with little drama then of course, the bird was always up and ready to go when he showed up.

On the other hand, prima donnas found it hard to find an aircraft or crew chief ready to go when they arrived. "Always something sir; we'll have it fixed in an hour sir; I have no idea how that happened sir; we are waiting on the part to arrive so we can fix it right now sir." And on and on and on we would go.

Rolling the dog was a time honored skill that was used on known pains in the ass until they figured out they weren't going flying that morning.

—

98% of the pilots just showed up in the morning, drove the bird around for the day without destroying anything expensive and then went home. Later in the evening they might bounce down the runway once or twice in an attempt to impress their fellow flying bus drivers with their aviation skills but this never amounted to anything serious.

These wizards of Naval aviation were always home in time for happy hour at the MMAF Officers Club. Getting back to the base early allowed them to get a good spot at the bar where they could hobnob with other aircraft drivers and tell inflated stories of their war fighting ability and aviation greatness.

A couple of the pilots in our squadron should have stayed in their civilian job which we assumed was driving the clown car for a second rate traveling circus. These people had no business operating anything mechanical, much less a helicopter with three other people inside of it.

You know the type, every mistake they made was the fault of someone else or the machine wasn't set up properly. In the corporate world they usually got promoted to a small desk in a far corner of the basement. In HML-167 we all just hoped that these jerks would be transferred to HML-367, the Cobra squadron down the road where it would just be themselves and a co-pilot onboard when they crashed.

Officers like that made it very difficult to go out and just kill communists every day.

Becoming a crew chief was always a long and difficult testing process no matter where the squadron was located. I had completed the same thing at my last base so I had no doubts about being successful at this location. The only noticeable difference was that here, little Vietnamese people

—

who didn't like you would shoot at your aircraft with evil intent using automatic weapons.

We also figured that we had been shot at more than once by little Vietnamese people who did like us and had no intent at all, but they figured it was the proper thing to do at the time.

Peer pressure from the visiting Viet Cong Cadre Commander and such.

It didn't take long for the little people on the ground with the straw hats to figure out that we never could see them in the jungle. Because of this everyone wandering around with an AK-47 and some extra ammunition used to shoot at us while we were flying along just for the fun of it. If we ever got a chance to see them, we would shoot back but that was a rare event.

At best, all you would ever see is a muzzle flash in the relative darkness of the tree line as you flew by. Unless you already had your machine gun pointing in their direction when they fired, there was no use in shooting back.

At most distances to return fire would be a total waste of ammunition plus you would get the pilots all upset for no good reason. Every time the pilots heard the door guns firing they would always forget what they were supposed to be doing and then start looking around franticly. Next they would begin asking questions about why were you firing and were there people shooting at us?

We learned early on that it was important that you never tell the pilots that anyone is shooting at them. First they get all excited and then they try to do some official evasive maneuver they were taught in basic helicopter school. The next thing you know all of your junk that wasn't tied down is rolling around in the back of the bus. The standard answer we always gave was, "We were just checking out the guns, we didn't see anything unusual and nobody was shooting at us, SIR!"

I was getting ready for a mission later on in the day when they asked me to smile for a picture.

Most of the time after that, the pilots who had been in country for a while just went back to whatever they were doing and didn't ask us about it again. On the other hand, new pilots kept looking into the back of the bus to see what was going on. Every FNG was very intent in finding out what kind of trouble we were getting into back there.

It was always the new guy pilots who used to get all upset about the extra weapons we used to carry. Fragmentation and white phosphorus grenades could always be found in the pouch behind the pilot's seat. Those things always made the FNG's wet their pants.

—

When they told us to toss them over the side I would toss a couple of smoke grenades out the door and put the fragmentation grenades in the aircraft's tool box. This was a location where no pilot ever looked. We figured that just because we are not authorized to carry certain items doesn't mean that they won't come in handy later on in the day.

Some people with rank have no imagination.

The only good thing about being shot at was that it was almost impossible to hit a moving helicopter, especially if the bad guys were any distance away from us. That's not to say it didn't happen, but it was a luck factor as opposed to a shooting skill factor.

The stupid ones wouldn't just hide in the jungle and shoot at us like they were taught in Viet Cong school. These idiots would hop out their own hooch door and shoot at us when we flew by their little tin shack village, outbound on a mission. Well we couldn't stop and take care of business on the way out but if we took the same route going home, that was a different situation altogether.

I had a single shot M-79 grenade launcher with 40mm. fragmentation rounds that the pilots couldn't hear when anyone shot it, along with assorted hidden hand grenades and the occasional 60mm mortar round without any of the powder bags attached to its fins. No one liked to toss the mortar rounds because you had to whack the base of the round with a hammer. (This would really freak out the pilots if they saw that).

The mortar shell whacking was required because they all had an inertia safety in their fuse assembly that requires a 4G shock load to make the round become armed. Smack the snot out of the round once on the tail with your hammer

—

then toss it at the shack where you saw the bad guy shooting from earlier. Mortar rounds would fly straighter than one of those 2.75 rockets and make as big a bang on the ground. All this without all those annoying machine gun noises, smoke trails and questions from the pilots.

Another useful skill was to put a hand grenade in a regulation mess hall water glass to hold the spoon in place, pull the pin and toss it toward the hooch. It wouldn't go off until it hit the ground and broke the water glass. It's not nice to shoot at me when I fly by because soon it will be payback time and I have lots of nasty things in the back of my bus that will not make you happy.

Nothing between you and the ground but humid air

Our helicopters were open gunships with no doors to close and no windows to look out of. We sat on a thin piece of nylon fabric stretched tight over an aluminum alloy frame with a single automotive seatbelt to hold us in place during normal events. These normal events ranged from rough landings caused by dumb ass pilots or an unannounced practice autorotation that caused everyone to lift out of their seat for just a second.

For emergencies we designed our own safety system. Our seating area had nothing more than regular passengers in mind when it was designed and that was why it only had a single seatbelt and not a seatbelt, shoulder harness and ballistic armor plating combination, like the pilots had.

Every crew chief, with any common sense, had a nice one-inch-thick plate of ceramic armor that he sat on to stop the AK-47 nastiness from below. We also figured that if we hit anything hard while still moving forward, that single seatbelt would tighten around our waist causing us to permanently bend in half like a greasy green fortune cookie.

To solve this problem, everyone took a second seatbelt and bolted it to the firewall behind our seat about shoulder high. This setup gave us one seatbelt around our waist and another one across our chest. At least with this makeshift system in place when the time came to recover our bodies at the crash site the team wouldn't have to go wandering all over the woods looking for the big pieces.

We were very thoughtful about these types of things.

Sitting in the rear seat you could turn your head and look over the side and there would be nothing but humid air and green tree branches between yourself and the ground, hundreds of feet below.

—

Now release your seatbelt and you were free to move around the cabin, as they say. In the center of both doorways was an M-60 machine gun mount attached to the aluminum helicopter deck by an assortment of anchoring pins. You always could count on that machine gun mount being there when you lost your balance and went flying through the air toward the space where the door used to be. You could catch the gun mount with your feet as you slid across the aluminum deck towards the gunner's door or you could run your helmet into it as you fell forward. You could even grab hold of one of the large holes it had in its side as you slid by.

HML-167 Crew Chief in his natural habitat

The most important thing was not the method of stopping yourself but the prevention of an undignified rapid exit from your workplace while flying along over the jungle.

As an additional workplace bonus, the helicopter's aluminum deck was always slippery as an ice skating rink due to the polishing effect of a thousand pairs of boots and the variety of lubricating fluids that wound up on it. Jet fuel or JP-5 is just a fancy word for kerosene and it was the primary culprit responsible for our slippery helicopter decks.

Refuel the bird and you are always stepping into puddles of that stinky stuff that had been spilt on the ground from past refueling. Then add three thousand psi hydraulic oil venting out from a never ending series of small leaks and hot gun oil mist that flowed into our work space every time our six machine guns were fired.

The M-60 machine guns always loved lots of oil. We found that, unlike the M-16, there was no such thing as too much oil in their moving parts. We would carry quart sized plastic bottles full of yellow gun oil with long flexible nozzles just for keeping the guns happy.

After two runs with all the external guns firing away, both of us in the back would lean out of the cabin while the bird circled around for another run and give both guns on each side a big squirt of oil. After this, the next time the guns fired thick white oil smoke would pour from the area around the barrel but the guns would chatter away all day with no problems.

It's a slippery world we had to work in and it didn't get any better after we had used the door guns for a little while. The M-60 would suck up belted 7.62mm ammunition at the rate

–

of six hundred rounds per minute. The ammunition would enter on the left side and spit out steel retention clips and expended brass on the right, tossing everything towards the rear of the gun. To help maintain our rate of fire I would take a large gray 20mm ammo can, toss the lid away and fill it full of door gun ammunition.

We would link about seventeen hundred rounds of 7.62 ammunition together and then layer them inside the 20mm can all the way to the top. With this I could just hold the trigger down and shoot because the door gun barrel hung out in the 100 mph airstream so the M-60 overheating was not a big problem.

Another important lesson that we were taught was to always remove any explosives and sit on your tool box whenever you are lined up behind your door gun. The soft aluminum skin and floor of the helicopter would do almost nothing to stop your basic AK-47 round from going in at the bottom of the helicopter and out the top. Your body will slow it down in its travels a little bit.

On one mission while sitting on my metal toolbox I had the good fortune to observe the interaction between an AK-47 round and one of my larger crescent wrenches. While it did an excellent job in stopping this copper covered Russian message of friendship and love it also provided me with a new meaning for, pain in the ass.

When we are hard at work doing orbit and shoot, the other door gunner would come over and feed your door gun while the pilots tried to stay on target. Pull back on the trigger and let the tracers fly. Theoretically you could grind away for three minutes without having to stop shooting but that never happened. The pilots would always lose interest

—

in the target after a little while and go off to find someone else to annoy.

Fire the door gun for over one-minute steady and you had a problem with scrap metal everywhere. The six hundred steel clips weren't bad because they never moved around. They stayed in one pile and you could get rid of all of them with one swift kick and out the door they went.

The expended brass rounds, on the other hand, would never stay in one place. They were always rolling around giving me a layer of brass ball bearings on top of the oily aluminum deck right where I had to work. We would always try to kick them out the crew chief's door while the aircraft was turning for another run but we never did get them all. If we allowed any of the expended brass to go out the gunner's door they might hit the spinning tail rotor which was on that side and then I would get yelled at again.

Between the oil, the bouncing around in the sky and all the little brass ball bearings we were always falling down, falling over or slipping on something. It got so bad that the pilots wouldn't even ask what was going on unless we slipped and rolled into the cockpit area. Now we had to listen to them flap on about what a big inconvenience this was until we managed to crawl back to our assigned station in the back.

The pilots, almost to a man, were very confident in the function and safety of all of the forward firing weapons. That included both the four fixed M-60 machine guns and the two nineteen shot 2.75-inch rocket pods. They would circle around searching for a suitable target that was deserving of their ordinance.

At the theoretical maximum range of their weapons our fearless aircraft commander would push the aircraft nose down, point the bird in the general direction of the enemy and pull the trigger. Not too close now because soon it's time to pull up and turn around for another run. Now was the time that the crew chief or his assistant, got to shoot up the target or a local tree line in case anyone survived this first massive assault.

During preflight the pilots always insisted that the left side door gunner have a cam lock placed on the swivel of his M-60 so he couldn't shoot up the nose or tail of the helicopter by accident. Some of them would also demand that the gun on the crew chief's side be set up the same way.

What they didn't know was that once we were airborne and they couldn't look into the back of the bus, I would release my gun from its mount and that would negate the cam. Then, when we were in the firing run with all the machine guns going, I would lean out a little bit and put the muzzle of my machine gun right next to the pilot's door frame and let loose.

The heat and gunpowder blast from a hundred rounds or so would be enough to knock off some paint directly across from where his right ear was. That activity would usually scare the snot out of most of the new guys and after that they would leave me and my gun mount alone.

Pilots always loved the 2.75 inch rockets that we carried. We didn't care for them so much but who cared what we thought. We carried nineteen rockets on each side which had to be hand loaded into the pods but that was taken care of by the ordinance shop people back at the base. Before each flight they showed up with their "DORF" tractor

—

127

pulling their little trailer full of rockets and cases of M-60 ammunition.

The "DORF" was just a standard small FORD diesel tractor that we had switched the letters around and the name stuck. They also had flare, flechette, (finishing nails with fins), and high explosive rounds for our M-79, 40mm hand held grenade launcher which we always carried around for close up work.

If they liked, you and there was something you had to trade then there was always a supply of AK-47 rounds stashed in the back if you needed some for your personal weapon. Some of the crew chiefs had personal AK's along with other official war souvenirs / trading material that had been purchased from the grunts at the forward fire bases.

After the 2.75 inch rockets were loaded into the pods, they had to be armed in a safe location. We would taxi out to the end of the runway and point the helicopter away from the base because sometimes the rocket pods had a nasty habit of going off when they were being armed.

The danger was due to a small static electrical charge residing in the arming switch which had killed some of our people in the past. Stand off to the side; stick the arming switch into the pod without looking at it and without getting any part of your body behind the rocket pod then wait two seconds. It there were no loud noises, you were good to go.

Sometimes I really hated my job.

These rockets had been designed in WWII and had to be the most inaccurate weapon ever produced but they were still in use at this time because they made a lot of smoke and noise. Both of which got the pilots all excited. In addition, they

—

were very cheap to make which got the manufacturer all excited.

The majority of the rocket blast splatters off the front of the rocket pod

When the rockets were fired, the motor would ignite inside the pod, shooting the warhead forward with lots of smoke and flames and it would stay burning most of the way to the target.

It was our good luck that we didn't have any dates to go on those nights.

Once free of the confines of the pod, these rockets had a set of stabilizing fins that were supposed to expand and stabilize the weapon in flight all the way to its target. Most of the time they worked properly but sometimes the rocket only got one fin to open up and then it made big circles as it went in the general direction of the ground.

There was that rare occasion when no fins would come out and you had no idea where that rocket was going. They had been known to turn around and come back towards the helicopter which provided a very exciting time for everyone involved.

—

One of the great inventions of our time came into our squadron after much testing and certification. This wonder weapon was a proximity fuse for the high explosive 2.75" war heads. This fuse allowed the rocket to explode about thirty feet above what it perceived as a solid object so that an air burst could be directed downward toward the bad guys.

I guess in all of the testing they had never fired these rockets out in what is known as ripple fire. This is where the rocket button is held down and all nineteen rockets come out of the tube about half a second apart. Ripple fire is very impressive, especially if you happen to be sitting three feet away from the tube and the pilot doesn't tell you what is about to happen.

The first time we used ripple fire with the proximity fuses, all of the rockets flew out in a straight line directly towards the target. The first one went off, thirty feet or so above the ground, exactly as advertised. The second one then mistook the first one's blast for the ground and it then went off, then the third and so on all the way up the chain.

Luckily we ran out of rockets before we ran out of room. They all exploded before they got back to the rocket pod where I was sitting. From my vantage point, those rockets looked like a chain of large dirty brown firecrackers popping off, one after another and heading directly toward us. As soon as we got back to base, our squadron sent out an emergency message about what had just happened and NATOPS restricted proximity fuses to single shot use.

Over there, sometimes even your own stuff was trying to kill you.

It was always good for us when the pilots had shot the last of their rockets into the jungle because then it was time to return to MMAF. We were now a lot lighter but not much faster due to the complexities of the UH-1E rotor system, a stunning lack of horsepower and its less than aerodynamic fat nose.

Your flying badge is your Nomex flight suit, also known as the green bag. The Nomex fiber is a form of nylon that was designed to make the suit fire resistant but by the end of any work day accidental spillage of JP-5, gun oil and hydraulic fluid has rendered useless all the work of those fine chemists at DuPont.

When a flight suit became worn and ripped to the point that it was useless we would gather around its final resting place and give it a flame check. Even with our longing for adventure this was always done outside of the hooch. Some flight suits smoked and only charred, as advertised but others lit up like a wax candle on a red hot stove top.

Unspoken between all of us was the realization that clean or dirty the flight suit was never going to be a survival factor in any of the helicopter crashes that we would be involved in. The true value of this green flight bag was in the multiple large zippered pockets that it possessed.

When the bottom has fallen out of your flying machine and you are now sitting on the ground that is not the time to be looking for some of the necessities of life. A military lensatic compass, extra pocket knife, waterproof matches, snickers bar along with a waterproof map were always tucked away in my pockets.

Depending on how bad the machine had broken up on impact with the ground, you should always be able to retrieve your rifle and some extra ammunition in case you had to walk home with just your flight suit survival kit.

—

If we were flying alone and the bird went down hard the unofficial plan was to set it on fire where it landed out in the woods. Use the ax to cut a hole in the fiberglass fuel tank and then stick a lit flare into the hole. It was always important to produce a nice smoke column and bright yellow flames so everyone could find you and remove all of the bodies and any survivors.

With luck, a nice CH-46 will come along and pluck you from the crash site so you could be back home in time to eat dinner and have exciting stories to tell everyone in the hangar. Common knowledge between us was that if the plane hit hard enough to be unrepairable then we would be unrepairable also.

Everyone always had a great survival strategy that they would talk about but we knew that there were not many wrecks in that jungle that any of us were going to walk away from. If the crash didn't get you then the NVA who shot you down would finish the job.

In 1970 we knew that there was not one single enlisted man who had been captured by the Viet Cong / NVA who was going to live long enough to be part of any prisoner release after the war. This was just a little something we kept in the back of our minds when we were a single ship, flying over the dark mountains at night.

Even to the NVA / VC our enlisted men had no value.

Three things happened all at once by the end of the first two weeks of flying. I passed my final check ride on the twentieth flight which elevated my status to junior crew chief. I was then informed by the Lieutenant in charge of the flight line that my advancement to crew chief proved that

–

Marine Corps Aviation standards had fallen to an all-time low.

This was also the general opinion amongst all of my fellow flight line worker bees. The twenty flights made me eligible for my first Air Medal and because we had documented being shot at least three times during those twenty flights I was awarded a set of Combat Air Crew Wings. Combat Air Crew Wings were the aviation equivalent of the Combat Action Ribbon that was awarded to grunts for being shot at while standing in the mud.

Another unexpected surprise that evening was my induction into the MMAF Helicopter Crew Chief's Protective Association.

Ok. I got what I wanted, can I go home now?

—

Chapter 6
Zone is Marked by a Burning CH-46
Total U.S. killed as of October 1970 in the Vietnam War: 54,166

Do you remember your first time? Your friends had talked to you about what it would be like. They told you how great it was and about the complete sense of fulfillment that you would feel after it was all over. The more stories you heard, the more you knew that this is what you wanted to do.

It was very important not to show any outward emotion beforehand because you didn't know if your first time would be all it was cracked up to be. Remember, you had lived with great anticipation about other events in your past but what you found was; wanting a thing usually wound up being more satisfying than actually having a thing.

So now all this anticipation was leading to self-doubt and you were kind of stumbling around on this road to your greatest personal achievement. Finally, desire overcomes doubt and the moment of your gratification arrived.

Flight in an airplane was not an unusual thing in 1969. This was a simpler time before lawyers found out they could sue small aircraft manufactures into bankruptcy because of the complete negligence of the pilot. By this time my total flight time was about twenty hours sitting in the back of an airliner and another fifty hours actually flying small Cessna 172's and others of their type.

But fly in any helicopter, no. That had never happened due to the incredible hourly cost of helicopter ownership. No business I knew back in the sixty's even owned a helicopter, much less gave out rides to high school kids. The USMC, on

134

the other hand, loved to give helicopter rides to kids of all ages.

As with everything else in the military, first time helicopter riding involves forms and documents. The HML-267 avionics shop in California where I worked back then, had to approve my request to skip work and ride for a couple of hours.

Next, after a grueling physical examination, the aviation medical people stated that I could indeed survive the slow rotary flight all the way up to three thousand feet. After all this was done, I was put on a list and waited impatiently to be selected. During this waiting time I would watch my friends and other assorted worker bees put on their flight suits and disappear for half of the day. This was exactly what I was looking for, especially the disappearing for half a day part.

When my name came up I was ready to go. The Huey's crew chief had just returned from Vietnam a short time earlier so he had his own set of rules. His words of wisdom to me were, "Forget all that crap you just learned and just do what I tell you". He knew it was my first ride so his instructions were very simple, "I want you to just sit in that seat, have a good time and don't say anything. If we crash you're to wait for all of the rotating parts to fall back onto the ground, then run like hell as far as you can and don't look back".

He sounded to me like he had been down this road before.

As the engine starts on a Huey it causes the main rotor and tail rotor to turn automatically. They turn slowly at first, which causes the aircraft to rock from side to side. As the speed picks up the rocking motion goes away and changes into a steady high speed vibration. I looked around and assumed that everything was going as planned because everyone was still seated and acting kind of normal. The big thing I realized was the difference between standing around outside watching, and actually being a passenger, is that this thing really shakes a lot.

Then without any effort, the aircraft lifted about four feet above the ground and a lot of the vibration stopped. If you have never experienced the effect of vertical flight the description of the event doesn't adequately convey that first time feeling. I looked out the door and we just sat suspended above the ground. Then without the slightest bit of effort we slowly drifted toward the runway. Still suspended above the pavement we turned onto the active runway, gathering forward speed until we lifted off and flew away. The rest of the flight was uneventful but as they say in the world of heroin users, I was hooked.

My first time was now just a distant memory for me at this point in Vietnam. To get flight time these days was simply a matter of sitting around the flight line shop during the day's aviation events. They always needed a warm body for an assortment of surprise missions that were dispatched to us from on high. Getting into the air was easy and so was I because my addiction had turned me into a true slut for flight hours.

The best time to be found for building up extra hours in the aircraft was in running the local courier flights around Da Nang along with aircraft maintenance check rides. Both of these missions had two requirements that I needed for my personal aviation fulfillment.

First they were long boring flights with no excitement and a predictable route to fly. Second, and most important, they only needed one real pilot. That means the old flight slut could get to fly in the co-pilot's seat and obtain that most prized of intangibles, actual helicopter stick time.

It was one of the more poorly kept secrets about helicopter aviation in Vietnam that all crew chiefs had to learn how to fly and navigate the bird well enough to drive it over and land at the 1st Medical Battalion just outside of Da Nang. We figured that this was in case something bad happened to both of the pilots at the same time and they couldn't aviate.

I always thought that this would be something much worse than the pilots dining on some bad chicken salad sandwiches for lunch, but you never knew. It was this discreet understanding between us that gave me the stick time that I wanted and gave the pilots a little more piece of mind.

Every crew chief understood completely the interconnected systems that made any helicopter fly along with each page of the NATOPS manual describing aircraft maneuvers and flight characteristics. It was learning how the aircraft responded to actual control inputs that took hours of stick time.

During the testing of newly replaced important parts, the pilot would always spend the first fifteen minutes motoring around six inches or so above the hover pad. This pad was a paved section of the field that was far removed from the active runways or even the normal helicopter parking areas.

This was in case something flew off the machine which would make it instantly less than air worthy. If you are going to crash it is always best to do so at a very low altitude while having the local fire department sitting two hundred yards away.

—

These words of wisdom were probably written by someone very experienced in such things.

The regular qualified pilot would hover around until he felt somewhat confident that everything important was going to hold together. Then he would gently set the bird down and the real fun for me would begin. With a smile on his face he would turn to his student, that's me, and say the magic words, "You've got it". It was worth noting that even though he said the magic words, his hands did not travel very far from the controls and he never took his eyes from the events that were happening before him.

His problem was, even though his student was in somewhat control of a half a million, 1970 dollars' worth of machinery he was the man who had put his name on the dotted line. That signature made him responsible to the Government of the United Sates in general and the glorious Marine Corps in particular for this aircraft, no matter who was actually flying it.

Learning to hover requires the coordinated input of three separate sets of controls. Very basically the rudder pedals control which direction the nose is pointed, the collective controls up and down and the cyclic does almost everything else.

While each control is independent of the others mechanically, controlled flight requires that each input be coordinated with a non-liner relationship to the input of the other two controls.

This is much harder to accomplish with an actual flying machine than it sounds.

The term for an uncoordinated relationship is called a crash and in the aviation world this was considered a bad thing.

The truth was the same then as it is now. Learning to hover and taxi a helicopter is one of the hardest things in flying to pick up and master. In 1970 there were no computer controlled inputs or regenerative buffering to smooth out your inputs. All aviating was accomplished with hollow aluminum rods, hydraulic cylinders and muscle memory.

At the end of my tour I had accumulated over forty undocumented flight hours in the Huey. These hours, combined with my Cessna time had gotten me to the point where I could make a satisfactory night visual approach into MMAF, land and slowly taxi over to the fuel pits. There I got to top off the fuel tank and clean all the dead bugs off of the windshield.

Those blast walls look mighty close when you are taxiing the aircraft at night.

I never wanted to try and drive the bird all the way home because that required the pilot to hover his rotating aluminum machine in between looming eight-foot-high thick steel revetment walls which were way too close on both sides for my skill level. There was nothing worse for your reputation among fellow squadron crew chiefs than

—

inadvertently using a spinning rotor blade to chip green paint off of one of those immovable steel blast walls.

The transfer out of experienced personnel and their replacement with FNG's affected both worker bees and pilot bees at every squadron. Old good pilots were replaced with people who should be made to sit on the helicopter's skids for a month until they learn some of the basics of life in any MMAF squadron. To get new pilots used to the airfield and talking on the radio, they would always be assigned to do test flights for minor component replacement after they had received a basic checkout with a real pilot.

Heading directly toward me from out of the hangar walks Nicky the New Guy, complete with his sparkling white helicopter driver helmet and two large buckets of attitude.

"One year ago this guy couldn't even spell helicopter pilot, now he are one".

His royal majesty spent thirty minutes doing a world class preflight inspection which included complaining in a loud condescending voice about each little oil spot or dead Vietnamese bug he observed.

Finally, after what seemed like a never ending display of his mastery of pre-flight procedures, he got in on the right seat and prepared himself for today's aviation adventure. He fired up the bird and did an acceptable job of not getting lost as we taxi out to the runway.

Someone has tipped off my fellow worker bees about this guy because they have all stopped repairing the squadron's broken aircraft and have lined up on the edge of the taxiway to wave at us as we go by.

—

Some do more than wave but my new guy never sees their symbolic hand gestures.

We lift off and enter the MMAF airfield traffic pattern where he does two careful landings at the field before he goes off and becomes adventurous. Lieutenant New Guy leaves the pattern, climbs to 800 feet and then flies south down the coast. We go past the stone monument known as the Marble Mountain and then the Korean Marine base comes into sight. He goes all the way south to the Hoy An River, turns the bird around and heads back toward home. We are now cruising along at about one thousand feet when he surprises me and asks if I want to fly. Of course I say, "Yes", and reach for the controls.

He almost makes me laugh when he says, "just take the cyclic and let's see how you do". He doesn't realize that he has the flying slut beside him, but I'm up for playing this game. I grab the cyclic and wiggle it around a little like I have never done this before and then we settle down. Then he lets me take the collective and I add too much then too little torque but soon we are zooming along just fine. Then I get the rudder pedals. Oh, this is too exciting. I click on the intercom and say, "see the black rocks on the beach about half a mile ahead"? He looks out then looks across at me with a question in his voice, says, "Yes?"

With a flick of my wrist the engine power gets rolled back to idle, I push the collective down till it hits the stop and the main rotors go to flat pitch. Then using the cyclic the airspeed is lowered till it reaches exactly eighty knots. Down we go in a standard engine out autorotation till we are a couple of hundred feet above the rocks. Now I roll the power back on, pull collective and stabilize in a hover.

—

He looks over and all he says is, "I guess you have flown these helicopters before". I thought, Yea, I guess so, Mr. FNG. But I was nice and didn't say anything smart ass. I told him that I did have a few hours of stick time and I hoped he didn't mind me shooting an autorotation because it had been awhile and I needed the practice.

Being a FNG and all, I bet he didn't even tell his fellow pilots about this great adventure back at the Officers Club that night.

Life for me at MMAF became an endless stream of gun cover missions for our friends in the transport helicopters. There were three squadrons of Boeing-Vertol medium lift helicopters known as CH-46's on our base and one squadron of heavy lift Sikorsky CH-53's. You could always pick out the CH-46's because they had a tandem rotor setup with three blades in front and three blades in back.

Just another day at the office for a CH-46

The CH-53's looked like a twin engine Huey from a distance except when you got close and found out that they were about five times the size and had ten times the horsepower. Both of these aircraft had the size and the lifting capacities to drop down into a restricted landing zone, fill themselves full of troops and still lift straight up till they were passing the tops of the trees.

One of the most important rules to follow when flying gun cover for one of the Sikorsky's was, never fly directly above one while it is sitting in an LZ. If they get shot at, their natural instinct for defense is to pull full collective and climb straight up as fast as they can go. There is no way your little Huey can move fast enough to get out of the way of a scared Sikorsky.

Our single engine aircraft was at or above its maximum gross weight each time we took off as a gunship with a full load of weapons. This meant that we couldn't lift into a hover and go, we actually needed a short scrape along the runway to get airborne.

The funny thing was that if we ever stopped moving forward in the sky when we were fully loaded, the aircraft did not have enough horsepower to hover. The pilots could pull up on the collective all they wanted to but the engine was at its limit and the bird would quickly lose rotor rpm which caused it to sink even while you are still at full throttle. The only thing to do at that point was to push the nose over and hope you had enough altitude to recover.

There were two ways to remedy this situation about the lack of horsepower. The first method was to yell at the pilots over the intercom about watching the rotor rpm's. When that didn't work then you had to go to plan B. This time you yelled the same thing as before only you first switched over

—

from intercom to the tactical UHF frequency so that all his pilot co-workers could hear firsthand about his bad flying technique. This would always provide many laughs at the pilot's expense when he returned to the Officers Club that night.

Do this UHF thing once or twice and even the densest aircraft driver won't ignore you the next time they are told to watch the main rotor rpm.

The second method involved a contact I had with the Lycoming aircraft engine technical representative or maybe it was one of his personal assistants. In any case it seems they were all fond of a certain brand of bottled liquid refreshment and more than willing to trade engine tuning secrets for a couple of bottles filled with their favorite sauce.

The trade was made, I had what I needed and so did they.

It seems that all of our engines were being run in a detuned state to extend engine life. This reduced power setting allowed the engine manufacturer to reach a certain agreed upon number of hours between overhaul at the expense of useful power available to the aircraft. As usual the truth was hidden behind the curtain where none of us field hands were allowed to see what was going on except for certain sneaky bastards, like me.

Adjusting a couple of set screws on the engine fuel control manifold brought the power up a notch or two and still kept the engine life in what we, the end user, considered an acceptable range. This adjustment did produce a minor issue with the exhaust gas temperature (EGT) going somewhat high on occasions. We resolved this small problem by resetting the EGT calibration screw back on the engine near its hot section.

—

This adjustment kept the pilot's temperature gauge within limits and the maximum allowable power level up where I needed it. More power is always a good thing for us and the pilots don't really need to know everything that is happening back there under the cowling anyway.

Just concentrate on the dead bugs stuck to the windshield and everything else will be just fine.

For the 24 hour shift when we were assigned to be the medivac gun cover, all of the aircraft and their crews would stay at the alert bunker. This was located across the field from our squadron's hangar and away from everything else. The hut designated for the officers had fresh linen on all of the racks and an air conditioner that worked like it was direct from the factory. The other hut was for the guys in back. No sheets on the beds for us, just mattresses with thick plastic covers and pillows without any covers.

The plastic mattresses actually came in handy on those days when the monsoon rains hit and we would spend our aviation hours stuck out in the rain with an eighty knot wet wind blasting you in your face. When we returned from a mission everyone, except for the pilots, was soaked from head to toe in cold rain water and shaking from the wind chill.

Lie down on the bed and the weak springs in the bed frame would sag badly toward the center. This valley allowed the water that drained from your flight suit to pool underneath you on the plastic mattress. When enough of a lake had formed, you would get up and pour the water out onto the ground. Do this for three or four times and your flight suit would be dry enough to allow you to go to sleep.

--

Hot food for the troops was provided in the form of large insulated steel containers that had the food separated into aluminum silos. Dig into the brown bag for paper plates, plastic forks and now dinner was ready to be served. Standby medivac always received the take out menu from the mess hall, which if you can believe it, was even worse than their regular food. Hot dogs, hamburgers and beans were a staple item on the medivac bunker menu.

For our added enjoyment we occasionally would be presented with some kind of mystery meat covered in dark brown heavy sauce for our dining pleasure. Dark brown heavy sauce was a specialty of the mess hall because it was simple to make and it covered the main dish so that its origins, smell or age, were undetectable. Because the bread was baked on the base and they went through a boat load of it every day, it was always fresh and actually tasted mighty good.

Try as they might, even the cooks were unable to make a stinky mess out of everything they touched.

All we did for the entire time we were in the medivac bunker was sit around and wait for the phone alert telling us to launch. Every day we prayed that there would be no call for us to launch.

This was not just because we had all turned into large couch sitting, food eating sloths that didn't want to do anything resembling work. More than anyone else, we knew that the only reason a call ever came in to the alert bunker was that some Marine was seriously injured and in danger of dying so we had to launch. When we got the call we would always launch, night or day and in any weather.

The only time we couldn't go was when a typhoon hit Da Nang and everything with rotary wings was tied down and grounded. That usually worked out ok because the bad guys were in hiding from the rain also, so contact with them was limited. There were always injuries from mines, booby traps and stupidity but unfortunately the troops would have to wait until the wind died down before we could go get them.

Daytime medivac was usually uneventful except on those mornings when the sea fog would roll in. Blinding white morning sea fog so thick you couldn't see the aircraft parked thirty yards away from the bunker. Fog or no fog the calls for medivac would still come in and we had to launch. There was a way to launch and make it back to the area where the medivac was needed but it was not approved by those on high and definitely not covered in the NATOPS manual.

Each of the low altitude aviation maps that we had covering our section of Vietnam also showed the road network along with all the mountains and radio aids to navigation. One gunship would launch out first and make a left turn till he found the bridge over the Song Han River. We turned at the bridge and followed the highway till we were out of the fog and could find the location of the medivac.

In the fog we would stay on the right side of the road and fly slow. This allowed us to navigate by sticking our heads over the side of the bird and look for crossroads and landmarks. Every once in a while another helicopter popped out of the fog going in the opposite direction. It would speed by you on the other side of the road and then quick as a flash, it had disappeared into the wet grayness. In all the time I was over there this was an acceptable way to fly blind in the fog.

—

We had never heard of a midair collision caused by flying this way but I don't know why.

On a normal day the call for a medivac would come in from Da Nang dispatch and we would launch. The first CH-46 would arrive on the scene and call for a smoke. The grunts would throw out a colored smoke grenade and the aircraft pilots would call out the color they saw. The bad guys were very sneaky and they were always planning new and improved ways to shoot down our aircraft when they thought they could get away with it.

Over time the NVA had learned that if one of our men was badly wounded, a helicopter was always called in to rush him to the hospital. They had a trick or two that they used to try and shoot down our medivac birds. The best trick was to fight hard only until one or two of our Marines had been hit and they knew for sure that a medivac had been called in. After the medivac had been called they would stop fighting and fade away into the jungle.

After the shooting stopped they would always pull back a safe distance from our lines. There in the bushes they would hide and prepare for the approach of the helicopters. They knew the direction that it would be coming in from because aircraft always approach for landing into the wind and take off in the same direction. Plus, they are so loud you can hear them approaching for five minutes.

They would now move to a different cleared out area large enough for the medivac to land and work to make it look just like the Marine's landing zone. They would wait until the grunts threw out the first smoke grenade to learn what the color was. This smoke color information was quickly passed to the bad guys at the false landing zone. The NVA had a complete supply of stolen smoke grenades in all colors so they would then just toss out the proper one.

If the CH-46 didn't see the double smoke in time he might land right in the middle of a big NVA trap. Their traps included rocket propelled grenades, land mines on the ground for the landing gear and thin steel wires stretching across the landing zone attached to hand grenades.

The aircraft would land; the blades would get tangled up in the wires and then wrap a couple of live hand grenades around its rotor system. Most of the time we would see the double smoke first and then go over and shoot up the tree line of the false LZ. This was where the bad guys were always hiding and we tried to make the survivors wish that they had stayed in their homes, up north.

In a hot LZ both of the gunships would come in right behind the CH-46 as it started to lift off. We sprayed the tree lines with our door guns in an effort to draw fire from the NVA while the medivac lifted out of the zone. Most of the time this action worked pretty well because we always diverted the enemy's fire coming from the tree line away from the medivac bird and towards us.

Maybe we even killed a couple of them while we were at it, kind of like a bonus.

The other little trick they had wasn't used as often because it was tough to get volunteers to participate. When the CH-46 took off it was always nose low and tail high to get forward airspeed built up and leave the killing zone as fast as possible. When they are able to, the NVA will have dug a tiny little hole for a single man in an open area and cover him up so well that they are invisible even if you are standing next to them.

—

When the CH-46 lifts off and the belly of the aircraft is exposed, the bad guy will pop the top off of his hiding place and put 30 rounds of automatic AK fire right into the bottom of the bird. Yes, he gets killed right away by the Marines on the ground but the damage done to the aircraft is impressive.

Moving an injured Marine into a CH-46

Night medivac was the same procedure except you couldn't see the smoke color and had to work with the absolute minimum of lighting on the ground. The grunts on the ground would set up a small strobe light, flashlight or even an ignited C-Ration heat tablet right where they wanted the front wheel of the medivac bird to go. There were no other lights on the ground and no lights on the CH-46 coming in to land.

The pilots or the crew couldn't see anything on the ground and had to rely on a magnetic compass and the skill of the people directing him not get him tangled up in a tree or land on one of our own Marines.

If we had enough time we could call Da Nang and order up the flare truck. This was an Air Force C-130 which was loaded with hundreds of parachute flares and was able to stay on station all night long. Everyone called those things basketball flares because that's what they looked like hanging from their big white parachutes as they floated for sixty seconds, down into the top of the jungle canopy.

Six flares would come out in a long string of white light and they turned night into day. Well at least a dim cloudy day for about sixty seconds, but it was a lot better than nothing. The C-130 would stay high up in the sky dropping row after row of white hot magnesium flares till all of our aircraft were out of the zone and we were on our way to 1st Medical with an appreciative customer.

Get in and get out because night time was no time to be hanging out in that neighborhood.

The only good thing about night medivac was when the bad guys started shooting; you could look straight down and see exactly where they were standing. No hiding in the bushes when you fired your AK-47 at night little bad guys. The muzzle flash from the weapon and straight orange line from the tracer rounds would always give their position away. Especially to those of us sitting directly above you.

We would return fire with our door guns and aim our point of impact to be about five feet behind where we saw the muzzle flash of their rifles. You know that you were doing a good job when the hostile fire shifted upward from the bird in the zone to you in the sky.

—

This was the truest form of instantaneous job satisfaction.

First thing in the morning the medivac birds would go out and pick up all the routine and the permanent routine injured Marines in the field. The permanent routine calls meant that the Marine was dead and to only remove him when it could be done safely.

During this time in Vietnam between three and four hundred US service men a month were dying and many thousands more were being wounded. Some recovered in-country and returned to the fight and others were shipped back to the states for recovery and then released from active service due to their injuries. Every single day in every single month of each year this death machine ran with incredible efficiency.

We spent a year of our lives picking up the broken pieces of what was and what will never be again.

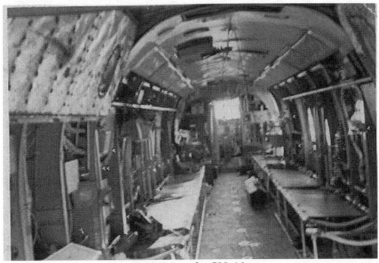

Interior of a CH-46

Inside the CH-46 medivac birds there was so much blood on the floor that it would seep through the plates on the deck and dry in layers on the inner skin of the helicopters. Damaged CH-46's that were sent to Japan for rebuilding caused the metal workers to get sick from the stench of rotting human blood when the aluminum deck plates were removed during repairs.

The regularly assigned medivac birds had lots of medical supplies on board along with a skilled Navy corpsman who would provide first class treatment to the critically wounded during the flight. On my UH-1E there was one small medical kit with enough supplies in it to handle a blister on one finger or maybe a paper cut but not both at the same time.

Unlike us, the Army had so many helicopters that they could assign entire squadrons of oversize Hueys to do nothing but handle the mission of medivac. Marine aviation did not have the luxury of medivac squadrons so any available helicopter could be assigned in flight to divert and handle an emergency call for help.

On occasion when there was no CH-46 available or the delivery was really small, our squadron would be tasked for the mission. We would use a cargo bird to take supplies up to a tiny mountain top firebase where there was supposedly no enemy activity. Occasionally, during that mission we would also be tasked with an emergency medivac after the supplies were out the door. We could never say no because we knew that there was no one else within an hour of our location and the life of one of our guys was on the line.

Turn in the direction of their outpost and get the cabin ready for the stretcher. Snap the M-60 from its mount and put it and two cans of ammunition next to my seat so I can get to

—

them in a hurry.   Unsnap the door gun mount from the floor, store it under the seat and get ready for someone's life to be placed in my hands.

On these missions we were always alone with no gun cover for our flying pickup truck. The Da Nang controllers would give us grid coordinates and a radio frequency to make contact with our future customers in their landing zone. As we climbed west into the mountains, Da Nang radio would fade out but we were still not close enough to contact the grunts.

Soon there would be a voice on the radio that would tell us to turn right or left as the troops on the ground could first hear us and then see our approach as we drew nearer. Climb high and circle around their tiny home of mud and rocks looking for a place to land. Now quickly spiral down in a hard right turn with a final flair to set down. These approaches were not for the faint of heart.

Welcome to fire base Nasty

The dust and rocks would fly when we sat down and just like you see in the movies, four men would carry a wooden handled canvas litter with their friend lying on it. He would be quickly slid into the open area on the helicopter floor by worn out men who had done this job too many times before.

The fire base's corpsman would yell something about treatment in my ear but it didn't matter what he said. We had no supplies and our only plan was to fly to 1st Med as fast as possible which would give this guy his only chance at survival. The door would slam shut, the bird would lift up and we would climb out and fly away down the valley toward his only chance for life.

Once the Marine had been slid across the floor and the door slammed shut, I stayed on the floor beside him trying to see what I could do, if anything, to help. Almost all of the time the guys in the field had done an excellent job of stabilizing the wounds and there was nothing I could do except talk to the Marine and try to keep him calm during the flight. When we were close enough that they could hear our radio we would contact 1st Med and give them an ETA so their crews could prepare for our arrival.

We would gently set down on 1st Med's gray steel helo pad and pop open the door. In what looked to us like organized confusion, the triage teams would rush out, load the casualty onto a wheeled gurney and quickly take him inside to the darkness of their medical sanctuary. He would never be seen by any of us again. There was no time to look around because more aircraft were on final approach to the pad with their cargo of dead and dying Marines. Now it was time for us to leave.

Some didn't make it. There were a couple of Marines that seemed to die as soon as they were loaded into my aircraft

—

for the trip. I never noticed that they were breathing during the flight and their eyes were usually open but never moving or reacting to changes in the light. We still flew as fast as possible and 1st Med was outstanding as usual but I don't think they ever stood a chance.

One thin Marine who looked about sixteen was carried on board without a canvas litter. Four of his friends carried him with their hands and slid him across the deck of my aircraft. This provided more than the usual amount of confusion and crush of bodies at the helicopter's doorway. The men who transported him across the field yelled words of encouragement to my new passenger and waved good bye as they backed away.

We lifted off with the usual blast of hot dusty air and small twigs being kicked up by our rotor wash. I looked down at my passenger as we began our trip and saw a puddle of bright red blood starting to seep out from under his body. Bright red meant that it was being pumped straight from the heart and the volume said that this was bad.

A quick check showed the flow was coming from a jagged wound on his right side that had not been wrapped with a pressure bandage. He may have been shot again as he was being carried over for all I knew.

I had nothing to bind it with except some cloths we used for general cleaning inside the bird and they were small and not very clean. Rather than try to fool with them, I took the skin on both sides of the wound and squeezed it together which at least slowed the squirting to an ooze. The blood flow lubricated the skin on the edge of his wound which made it even more difficult to hold the ripped flesh together. What I was doing seemed to be helping, but how do you really know. I was only a glorified mechanic, not a Corpsman.

—

The wounded Marine had his hand on my shoulder and he was praying to God not to let him die. At this point I was praying along with him because for the rest of the ride there was nothing else I could do. Towards the end of the flight his strength started to fade, his hand relaxed its grip and fell unrestrained to the deck.

Our aircraft started our final turn for landing and quickly flared to land. As we touched down and the door opened he stopped moving his lips and he eyes didn't follow me when I moved. One of the litter team from 1st Med switched places with me and applied pressure to the surface of the wound. I got out of the way while my passenger was carried off into the inner sanctum of the hospital to meet his fate.

My hands and flight suit were smeared with the clotted brown clay from his uniform and the fresh red blood from his probably silent heart. I never knew this Marine's name; in fact, I never knew any of their names or what finally became of them. All of the aircrew thought it would have been nice to have some kind of score card to know if we had actually made a difference in someone's life.

To a man we believed that we had made a difference, but even to this day none of us will ever know for sure.

One day the monsoon weather moved on and gave us a break from the wind and low hanging clouds. This allowed the medivac crews to go out and do delayed pick-ups at all the outlying fire bases. Two CH-46's and two gunships would leave in the morning and spend all day going from one location to another.

—

Within a half an hour bird number one was filled to capacity with dead and wounded, it then headed back to 1st Med. The remaining 46 took the lead and we proceeded to a fire base way out in the middle of nothing. This was a five-hundred-foot high bare hill of just dirt and large round rocks surrounded by thick green jungle.

There was not a single growing plant on the sides or top of this outpost. The entire thing looked like someone had taken a load of big round boulders and made a cone shaped pile of them in a long lush green valley. The Marines had made their home on the top of this pile of rocks and today they requested that we transport two of their employees who had received on the job injuries.

The area where the CH-46 was to set down was highly restrictive due to the piled up rocks on one side and a sharp cliff drop off on the other. The driver of the CH-46 decided to do what is known as a ramp job near the top of the hill.

This is done by backing the helicopter into the landing zone and letting only the rear wheels and ramp have contact with the ground. This maneuver keeps the aircraft's nose sitting out into space but the pilots are blind as to what was happening where the action was. In the past I had seen it done on a number of occasions and it is quite impressive to watch.

Not so much this time.

The crew chief had the pilot back the ramp into the side of the mountain but forgot to watch the rear blades like he was supposed to. Riding around the zone and watching all the action I was about three hundred feet off to the side when the spinning blades on his rear rotor system edged into the rocks. At first the rear blades started hitting small rocks and clumps of dirt which shot off in all directions.

People on the ground started to run up the hill as the amount of rocks and dirt in the air increased. The repeated impacts with the ground caused the blade tips to break away from each rotor as they began to come apart under full power. With a shattered rear rotor system, the back end of the helicopter lost lift and settled down onto the rocks.

At this point the rear rotor and the front rotor meshed. The entire aircraft rolled over onto its side causing the now broken front rotor blades to also impact the ground. Dirt, dust and broken aircraft parts hung in the air obscuring the scene below for a fraction of a second.

What used to be a multimillion dollar Boeing CH-46 now lay broken and on its side. Black smoke poured from its engine exhausts while its two blade-less rotor hubs still spun uselessly digging holes in the dirt. It was seemingly attached to the steep hillside for a long second or two but then the law of gravity took over.

The radio was silent as we watched this former aircraft begin its death roll down the hill. It went slowly downward in fits and starts, throwing up rocks and helicopter parts all the way until it struck the trees at the base of the incline.

About five minutes away from the crash site was a larger firebase with an actual steel mat landing area. Our gunship set down there and as quick as possible we dropped our rocket pods, both door guns and all ammunition. To save weight we also removed the co-pilots armored seat and left it, my gunner and the co-pilot behind.

By the time we had dropped off all of the excess weight and returned to the hill, the grunts had gone down to the crash site. Somehow they extracted everyone out of the destroyed 46 and helped them back up the hill. The impact had split both of the bird's fuel tanks and the broken engines had set the jet fuel on fire. As we approached we could see that the fire was localized in the rear but there was no way that thing was going to fly again, ever.

We set our little Huey down on that tiny opening at the top of the hill with inches to spare. The wounded were loaded onboard except for the CH-46 co-pilot who could still walk, even after that ride. There were a number of CH-46 air crew who were injured pretty badly as a result of the crash but no one looked like they were going to die. The Navy Corpsmen assigned to the medivac bird was not hurt too badly in the accident so I stuck him in the back of my Huey with the rest of the 46 crew. He could make sure everyone survived the ride over to 1st Med.

My aircraft was loaded at or near maximum for this location so I told the pilot I would stay behind and try to salvage what I could from the burning Boeing. My staying behind would also save 200 pounds of weight on takeoff. I reminded him that when he went off the top of this hill the bottom would fall out of his flying machine. Just push the nose over and use the altitude to pick up airspeed and everything would be alright.

I stood off to one side and launched him off the top of the hill. He lifted off, lost ground effect, swooped down the hill, picked up lift and flew away towards Da Nang. My aircraft went slowly out of sight and sound as it flew down the valley. It looked like I would have lots of time to talk to my new best friends whose home was on top of a pile of rocks, dirt and burning helicopter parts.

—

I met with the head grunt and talked with him about going down to the crash site to do a little equipment salvage. Myself along with a small squad worked our way down and got close enough to the front of the aircraft to see inside. By this time the kerosene fed fire had started to melt the aluminum in the rear of the aircraft and the flames were traveling through the inside of the cabin.

Smoke was pouring out of each round side window and fire was licking at the inside of the cracked front windshield. The nose was too high off of the ground to reach the KY-28 cipher radios and at this time they looked to be too hot to touch even if we could get to them.

While we were thinking of a way to get to the radios, the fifty caliber ammunition inside the cabin started to bake off from the heat. This was the time when everyone decided that we had done enough. It was time to climb back to the top with the little bit of hardware that we had been able to salvage from this latest disaster.

It took about two hours of sitting around trying to look insignificant before another CH-46 showed up to remove myself and the CH-46 copilot from the now smoky firebase. As he approached in the darkening twilight I took the radio and provided him with a situation report for the landing zone.

"Winds are calm at the zone with light haze due to smoke. There has been no enemy fire for the last twelve hours and the zone is marked by a burning 46."

He circled close to the hill once to inspect the crash site and parked his aircraft on the top of the hill like he was stopping off to pick up a loaf of bread from his neighborhood grocery store. It was obvious that we had the "A" team driving this machine.

Without bending over we walked up the ramp and into the cabin. Then without a thank you very much from anyone, we flew away. It was late by the time we dropped all the wounded off at 1st Med and returned to MMAF. I found that I had to explain everything that happened to at least five different groups of people from two squadrons. Because of this I ended up missing my favorite TV shows that night.

The war ground up young men and changed the lives of everyone who touched it. The three CH-46 squadrons at Marble Mountain were the heavy lifters in the daily battle to save lives with rapid air medivacs. Every day these crews went out and loaded those birds with our dead, dying and badly injured Marines. They answered every call, filled their aircraft to the limit and brought these damaged bodies back to the only people in our world who could help them.

HML-167 took in just a small portion of the overflow and then only as a last resort; our lives were touched by only a small leak from this high pressure fire hose of death.

On rare occasions we would be directed to take our medivac to the USS Sanctuary which was always floating in Da Nang Bay or just along the coast of the South China Sea. The USS Sanctuary was an all-white Navy hospital ship with big bright red crosses on its top and sides.

The ship came complete with a helicopter landing pad on the back of the boat and lots of people who were actually glad to see us. All the pilots loved to be diverted to the Sanctuary because they got to list a ship landing in their log book plus there were always lots of nurses standing by the rails, waving at the helicopter crews.

—

The crew chiefs also liked it when we were directed to land on the Sanctuary but for a totally different reason. During that short time when the ship's medical personnel were removing the Marine for treatment, we would get out of the helicopter and run to the front of the landing zone where there was a big white plywood box.

Before a patient was allowed to be taken inside the ship he was always searched for weapons, explosives or other tools of the trade that he might have had on his person. The explosives always went directly over the side of the ship into the deep salt water never to be seen again.

The USS Sanctuary adrift in the South China Sea

All firearms were placed in that big white box for later removal by someone from Marine Corps ordinance. Actually the officers of the Sanctuary didn't care who took the weapons away as long as they were removed from their ship.

Upon landing we would always run to the box and see what kind of goodies there were inside for us. If there was a Russian AK-47 or a .45 caliber Colt pistol in good shape, we would keep them for our personal use. A Chinese SKS semi-

—

auto or some other off brand weapon would always be fine for trading material at the Da Nang Air Force Base.

You had about sixty seconds to grab all the goodies you could carry, wave at the pretty nurses watching you from the railings and get back into your bird. The pilots would always take careful note of your recovered contraband as you ran by and later in the day they always requested an obscene percentage as their personal share.

This request was kind of unfair if you ask me because they always got a percentage of the weapons but we never got a percentage of the nurses.

Chapter 7

The Korean Marine Corps
Total U.S. killed as of November 1970 in the Vietnam War: 54,552

One of the most interesting experiences that happened to all of us in Vietnam was the loss of calendar perception. From the time you experience self-awareness as a little kiddy, you learned calendar perception mostly based upon watching the actions of your parents. Before you even started school you knew weekdays from weekends and the changes in rhythm that the different days of the week would bring into your life.

This was reinforced later during your formative years in school when the calendar would bring everyone five days of misery followed by two days of weekend fun. Once in a calendar year there was a Christmas holiday and then after many months had dragged on we got a nice three-month long summer vacation. Even at that age we realized that the calendar controlled our lives. That is until we hit the shores of Vietnam. In our new Asian home there were no vacations, holidays or weekends to look forward to anymore. This war ran 24 / 7 / 365.

No songs about, "working for the weekend", in this place.

Every single day on Marble Mountain was Monday with a very long week ahead to look forward too. Hump day was one hundred and eighty-two days away in an unreachable futuristic haze. There were only two things sharply visible to you on your personal time horizon. The first was your date to go away on an out of country Rest & Relaxation and the other was day number nine on your short timer's calendar when you were reverently referred to by all as a, "single digit midget". That was the day you stopped flying, walking alone at night or going to the enlisted men's club for any reason at all.

If anyone wanted you during these last nine days they had to crawl into the reinforced sandbag bunker outside of your hooch because that was where you had moved. The general consensus was, after we had put up with all of this crap for over a year, there was no sense in taking any chances in not going home upright. That being said, all of us who still counted our time left in country in double or triple digits, always made it a point to talk loudly outside the short timer's safe bunker.

Stories about all the guys who got killed in vehicle accidents while driving to Da Nang for the flight home to the land of the big PX were always good. My personal favorite was the story about how the local VC was always trying to put ground up glass in the food or drink of everyone nearing the end of their deployment in an effort to destroy moral. We had it on good authority that they made the glass look like white beach sand that blew around and normally got into everyone's food or drinks.

Single digit midgets tended to lose a lot of weight during their last week on base.

At first we didn't feel the effects of not living by the calendar. We went to work when it was dark, ate over-cooked bad food for lunch then returned to our communal living facility at night. If we were lucky we got to drink all the alcohol, we could find till we got sick then slept for five hours. This was our daily work schedule and we did the same exact thing each and every day of the week, each and every month of the year.

—

What brought this into sharp focus was a weekly event which occurred during our normal daily walking commute. After breakfast we would wander down the road from the base mess hall towards the flight line so we would always pass by the base chapel.

This building was the size of a standard ugly hooch but it had white walls along with a small white steeple which provided a marked contrast to the rest of the Marine green base. Out in front of the building by the road, once every seven days, the chaplain or one of his assorted flunkies would put out a small "A" frame sign that said, "Today is Sunday and everyone is welcome to come inside for services".

We were so far off planet earth that each week when we saw that sign there would be an argument between us about whether it was correct or not. It made no sense to argue about the sign but we did anyway. First, the chaplain was probably the only person on MMAF who had a real calendar and second, why would he lie to us about the day being Sunday unless he was getting paid by the soul.

These are some of the big things we would never know.

Working with the U.S. Army on any combined project was always an exercise in amazement. What they lacked in discipline, organization or enthusiasm they made up for in the total volume of men and equipment they brought to the game. One day during the rainy season I got a firsthand look at our new action Army.

The day before this event one of their mechanical units had been out on some kind of patrol in an area about twenty miles south of MMAF. One of their highly skilled drivers in an armored personnel carrier, (APC), had driven it off the

—

only hard surface road in the area and right into a rice paddy. Not being content to wait for a tow from another APC he spun his tracks until the water was halfway up the sides of the machine, the engine was flooded and it was now immovable. They tried to pull him out with another APC but they only succeeded in burning out the second machine's transmission. Now they had two dead tracked people movers, all without assistance from the local NVA.

They managed to tow the road kill APC back to their camp but the one in the mud looked like it was going to turn into a large green obstacle during next year's rice harvest. In typical Army fashion they left it there in the mud and called for help. That was where we came in. Their plan was to hook cables onto this dead beast and fly it out of the mud using a special heavy lift helicopter. They only needed us for gun cover to protect the only heavy lift helicopter anyone had in this section of Vietnam.

During my short time in the military I had been witness to a number of unusual things and given the extensive show preparation I felt that today's adventure was going to be extra special. An Army APC in those days was designed to carry fourteen people and weighed around twenty-five thousand pounds' empty.

This one didn't have any people in it but it was not empty because by now the stinky rice paddy mud and brown water had filled it half way to the top. I didn't think there was a chance they were going to lift their APC out of the swamp, but who was I to cast a shadow of doubt over this U.S. Army aviation operation.

We flew south to the Hoi An area to meet with the heavy lift helicopter and then together all three of us aviated down to the location of their latest disaster. The Army had trotted

—

out their big gun for this event. Flying in front of us was the undisputed king of the Sikorsky helicopter family, a CH-54, flying crane. All of us had read about them in books with lots of pictures but this was the first one any of us had actually seen in the air.

Without a doubt, this was the strangest looking flying machine that we had ever looked upon. It had a small cockpit up front for the two pilots and a third rearward facing seat for the crane operator. This machine was nothing but engines, transmissions and gearboxes all the way back to the tail rotor. There was nothing else visible except wheels offset from the frame and a drum of thick steel cable attached directly under the main rotor.

We buzzed over to the rice paddy where an Army ground crew had already attached four lift cables to the top of the APC. The crane lowered its hoist cable and the APC was hooked up. The ground crew waded through the water to the roadway and then ducked behind their vehicles as the crane started to take up the load.

—

I still had my doubts as the lift started but soon the main rotor tips of the CH-54 started to rise with the increased strain of the load. The CH-54 was at full throttle now with both engines pouring out black smoke and the main rotor system producing hurricane force winds below. This blast from the main rotor knocked over a small Buddhist shrine, someone's house and two or three grass shacks that were close to the rice paddy. The crane was lifting as hard as it could and the APC was still in the mud and for the longest time it looked like it was never going to move.

As we watched, brown water slowly started to pour out of the open doors of the APC as it grudgingly inched upward just a little bit. Slowly at first and then with what must have been a loud sucking sound, the mud released its victim and the APC cleared the water's surface. The crane carried its load sideways through some roadside shrubbery and stopped over the hard road surface. The APC stopped its slow rotation at the end of the lifting cables and was set down with a road damaging thump from about three feet up.

It was a good thing for the flying crane that there were no NVA in the general vicinity. We became so absorbed with the actions of the crane that we stopped paying attention to what was going on anywhere else.

To this day I can still remember the sight of their Sikorsky Sky Crane pulling the Army APC out of the mud like it was a green cork in a brown wine bottle.

The one single defining word to describe South Vietnam was disorganization. By observing the layout of its roads, towns and farmers' fields it was obvious that there was no central planning. Nor was there any desire by the government to improve either the productivity of the land or the lives of the people.

Things had been allowed to settle into a patchwork quilt of societal norms going back thousands of years. This was now being directed by an inept governmental system that was also incredibly corrupt at all levels.

In South Vietnam your basic water buffalo had greater motivation to improve the status quo than did the general population. When you think that it couldn't get any more confusing, you find that South Vietnam had used as its model for entry into the modern world, the criminal laws, civil rules and complete bureaucratic system of its former colonial master, France.

About twelve miles south of MMAF on the banks of the Hoi-An River was the headquarters of the Korean Marine Corps detachment in Vietnam. This was going to be my island of sanity in the surrounding Vietnamese countryside. Inside the walls of this compound was organization, discipline and a first class standard of living.

As an additional bonus there was not a stinky water buffalo in sight.

The first time I was assigned to this detachment, I flew with one of the other crew chiefs who had been assigned this job a number of times. There were a few new rules to learn about dealing with a group that had a really good attitude and took care of business. The first important item of business was not to eat at the MMAF mess hall before you showed up for work here.

The USMC had provided an independent detachment who were assigned as liaison officers for the Koreans and they

171

gave us the tour. First on the stop was the detachment mess hall. This was a first class operation with independent authority to procure what they wanted in whatever amount they needed.

Let me put it this way, they had printed menus in the mess hall. Blueberry pancakes or French toast with link sausages for breakfast and grilled steak sandwiches for lunch either served on real plates or prepared to go in case we had to be in the field. I was in double bacon cheeseburger heaven in this place. Two things happened after spending time on this base. First, I developed an even worse attitude towards the ability of the cooks at MMAF and second, I started looking for larger flight suits.

The Korean Marines were all volunteers and it showed. These guys were all business and totally committed to the job at hand. Discipline for most minor infractions was handled at the local unit level by the next highest rank and these guys did not fool around. There was none of this hauling your basic offender to the brig and later in the week bringing him up before the commanding officer for minor infractions.

When one of their boys screwed up the entire unit would stop what they were doing, take the offender to a quiet place that was out of sight, and proceed to provide him with an education in the latest karate moves. The interesting thing was the offender would just stand there and accept his punishment until he collapsed and was dragged back to the location where the transgression had occurred. If the person of higher rank observed the transgressor and felt that the punishment was sufficient, then activities would resume as though nothing had happened.

These were tough dudes, every one of them.

—

Our number one duty was Korean General Taxi Service. For this assignment we kept one of the non-gunships as clean as possible and then placed a red cover over the back fire wall that said something in Korean along with padded red leather seats for the Korean General and his girlfriend to ride on. Most of the time our duties would be limited to taking the general out for monthly inspection tours of the larger Korean Marine outposts so that he could impress them with his style.

Always a little after the scheduled departure time, the general would arrive at the head of a long procession of military vehicles, all properly polished and shining in the sun. All of his underlings would get out and everyone on base within visual range would salute and bow. God help the poor private who didn't see the general in time and was slow to salute or bow properly.

A special hell awaited him along with each of his supervisors because in Korean Marine land, punishment starts at the very top and rolls all the way down hill and when it hit the bottom it was big and nasty.

So off we go with the general on his throne, his aides securely belted into the rear seat beside him and me sitting on the floor, facing backwards. I have my visor down and my AM radio (LFADF) turned on to the Da Nang armed forces station which was blasting away music in my ears.

During the course of the day we would make six to eight stops with the same activity at each one. We would land and shut down; at which time everyone in the outpost stops what they are doing, salutes and then bows. Only at this point will the general hop out of his flying taxi and proceed to walk around the base being followed by all of his aides and the outpost commanders.

—

Somehow they had the rank and seniority thing worked out ahead of time because at each base the general's aides would be interspaced at a different location in the parade. Sometimes everyone would stop and fingers would be pointed and voices would be raised but by the end of the tour everyone seemed satisfied. Then we would load everyone back up and fly off to the next base where this parade would be repeated.

When the general wasn't inspecting his outposts or leading his troops, we would all go shopping. The general and his girlfriend / executive assistant, would call up the HML-167 taxi service and we would fly him over to the USAF side of the Da Nang airfield. At that point, he and the little sweetie would go into the main PX for hours.

Now time on this side of the base was never wasted because earlier I had made some business contacts on the Air Force side. It was possible to obtain quite a few interesting items on the Da Nang airfield if you had proper trading material. Nothing said let's make a deal like a new Chinese SKS semi auto rife or maybe a slightly used NVA helmet which I always kept stashed in the tail.

Air Force officers would gladly trade many gallons of bottled scotch or a nice Colt 45 for one of those weapons and I was more than willing to be a participant in this improper activity. As usual our pilots would always take a more than adequate cut of the action. After a couple of hours, the general would return with lots of bags, boxes and a smile on his face. We would gently load the goodies along with him and sweetie into the aircraft for return trip to his base. This allowed time for a late lunch at my favorite restaurant.

All of the major Korean outposts were given the call sign of "Lemon" something or other. There was Lemon Alpha,

—

Lemon Bravo, Lemon Charlie and on and on. Before landing at any of them you were supposed to call for a situation report. The US Marines at each one would come back and report the local weather, when the last time that they had received incoming fire and where it had come from. Each and every time it was the same report except for the weather. The standard report went something like, "Last fire taken was small arms rounds from the east about eight months ago".

Every day the same thing and every day we ignored it.

We got to the point where we didn't even ask for the report any more, we just showed up and told them we were on our way down. On one bright sunny morning we are doing our standard circle to land thing when the Marine in the outpost comes on the radio in a high pitched voice and says, "Last fire taken was 81mm mortar fire from the west and it was twenty minutes ago".

We looked like one of those old Road Runner cartoons where Wile E. Coyote stops in midair and tries to turn around. It took about three seconds for this unusual information to travel from the earphones in the pilot's helmets to their little hands now tightly clenched around the aircraft controls. They were yakking on the radio and pulling on everything they could think of to stop our descent. We drove off about half a mile and were finally told what had happened.

It seems the local ARVIN, Army of the Republic of Vietnam, base down the road had been infiltrated overnight by the VC. They got into the ARVIN mortar tube area and early in the morning launched a couple of live rounds toward the Korean base. By accident, during the fighting on their base, the ARVIN soldiers killed all the V.C.

—

175

We were as shocked by this unexpected event as were the Koreans.

We were to learn that a little later, the Korean Marine General gave the ARVIN commander a nice medal for doing such a fine job in killing all the bad guys. It didn't hurt anyone's feelings that the VC's aim with the mortar tube was so bad that they missed the Korean Marine's base entirely.

Well such are the fortunes of war.

Along with the general we also did a taxi service for other US Marines who had to be quickly transferred to some of the other Lemon bases during the day. We would also bring out the week's mail and on special occasions a birthday cake from the Hoi-An restaurant for one of our guys stuck in a forward outpost.

During one of those deliveries we had to shut down and wait for the Korean's to dig up something important that had to be returned to their headquarters. While we are sitting there doing a little trading with the locals, a call comes in for an artillery fire mission. This call sparks an immediate call to action and soon Korean people are running everywhere around the outpost.

The main Lemon base weapons consisted of three or four 155mm howitzers as the main artillery battery along with a couple of smaller 105mm guns for the light work. As soon as this latest fire mission is called in, our aircraft is grounded due to shells in the air. We leave the bird safely parked in the brown mud while I got to wander around the compound trying to stay out of everyone's way.

People are yelling different settings for the guns and others are repeating them and this is all in Korean so I don't understand a word they are saying. But they look good doing it and for the most part everyone is having a grand time with lots of arm flapping, ammunition carrying and gun pointing.

The call comes in to fire and away they go. The blast and recoil from a 155 mm howitzer is quite amazing if you have never been close to one when it goes off. All the guns and their crews are in a rhythm and things are looking pretty good on our end. The point of impact for all of these rounds is miles away so I can't see the results of all this activity. It doesn't take too much imagination to realize that high speed red hot steel shells filled with explosives were landing with great accuracy in someone's neighborhood.

In between shots one of the Korean lieutenants asks me, in English, if I want to shoot off a round from one of the 155mm howitzers. A 155mm round is about 6.1 inches in diameter and around two feet long. "That would be very nice, thank you", I said. I give him a little bow that I remembered from my Judo classes and his face lights up with a big grin.

He has his boys stick a nice fresh shell into the chamber of the gun followed by a couple of bags of powder. In the breech of the gun they screw in a new primer or igniter device for the powder and lock everything closed. I am given a lanyard that looks like a heavy duty lawn mower starting rope and told to stand off to the side and pull.

I do exactly as I am told and this thing fires off just like I know what I'm doing. The really interesting observation about the shot was that when you are standing directly behind the weapon when it goes off, for a very short time, you can watch that round flying off into the distance.

Now there is something you don't get to see every day.

—

As I watched the round go sailing off to do untold damage in the Vietnam countryside, my hopes were that it would land on top of Ho Chi Minh and this would end the war. The reality was it probably fell off target into the middle of a rice paddy and only killed someone's four legged dinner.

The Koreans were very used to doing things their own way because they grew up in a land where safety was not first on the list of things to worry about. My flying general's primary dislike was the seatbelt which was in place for him to use while flying. Every time he would get into his assigned seat I would pull the seatbelt out for him and smile. He would smile in return and stick it back behind his seat. As a form of privilege he would always demand that all of his staff and junior officers always wear theirs.

Oh well, what are you going to do with an unsafe general?

Most of the flights were short and we usually spent the rest of these days sitting around eating and being amused by the activities going on at the Korean Marine base. Volleyball games were a favorite activity between competing units there because in Korea volleyball had become a contact sport.

An argument would break out between teams and then the fights would start. Fighting was something that was not prohibited between the enlisted ranks because it was considered to be hand to hand combat training. The fights would resolve themselves out by matching one guy from team A and one guy from team B. Bets would be placed by the helicopter crew and the action would start.

We observed that they were all quite good at that karate stuff and we went out of our way not to piss them off.

—

When the flight schedule was heavy, we had to fly the twelve miles back to MMAF land and refuel the taxi so we could complete all of our missions for the day. One time we had a full mission schedule and it extended way into the night time hours. Our problem this night was that even though we had the general in the back, we had to refuel at MMAF or he would be walking home. We have done this before so it was no big deal for either us or the general.

It was later than normal when we parked at the fuel pits and the moon was still below the horizon so it was extra dark. Fuel was provided by a tanker that was parked next to the pits outside of the arc of the rotors. We showed up as the truck started its diesel engine and pressurized the two-inch fuel line that was on the ground next to where my bird was sitting.

That night, like always, we did what was known as a hot refuel on the aircraft. This is where we kept the aircraft engine running at idle with the blades turning while we pumped its tank full of JP-5. The standard procedure was for the two pilots to stay in the aircraft while all passengers got out and stood outside the rotor arc in case there was a problem. Rules for everyone, that is, except for the general. He was not about to get out of his seat and show fear of the refueling to any underling. I always asked him nicely and he always refuses with a short shake of his head.

This Korean general didn't actually speak to peasants.

In its normal operation the fuel truck puts enough pressure on that two-inch hose so it feels rock solid even when the nozzle is wide open and the fuel is flowing. There are two brass locking lugs on the side of the nozzle that are designed to prevent the recoil of the flowing fuel from pushing the hand held nozzle out of the fuel tank opening.

—

179

Because there was no venting system the only escape for the displaced air was the small opening between the nozzle and the locking cap rim. The air inside the tank mixed with the incoming fuel and would just scream out of this restricted opening. This jet fuel mist would cover you and everything within ten feet. The aircraft fuel tank carried over two hundred gallons of JP-5 and with this hose delivery volume it took a little more than a minute to fill it up.

We are talking about a lot of jet fuel in a short period of time.

The tank was filled and the nozzle handle released but the fuel delivery did not stop. The delivery nozzle had just failed to close and the aircraft fuel tank immediately overflowed shooting a geyser of fuel off to the side of the plane. I was instantly soaked with jet fuel and so was the ground around me. The fuel truck driver ran back toward his truck to hit the emergency shut off but he didn't make it in time.

The fuel flowed into the now filled tank and forced the nozzle sideways kicking it out of the tank. During all this I was screaming on the intercom for the pilots to get out and run. The nozzle kicked out and the high speed stream of jet fuel one and a half inches in diameter hit the red hot jet exhaust pipe and just boiled off as a white cloud of kerosene steam. For some unknown reason it did not ignite and kill all of us in a ball of flame. I wrestled the twisting nozzle into a nearby ditch and within seconds the fuel truck driver shut off the flow.

The pilots figured out what was happening in less than three seconds and they were, "feet don't fail me now", running as fast as they could away from the scene. On the outside our refueling world was going downhill rapidly but inside the

—

helicopter the general still hadn't figured out exactly what had happened but he knew it was not a good thing.

Leaving his girlfriend behind, the general jumps up from his throne and leaps from the aircraft cabin. He hit the ground safely but landed in a deep puddle of hot jet fuel mixed with mud with his shiny general shoes and almost fell on his general face. At this point he figured out what was happening and he became very upset because no one had come back to inform him of the refueling problem before the pilots had run away.

The base crash crew showed up with their ugly green fire truck after about 30 seconds to help out. They sprayed down the still idling aircraft and washed all of the puddled JP-5 into the ditch where the broken nozzle was sitting. Before they left I got a long deluge shower from one of their fresh water sprayers to wash most of the JP-5 from my hair, mouth and flight suit.

We checked the engine exhaust; put the cap back on the fuel tank and then we were ready to leave like nothing bad had happened. I coaxed the two pilots to come back but first they had a long talk with the fuel truck driver about checking his equipment. They both climbed back into the helicopter, which was still idling with the rotors turning and got everything spinning again, just like normal.

During this entire event the general's little girlfriend sat patiently in the back of the aircraft while pandemonium reigned around her. It had been observed on numerous occasions that his little sweetie would not ever move from her seat until she was directed to do so, by the general. We all came to the same assumption that she had stayed, facing death by fire because she had not been personally directed by the general to leave. Wow!

It took about five minutes to coax our upset general back into the bird after that event.

There was no doubt that someone was going to spend all of that night shining his shoes and getting the smell of JP-5 out of his uniform. Needless to say our general got out of the aircraft and waited outside the next time we had to refuel.

The most interesting thing about the entire event was that I was still alive to talk about it. I had never seen JP-5 flash to steam and not ignite before. The second most interesting thing was that in times of high stress and much excitement, our Korean General exhibited an unexpected proficiency in the English language.

Christmas time was really special for the Koreans and they tried mighty hard to get hot dinners to their Marines who were stuck on some of the far outposts, way up in the mountains. Their chow hall would make up hot Korean food and place it in the standard military insulated containers, drive it out to us on the landing strip and then we would do our helicopter taxi thing.

Up into the mountains we go through the inverted layers of temperature fog and try to find one hill top out of hundreds. What happened in those days is our guys on base could always hear us coming up the valley and tell us when we were close. When our aircraft got close we would see them on a cleared mountain top about the size of a 7-11 store and parking lot. Everyone would be standing around with smiles on their faces waiting for the food truck to arrive.

It felt good to do something nice for a change over here.

Later that day we made it back to the strip at Hoi-An where there was another delivery truck waiting for us. We checked and saw we had plenty of fuel for the run so we said, "Let's do it". They told us that this time we are taking a special load to another fire support base that is really high up in the mountains. "Special load", they said, there's no telling what this was going to be.

Three Korean Marines quickly loaded all of the big hot food containers and ten cases of their own special Korean food into the back of my helicopter. Once they hopped in and sat on the rear bench pretty much all of the available room was gone. There was a little space on the floor behind the pilot's seat for me to sit, but that was all. I started to slide the door closed when I was told by the ground crew that we had one more menu item to go.

Before I could say anything they reached inside and dumped ten live flappy chickens onto my lap. These were live fat chickens all tied together by cords wrapped around their feet.

These were not happy chickens.

All of the chickens were unceremoniously dumped onto my lap and the ground crew quickly slammed my door shut. There are now ten chickens squawking, flapping and clawing their way toward freedom. Feathers are starting to come loose and float through the air. The Koreans in the back are just rolling around laughing as hard as can be while I try to control tonight's lunch on a rope. The pilots were five hundred feet in the air before they finally figured out where all the feathers were coming from.

I wasn't able to move because of all the boxes and the chickens are trying to do the great escape by flapping their way forward and using the pilot's radio console as a roost. The pilot kept flying while the copilot grabbed escaping chickens and kept tossing them over to me.

—

It took a while but finally I got all the chickens rounded up and under control for the remainder of the trip. Everyone on the outpost had been told to expect live chickens for dinner, so when we landed, the aircraft was surrounded.

Pilot's radio console / chicken roost

The boxes got unloaded, the three Koreans walked away and finally someone leaned in and took possession of my flock of flappy chickens. Looking down I could see that my flight suit now has multiple wet white spots on it along with everything else in the cabin. The pilots thought that this is the funniest thing they have seen in months.

They can laugh all they want to but it took me two weeks before I got rid of the last chicken feather from that cabin.

Every once in a while someone new would come down from North Vietnam and decide that the way to fame and glory was to attack the Koreans around Hoi-An. The Lemon outposts would start getting hit first and there would be word in the villages about what was going on. When there was enough information about what was happening in the area, the Koreans would use air strikes and artillery to take care of the new guy and most of his troops. After the major action was completed, there was the Korean version of mopping up that was unique in execution.

Everyone has seen troops on line moving across an open field in an effort to dislodge and eliminate an enemy. Think Napoleon Bonaparte and the French army without any horses. These guys brought this open field operation to a whole new level.

Early on the morning of this grand event the Korean general would truck his boys out to the area where everything was going to take place. He would order up the taxi and take his place in a special jump seat that we installed so he could look out the right door and provide direction for the day's activities. We would then launch with the general and his aide in the back.

I am sitting on the floor, tied down to the deck with a seatbelt and my feet outside, resting on the landing skid. In my hands was my favorite M-60 machine gun suspended from the roof with a couple of bungee cords so it wouldn't fall out the door if I got shot. There were also a couple of cans of belted 7.62mm ammunition sitting on the floor beside me.

The way it worked was like this:

The Koreans would all line up on one end of the open field that they wanted to inspect and wait for the general to fly up. At this time the troops would move forward on line searching for any NVA troops who might be stupid enough to still be hanging around.

Our job was to drop down to about thirty feet above the ground while the general pointed out where he wanted the aircraft to go. I would tell the pilots and we would then zoom over there. This guy would have us fly about fifty yards in front of the line of approaching Korean Marines and look for camouflaged bunkers or other likely hiding places. When he found one, and he found plenty, his aide would toss a smoke grenade inside it and we would move out of the way.

With lots of shooting and yelling his troops would run up and secure the bunker. When the general had run out of bunkers at this one location he directed us to a new location where he had another group of Marines just waiting for him to arrive. When the general made his appearance at this location we started doing the same stuff as before.

We would spend the entire day doing this aerial leadership stuff with an unarmed helicopter and a general who loved to toss smoke grenades. If there had been even one NVA with an AK-47 or an RPG (rocket propelled grenade), ourselves, the aircraft and the general would all have been history.

—

This had to have been the dumbest thing I had ever done, drunk or sober, in the entire time I was an enlisted man in the glorious Marine Corps.

The Koreans always had their own style when it came to handling problems and sometimes you could even watch them in action and still not believe it. One of my favorites was one day when we were assigned to be medivac gun cover. A call came that one of the Korean Marine units on patrol had been shot up and they had requested a medivac. First off you knew it had to be very serious if the Koreans called for a medivac. Most of the time they would just bandage the bullet hole in the field. This allowed the wounded guy to stay in the area and continue to fight.

This was the Korean Marine version of light duty.

When we arrived on scene we saw the lead CH-46 break away and start its approach into the zone for the pickup. As soon as he started his descent, one of the Koreans got up and started running back and forth around the area where the medivac was going to sit down. We found out later that the plan was as follows. The Korean officer leading this patrol had lost face in front of his superiors because one of his men had been injured and a US medivac had been called.

This officer did not intend for anything else to go wrong with the pickup because he was now personally responsible for the aircraft he requested along with his original mission. What we were observing was the least favorite grunt in his patrol running around in the landing zone looking for landmines to set off. The Korean's always figured that if the bird had to come in for one of his charges, it was no big deal to take two injured men out, as long as the aircraft was not in danger. He did not intend to lose additional face by having the CH-46 set off a landmine at his LZ. Makes sense to me.

In those days I could think of three or four people over at Marble Mountain that I would like to send out into an NVA mine field for a status check.

During the time I was there, the Korean Marines had a change of command where the old general was replaced with a new and improved general. All of these generals were like peas in a pod as far as I was concerned. We found it to be a spectacular ceremony with rich symbolism, a nice band and lots of flags.

We also had the good taste to observe the event from the enclosed dining room of our personal mess hall so as not to interrupt the formal proceedings with our less than gracious comments.

Of course as soon as the new general came on board he had to fly around and look at all of the official mud holes that he had just inherited. More saluting from the enlisted men and junior officers was required which led to additional Korean downstream ass kicking. This happened more often than before but I guess this is a normal thing during their change of command events.

One thing that was different between the two generals was that this new one did not take unnecessary risks with either himself or the aircraft. He did one tour of the outposts when he first showed up and that was enough for him. Also there was no more flying around like a big rotary target searching for VC bunkers or hidden NVA soldiers with smoke grenades with this guy.

Searching for the NVA is what Korean captains are for and Korean captains don't get to use my helicopter.

.

Another thing that was different; this one would speak English to us directly. The other one never did that, except for that one night we almost killed him. The old general always used an interpreter when he wanted us to take care of something that couldn't be understood by finger pointing.

There was no doubt that the original general spoke English as well as anyone else at that level of power. I also knew that he liked to listen to what people were saying when they thought he didn't speak English.

I always told any new pilots ahead of time that the Korean general did speak English and not to say anything stupid or we would get in big Korean trouble.

He was a very slick guy with his hiding the language thing, but he sure understood English for about ten minutes that night when the fuel nozzle broke!

Chapter 8
The Ho Ho Hope

Total U.S. killed as of December 1970 in the Vietnam War: 54,823

Jingle Bells: Mortar Shells: V.C. in the Grass: Take your Merry
Christmas: And Shove it up your Ass
A day or two ago, we went out on patrol, it was search and destroy, this
plan we did employ
The bugs were thick as hell, the weather it was hot, we got into a firefight
and all the gooks got shot

Nothing says Christmas in Vietnam like monsoon season. For about three months starting in November, black rain filled clouds form an unbroken ceiling at around fifteen hundred feet and the world turned wet, grey and extra nasty. The feeling was almost like a low grade Florida tropical storm that just went on forever and ever.

Because there was no motorized transportation for any of the peasants inside the fence at MMAF, everyone had to put on their hooded rubber tarps before being able to traipse around the Marine side of the base. We looked like a herd of faceless green bags with legs.

These things were actual bags that the military called ponchos. They had no arm sleeves or closures of any sort other than a cord around the face hole which we believed had been designed for ease in our suicide attempts. Instead of plastic, these things were made of some kind of industrial fiber which was too stiff for tire tread and then coated with three layers of inflexible green rubber goop.

Make your way through the early morning wet darkness for breakfast at the mess hall and now you have to find a place to put your rigid rubber bag. It is best to pick a location where your bag wouldn't get stolen and the collected rainwater doesn't run onto your seat or your neighbor's

—

food. At 0500 hours we sat observing our official Marine Corps breakfast in the blue/brown glow of worn out fluorescent lighting. Adding to the dining pleasure was the odor of fresh floating mold spores and warm wet rubber from the green bag sitting at your side.

It just didn't get any better than this.

Enlisted Men's Mess Hall Breakfast   Yum Yum

After our allotted time at the feeding trough, we needed to make our way to squadron hangar row to start our work day adventure. This meant we had to walk along the edge of the pavement because there weren't any sidewalks at MMAF. Large puddles formed on the edge of the roadway which always meant you were going to get splashed by passing trucks.

Well splashed isn't exactly the proper term. Drenched with a mixture of rain water, beach sand and assorted petrochemicals that were floating on the puddle's surface is a more accurate description. Look away quickly mister

—

pedestrian or you're going to get a face full of nastiness. These multi-wheeled tarp flapping noise makers were always in a great hurry for some unknown reason and we were just another insignificant obstacle in their daily schedule.

Slog through the wetness to arrive at our squadron hangar and who do we find waiting for us with an impatient look on his face? It is none other than the thoughtful duce and a half driver who tried to drown us with his vehicle while we strolled into work!

Work on the flight line will have to wait because it's time to drag this jerk out of his truck cab and have him roll around in the wet sand for a little bit. He loudly proclaimed his innocence while we worked on turning him into a fat sand crab. As a bonus one of our fellow drowning victims grabbed a shovel from inside the hangar and started tossing large quantities of wet nasty sand into his cab until the seat was full and it began to pile up on the truck floor.

Take that, motor transport boy!

After we had vented our frustrations, with him in particular and life in general, we strolled into the relative dryness of the flight line office and tossed our green rain bags into a safe corner where they wouldn't soak any of the still functioning electronic equipment. Everything below our knees was soaking wet and our boots would not dry out until February. The cold monsoon wetness of Vietnam seeped into every crack and crevice of our being and seemed like it will never go away.

Our daily existence shuffled from having the best and most modern aviation equipment available to fight the war, to having to light a wood fire to get heat so we can dry off at

—

the end of a day. There is no middle ground here on the base and for months there will be no relief from the full body clammy feeling of wet air stickiness.

Because there was no air conditioning, the sheets of everyone's bed would always be at the same temperature and humidity as the outside air. Surprisingly enough, during the summer months this was bearable because the hot winds would dry off the bed during the day and a fan blowing directly on us would cool us enough at night for sleep.

During this excuse of a wet winter, the cold air and high humidity never went away. This was especially pleasant when retuning to our green plywood home through one of the frequent monsoonal downpours and then trying to go to sleep. Because the plywood awnings had to be nailed down to keep them from flapping open and letting in liquids, there was no air flow through the hooch. This did not help with the humidity problem. It was cold and wet enough that we would have turned on the heat if we had any but this item was not included in the standard hooch blueprints.

There were two large problems to overcome in hooch air temperature management. First it never stayed cold enough, long enough for us to invest the time to design an electric heater which would warm up our little house by the sea. Second our shack had at least two-inch air gaps around the areas where the windows should go and the cold humid wind would just whistle through these openings at night.

The burning of scrap wood inside an empty 55-gallon steel drum helped a little with the cold but after a while we couldn't take the smoke and fumes anymore. The smell of pressure treated wood smoke got into everything and really left every item we owned stinking of whatever it was that we burned that night. Looking back, the thought of carbon monoxide or lead poisoning from the painted wood we burnt never entered into anyone's thought process on the nights when we left the fire burning till morning.

In the part of Vietnam, we were now occupying, rainy season inevitably led to rat season. This wasn't because all of the rodents had waited all year to come out from their hidey holes to take a nice shower in the rain. Our original assumption was because it got darker earlier, the base rodents figured it was ok to come out and walk around when no one could see them.

What we learned, was that for thousands of years the rats of Vietnam had their reproductive cycles tied to the rice planting seasons and the rain told them that the start of their season of love was now at hand, or at paw, if you're a rat. So out they would come by the hundreds. One by one, out of their rat holes and into the darkness they came, sneaking around the unlit edge of the human's world.

They were always looking for extra food, love in the bushes, or something to chew up and destroy with their big yellow rat teeth. When we were trying to go to sleep at night, everyone could hear their little sharp rat claws scratching and sliding on the galvanized steel roof of our home. They would run across our hooch roof with wild abandon having no consideration for the residents inside trying to sleep.

Our base rats had started to adapt because they were not tied to any rice cycle like the swamp rats outside. We figured that this was due to the ever present volume of edible garbage that was thrown out in unsecured locations around MMAF. Base rats bred all year long and they grew fat and insolent due to the lack of any natural predators.

—

Outside the base, in the real world, big birds with sharp beaks and thousands of snakes would gladly eat slow, fat and nonchalant rats. In addition, the local farming population had been trapping rats for thousands of years both to protect their rice crop and to add tasty rat protein to their meager starchy diets. Hungry predators always kept the rat population thin, fearful and under control.

What happened outside the gate didn't help us one little bit with our ever increasing rodent population. The people who sprayed for bugs came around and set out poison bait but our base rats turned their whiskered noses up at these unsuitable offerings.

This bait must have been quite a bit less tasty than the mess hall food because it was never nibbled upon while the rats just got fatter. Late at night when most human activity on base had slowed down the mess hall rats could be seen running around in packs like large feral cats with long hairless tails.

Small base rats could always be caught in regular spring operated traps if the food offering was both extra tasty and difficult to remove from the trigger. Wedges of a Snickers candy bar worked best with chunky peanut butter coming in second.

The base rats had quickly figured out the functioning of the standard spring operated trap and this knowledge was passed on down the line to future rat generations. They found that by playing around on the outside of the wooden base they could set off the spring trap. Once it went snap, they could get the goodies inside without getting hurt.

The trick to catching and killing a MMAF rat was to nail the trap down to the floor. If the trap wasn't nailed down, a

—

large base rat caught by his tail or one foot would simply drag itself and the trap out the screen door and then go under the hooch to die. Within days the liquid smell from this fresh dead rat would filter up through the floor, into the hooch and odorize your flight suit and bedding for a week.

This smell was so sickening that we could never get anyone to go under the slum and remove the rat, no matter how drunk they were. With a nailed down trap the rats couldn't set off the trigger and they couldn't drag the trap away after it went off. This would give us time to run over to the trap where we would kill the rat with boots, sticks or bayonets.

Needless to say these were some bad ass rats.

Late one evening I went to sleep in my bed after finishing off a frozen snickers bar which I kept in our tiny hooch refrigerator for nighttime food emergencies. The after action report and general consensus was that I didn't get all of the creamy chocolate and caramel goodness from my fingers before falling asleep. This was bound to happen because there were those rare occasions when I would have too many cans of Budweiser brand medication before I went to sleep / passed out in my plywood home.

Much later that night I woke up with a sharp pain in one finger. I opened my eyes and there, standing on my chest, was a large black base rat eating the Snickers bar residue off of my fingertips. He must have gotten greedy and bitten in a little too deeply because he had just hit the nerve bundle on the tip of my finger.

My waking up caused the rat to stop eating my finger but he didn't take off right away. He stood there, six inches from my face, licked his rat lips and looked right at me while I

—

slowly reached down with the other hand and got my .45 caliber Colt pistol from beside my bed.

When I cocked the hammer mister rat turned, leapt off my chest and ran to the end of my bed. He headed directly for his small rat hole in the side of my hooch in an attempt to make his escape.

Just as he stuck his furry head into the hole I let loose with the first round from the hand gun, followed quickly by three more. He escaped with most of his entire fur covered body intact only because of the documented sloppiness of the Colt .45 internal assembly and not because of my semi-inebriated state.

Actually I was lucky I didn't shoot myself in the foot and take off a toe.

In those lawless days you could get away with a lot of things in hooch land without causing any excitement. Shooting four rounds inside your closed-up tin building at 0200 hours with a .45 caliber Colt was outside even these widely spaced boundaries.

Immediately lights went on and people were screaming and running everywhere. Everyone had a terrific assortment of personal weapons which were locked and loaded. They were ready to fight the enemy at the wire.

The person most excited about these events was Rick who was sleeping in the rack directly above me. Between the noise, the flashes and our small room filling with gunpowder smoke, he knew the end was near. I started to get out of my rack just as he jumped out of his and we both went down onto the floor.

—

This added to the confusion of armed people yelling and running all over the place trying to find the enemy. I looked down and saw to my dismay that my finger was bleeding from the rat bite. I figured at that point if the NVA didn't get me or my helicopter didn't crash and burn after falling from the sky then I was going to die of rabies from a wild Vietnamese rodent.

The next morning, I went to sick bay and lined up with all of the other malingers who unlike myself, were just trying to get out of work for the day. When I told my tale of woe to the corpsman he just laughed and sent me in to talk to the doctor. Everyone in the office had to come in to look at my gnawed off fingertip and have a good laugh about North Vietnamese trained attack rats. At least someone was enjoying my unpleasant situation.

MMAF Sick Bay

They gave my finger a quick spray of disinfectant and then covered the wound with a tiny Band-Aid with pink hearts on its outer cover. Everyone in sick bay got into the spirit of the times and became creative in trying to write-up my

—

injury so that I could be awarded a Purple Heart for my latest indignity.

The general consensus was, that while there may be a multitude of diseases carried by rats, at least in this location, rabies was not one of them. I was told by the medical staff that I would live a long and unproductive life drinking beer and eating frozen Snickers bars.

The Corpsmen then told me it was time to get out of their air conditioned office and go back to work. It was a long time before the people in my hooch forgot about that night's adventure and even longer before they let me have any more ammunition for my .45 caliber Colt.

During the long monsoon season there were only a limited number of things you could do for entertainment. The perpetual card game was number one. The game always included a reasonable consumption of alcohol but never any drugs. The professional card players found that they lost too much money when they consumed large quantities of alcoholic beverages or drugs of any kind except for amphetamines.

Little white crosses (amphetamines) were a fact of life at MMAF with its odd shifts and night operations and were never thought of as drugs like marijuana or heroin. A single upper was kind of like a quick two cups of coffee without the sugar. Three or four would keep you going all night and the next morning.

We were only provided with 3.2% alcohol beer so we had to consume the contents of a large number of steel beer cans to produce an adequate buzz. Because of this, the big beer drinkers found they had to go outside a lot, to use the pirate plank urinal extending behind our hooch.

—

When they got too drunk they would always walk off the end of the plank which caused them to land in a piss soaked sand trap of smelly nastiness. Anyone who did that was not allowed to come back into the hooch until they got a shower or went for a quick swim in the South China Sea.

Even we had a certain level of hygienic standards.

The super heavy whisky drinkers didn't play any card games but they sure had drinking down to science. Their days would be spent in the pursuit of their favorite bottles of joy juice and their evenings would be spent consuming the day's catch as quickly as possible.

The true alcoholics in our group would have one for the road in the morning before they left for work, drop by their hooch for a shot or two before eating lunch and then at the end of the work day they would finish up the bottle. As the night progressed they would usually pass right through being a loud and bothersome person to quickly become a non-functioning sloppy drunk individual in the corner talking only to his bottle.

The big drinkers would tend to congregate in the same hooch and that was where they would throw up and pass out. If they were involved in early morning operations the wake-up clerk always knew exactly where to find them when it was time to start a new day of aviation excitement.

We had heavy duty alcoholics back on my last stateside base so it was no big deal seeing them here at MMAF. The only problem we ever had with this excess consumption of alcohol came when we were unable to bring them back to life early in the morning.

—

If we couldn't get them back to consciousness, then they would be carried out to the roadway and tossed into the back of a passing truck. We would have them hauled over to sick bay where they would be treated for alcohol poisoning. The next day the HML-167 Commanding Officer would give everyone another big sermon about being responsible individuals and how our excess drinking was letting down the rest of the HML-167 team.

No one listened to him then and no one ever cared what he said. We all had our own set of problems and alcohol helped minimize the nightmares. Booze allowed most of us to sleep through part of the night. On the very same day that any of the drunks were released from sick bay they would always go right back to drinking with their buddies. They all said they were going to drink in moderation but they never did. We were all quite surprised that no one died from alcohol during the time we were at MMAF.

I personally know there were more than a few close calls.

Living on the other side of the intoxication bridge were the dopers. These were not the pass a little weed around inside of your closed up 1959 Oldsmobile kind of dopers. Nope. We are talking about, I am a very bored person, lots of people are trying to kill me and super high potency marijuana is $5.00 a pound, kind of dopers.

We are talking about so much weed that it would normally be left in unsecured locations inside of unlocked hooches and nobody stole any of it. We are talking about puffing away openly with your buddies till the smoke was rolling out of the openings in the hooch and the place looked like it was on fire, kind of dopers. Large scale marijuana use was such a daily occurrence that nobody ever said one word about it.

–

During the entire time I was there, our overseers did not inspect hooch land even once for anything that might be illegal. No sergeant major, lieutenant or general ever left the paved road and walked around through the sand to see what was happening in enlisted hooch land. The only time they even threatened to inspect us was when the electrical power usage went too high, and even those inspections never happened.

The problem that all of the squadron commanding officers faced was what to do if they were ordered to conduct a surprise inspection of the enlisted living quarters for illegal substances. The squadron weasels had to be telling them that marijuana was being used on a daily basis by a substantial number of the enlisted men and some of the NCOs.

So they faced two choices should an inspection ever be ordered. They could either let the rat out of the bag and tell everyone that an inspection was coming, giving everyone time to clean up their act and hide the goodies or risk losing thirty-five percent of the enlisted men to court marshals.

It was a very good thing that at this time there was no chemical testing for drug use like there is today. Between the people who actually used marijuana as a form of recreation and the people who didn't smoke but got caught downwind in the billowing clouds, there might be fifty to seventy-five percent who would have tested positive for THC.

It was lucky for us and lucky for them that no one ever pushed the issue and no inspector's nose ever tried to sniff out the evil weed inside our plywood village. The interesting thing was that all of the national news operations in Vietnam were spending their days talking about how bad

–

the drug use was among the troops and we knew they were correct.

The only thing we could ever think of was that the generals and their staff, who lived high on the hill outside of Da Nang, had to believe one of two things. Either they thought that the drug use was only an Army problem and the Marines would never do something like that or they knew about it but were willing to turn a blind eye to the problem as long as the daily flight schedules were met.

There are lots of things about this war that we will never know.

The secondary substance issue was heroin. We figured that this drug affected about five percent of the enlisted men. Like marijuana, heroin was easy to obtain, almost totally pure and quite cheap. The going price for a one-ounce glass container of the white powder was usually less than $10.00 in US armed forces play money. Because it was always obtained from the same person who delivered your weed there never was a problem with ordering or waiting for two shipments.

The heroin purity was so high that most of the first time users didn't have to worry about needle marks or even shooting up. This helped to get them hooked and once hooked they didn't care what they did to get high. The primary way to use this grade of heroin was to smoke it.

You would take a standard Camel non filtered cigarette and pull about ¼ of an inch of tobacco out of one end. Then fill the ¼ inch with your china white heroin and then snap the side of the cigarette tube with your finger till the power started coming out of the other end. Now you were ready to light up. The added bonus was that you could walk around all day with your super camels stashed in your regular cigarette pack and no one would ever know. Light one up though and everyone around you knew exactly what was in that paper tube. The heroin would burn with a sickly sweet smell that would let everyone know what you were doing and make most people walk away, quickly.

It was an unwritten rule that the dopers in any squadron always had the best music and the best equipment to play it on. This was the time when music came on vinyl records with only five or six songs on a side. We spent many an evening transferring vinyl recordings over to a seven-inch reel to reel tape deck so we could listen for hours without having to flip records.

The best high tech system in those days was a large reel to reel tape deck, a standalone amplifier and two big speakers. Through the armed forces PX system we were able to have all of this equipment shipped directly to our squadron from Japan.

In those days we were the envy of hooch land.

The problem with the dopers was always the billowing clouds of smoke. Smelling it made me sick after about two minutes but they always had the best music collection around so you learned to live with the smell. Luckily there was always a breeze blowing from the sea at night so I found a solution by sitting at the East end of the hooch and let the night wind carry the smoke out and away from me. They could smoke, snort and shoot up while I drank my Budweiser's and listened to the tunes of the late 60s.

The one nice thing that came out of the big anti-war movement back in the states was all the great music. We didn't care at all about the protests back home, in fact

—

halfway through the night we would all start singing along about the evil war in imperfect harmony.

It's funny how some things never work out like you thought they would. Here we were sitting in the middle of marijuana heaven. Incredibly cheap grass is freely passed around that is a superb quality unseen on the shores of the United States. In this place there is no law man hassling you every time you light up and all of the tunes are mellow and commercial free.

There is only one big problem. There is no grocery store on base, no 7-11 and no McDonalds or Jack in the Box, with or without a drive thru. Super grass means super munchies. What are you going to do?

You could pre stock your munchies with items from the little PX on base or you could steal food from the mess hall and have it there when you and the boys needed it. The problem was that the use of this high quality dope also came with a high quality lack of planning and preparation. These guys were either stoned out of their minds or always thinking about getting stoned. The thoughts of food only occurred after the weed had been lit but then the cupboard was bare. There was only one solution to their late night munchies problem.

On our base for those times when the mess hall was closed there was a little fast food restaurant with a single walk up window that served hamburgers, cheeseburgers and plain hot dogs. Because like the barber shop and a few other businesses it was run by the local Vietnamese citizens this place was known to all as, "Gook in the Box".

We never asked where they got the fresh meat for the burgers but then maybe we really didn't want to know.

—

Smart members of our group always asked for their burgers to be cooked well done and then they would look to see if the burger has remnants of a hairless tail under the bun before eating. All we really knew was that the snacks were cheap, quick and almost as tasty as the mess hall food. But most important to us, "Gook in the Box", was open when the munchies struck late at night and we needed ten cheeseburgers, right now.

Your first haircut in Vietnam was also something that will never be forgotten by anyone who was there. The barber shop was run by a crew of all Vietnamese barbers who were quick and good at what they did. That being said, what they did was the basic Marine haircut which could be accomplished by a ten-year-old kid with hand clippers and a soup bowl. Hop up onto the chair and the clipping starts. Hair flies and soon you are mission accomplished, looking ready for inspection. Now the fun part begins.

The barber asked you something when the cutting was done which you did not understand because you have not been in country long enough to make sense of what the locals are saying, and you're not drunk enough to be totally rude. So you figure that he was asking you if you liked the haircut or something like that and you say, "Yes".

Bad move, FNG. The barber puts his arm around your neck and as quick as a snake he twists it sideways and your neck bone goes, "CRACK". Then he asks you if you are ok and do you want it cracked in the other direction?

Everyone in the shop, including the other barbers are laughing just as hard as they can about this. Welcome to Vietnam, new boy, they all say. Here you get a number one neck crack with every haircut. I know that no one has ever

–

died from this but it is still scary just to think about it even today.

On MMAF, the airfield control tower was located right on the edge of the runway, a little bit to the north of center. It was the most imposing freestanding structure on the base due to its height of fifty feet and central location. At the base of the tower was the meteorological shack which was full of weather guessers and other buildings that housed the crash crew foam sprayers and their ugly trucks.

This was kind of a self-contained, all in one package deal for your instant military airfield needs. These groups lived and worked together and the normal people on base rarely ever came in contact with them in person. They were just voices on the radio to us.

One evening as it was just starting to get dark, "someone" got their hands on one of the very large weather balloons

—

from the weather clowns. They put a small lit flashlight inside of it, and then filled the balloon up with helium.

Once it was nice and round they attached a seventy-five-foot cord to the balloon and tied it off so it was about thirty feet away from the tower. Up went the first MMAF-UFO into the ever darkening skies of the airfield till it ran out of rope and it was left hovering a little bit higher than the tower. The little light inside it illuminated the entire exterior of the six-foot balloon making it bright enough in the darkness so that everyone on the base could see it.

It took about two minutes before everyone within half a mile of the tower had run out of their plywood shacks to see the illuminated balloon swaying around in the light breeze. It took a little more time before someone got the bright idea to shoot the balloon down.

From the darkness of hooch land, the first rounds were fired from the little single shot flare pens that every air crew had on their person at all times. First one, then another, then soon multiple flare pen rounds were arching up trying to knock the balloon out of the sky. Through all of this the balloon remains untouched and flaunts its invulnerability. By doing so it becomes an unspoken challenge to everyone on base.

There was a slight break in the action, and then the first of the .38 caliber flare rounds went off. Everyone stopped what they were doing and ran inside their own little shack to grab their own little pistols and all of their flare rounds. Within minutes there are dozens of orange flares arcing in the direction of the tower.

These flare rounds were never designed for any type of accuracy and flare rounds being fired by drunken aircrew

—

were even worse. A couple of the flares hit the control tower windows and bounced off into the night sky. Some flares went straight up and others not so much. We watched as flare rounds bounced off of hooch roofs into bushes and onto parked vehicles.

Every one of us were surprised that nothing of any value caught on fire that night.

At this point the tower shut down MMAF for all air traffic. Even though there were flares flying everywhere it wasn't too bad for the guys in the control tower. Most of the flares that were in the air at this point were harmless. They continued to bounce off the thick tower glass and not do any serious damage inside.

It didn't take more than three or four minutes before all the flares on the Marine side of MMAF were used up and the volume of shooting dropped off to almost nothing.

Thirty seconds went by and then the first tracer round from an M-16 sailed between the balloon and the tower. Soon a second one is on its way in the same general direction. Along with the sound of M-16s you could also hear the occasional AK-47 being fired in burst mode. Even with all this gunfire, the balloon stood defiant and untouched against the horizon with its little light burning brightly.

There was a break in the action as all of the drunks decided to reload at the same time. The crew manning the tower figured that things are not going to get any better for them in the near future. They stayed low and crawled outside onto the catwalk surrounding their enclosed glass office.

Here they found a two-inch rope tied onto the catwalk railing which was there for making an emergency escape

—

during rocket attacks. This may not have been a rocket attack but the air traffic control crew abandoned ship anyway. They reached the ground safely and hid behind one of the crash crew trucks where they were protected from the rifle fire assault on the illuminated balloon. The volume of rifle fire increased now from both sides of the base, but still the balloon continued to glow defiantly at all of its tormenters.

Soon after the tower crew hit the ground, one of them broke from cover and cut the balloon free from its mooring. Everyone watched in sadness as it sailed off into the west towards the Quang Ngai Mountains with its little light still burning.

I wonder what the NVA hiding in the mountains thought about that when it flew over?

Bright and early the very next day the MMAF Base Commander sent down one of his screaming letters of outrage addressed to all personnel in his command about the events of last night. The letter stated that the use of, or improper possession of firearms on the base was expressly forbidden; and anyone found with one would be severely punished. The letter was read to all members of each of the squadrons and to a man, no one had any idea what the Base C.O. was talking about.

It seems that on the night of the great balloon shoot, the MMAF brass got a firsthand lesson in how many illegal weapons and stacks of ammunition were being kept in hooch land by the peasants. They also found that no one was afraid to crank off a couple of rounds if the target was worthy enough. The brass also knew that the letter would be laughed off, but what else could they do. Remember what we learned early on about their threats.

—

What are you going to do to us, shave our heads and send us to Vietnam?

Christmas time in Vietnam brought boxes of cookies from home and marginally talented USO tour groups to brighten up our miserable existence. It also meant that Bob Hope and his entire entourage was coming to Da Nang. Not that you could ever get close enough to actually see a live person on his stage, but the thought was there and that was what counted.

The Pentagon had sent word down to the local general who passed their message down to us. Anyone who flies a helicopter within two miles of the Bob Hope show would be court-martialed and transferred to Hanoi for the remainder of the war. Nothing would give the military brass a black eye faster than someone crashing a helicopter in view of the stage and all those news cameras. Those news guys were just sitting around looking for something interesting to film.

Some things they did not kid around about.

Well if we couldn't fly over to see Bob then we would welcome him in our own little way, with or without Pentagon approval. The squadron took one of the non-gunships and decided that they would repaint it with the traditional Christmas colors. This meant they wanted it painted red and white with a candy cane stripe on the tail with the words, "HO HO HOPE" in large white letters.

The only problem we had was in finding the red paint. White was no problem because it was used for lettering on buildings and even aircraft. We found that nowhere in all of Vietnam were there any quart cans of automotive grade bright red paint to be bought or stolen. We even tried the Air Force's secret stash of goodies in Da Nang, but no luck. Rather than admit failure we went into plan B. We picked

211

up, at a fair market price; five cases of bright red paint in little hand spray cans, kind of like you get at the hardware store. Twelve cans to a case. At long last, we had our red paint and our mission could continue.

The late night painting of Ho Ho Hope

Metal shop tried to remove the helicopter's marine green paint that was covered with layers of JP-5 exhaust but that didn't work too well and it kind of left the surface blotchy. After that they primed the bird with zinc chromate and that just made the blotches stand out even more.

While the primer was drying all of us got together and punched a hole in each of the red spray cans with beer can openers to let out the propellant. Next we had to pour the paint into a regular automotive paint sprayer so it would have a smooth coat. Then using that stuff, we painted a Marine combat UH-1E helicopter cherry red with white stripes, put on the lettering and rolled that thing out of the hangar. Everyone got out their cameras and took pictures but no one in the squadron wanted to fly it.

—

Talk about your basic flying target.

Everyone got together and elected the squadron commanding officer to fly the stupid thing but he refused. He said that he was giving the privilege of flying HO HO HOPE over to the newest aircraft commander. Because he was the most junior aircraft commander in the squadron this was one of those things he could never say no to unless he wished to spend his remaining months as a permanent co-pilot.

They quickly picked two crew chiefs who were too slow to run out of the hangar in time, to man the thing. So with a full crew of semi-volunteers they flew off with much single finger waving and the flashing of press cameras.

The big plan was to fly a couple of miles south of Marble to a couple of the local villages that didn't shoot at us very often. There we were to hover at fifty feet and drop lots of little bags of candy to the local population of villagers for Christmas presents. This was kind of an aerial Christmas gift to all the little children we hadn't tried to kill lately.

This was a great idea in theory. The big brass at MMAF had contacted all of the military newspapers. They had a great time taking photos and writing what a wonderful thing this was going to be for our squadron and for the children.

The entire operation had a flawless execution on the parts of the painters, the candy droppers and the pilots, but as with a lot of things in life, final results were found to be a little less than spectacular.

The villages we were visiting had been advised ahead of time to be ready for a surprise. This information had been

—

passed down to the village people from their chief who got it from the district chief who got it from someone in the South Vietnamese government. You can see where this is going. Whatever the original message had been, was lost in translation twenty times over. Who knows what they were actually told other than stand in the middle of your village at a certain time and don't shoot at anyone.

7 Marines Launch 'Santa Bird'

Vietnam, There's Santa Cl

So when the time came for the big event every Vietnamese citizen, old and young, was standing around the middle of the village clearing and waiting like they were told to do.

Without any warning this bright red and white helicopter pops up and hovers above them. They had never seen a red helicopter in all of their lives and had no idea who HO HO HOPE was, and they didn't care to find out.

Each person, in every village we visited scattered in all directions like they had seen the devil. Actually, as we found out later, all the villagers thought it was an NVA helicopter because all of the communist stuff was painted red. The end result was that the population of every village hauled ass and would not return for the mandatory photos. Ho Ho Hope spent the morning dumping a couple of candy bags in the middle of each of the empty village centers. After that uplifting adventure our red helicopter headed home to MMAF before some enterprising young Air Force F-4 jockey out of Da Nang tried to shoot it down.

The remaining bags of candy were taken back to enlisted hooch land and were passed out to the troops. These sweets wound up being the only Christmas present from MMAF that anyone was going to get that year. The helicopter formerly known as "HO HO HOPE" was repainted back to Marine green soon after this failed candy drop escapade.

This HML-167 aviation adventure only lives on in a few faded photographs and the memories of those of us who had red spray paint on our fingers.

Chapter 9
A Present from the Hoi An River
Total U.S. killed as of January 1971 in the Vietnam War is: 55,081

Flying always means lots of fixing, and did we ever do a boatload of that. Every hour of flight time took something like eight to ten hours of repair and adjustment just to keep the machinery functioning at what we would consider a minimal MMAF acceptable level.

Now, not all of those repair hours were done by our fellow flight line serfs or even our brothers in pain toiling alongside us in the other squadron shops. If a major component went bad, we just took out the old and stuck in the new. Well not exactly always new because replacement parts ended up being a mishmash of quality factory parts from Japan, locally rebuilt stuff from some dim workshop in Da Nang or a functioning goodie plucked from one of the wrecked birds we always had lying about.

It was expressly forbidden back in the States to use any component from a wrecked aircraft but here at Marble Mountain it was like picking ripe fruit from a dead aluminum parts tree.

When an aircraft fell out of the sky it became an organ donor. This crash could have been caused by the local bad guys shooting a vital component full of 7.62 mm holes or one of our ace pilots placing some of the aircraft's high speed rotating components into a tree. At this point all that mattered was its ability to supply us with prime parts so that we didn't have to enter into the dark musty world of the Marine Corps Aviation Supply System.

After any kind of a crash landing it was important to wait for the cessation of rotary motion and then for all of the

—

unattached parts to fall onto the ground. Next, everyone inside the wreck would just sit still for a second or two checking to make sure all of their attached personality was still functioning. Then we would climb out of the wreckage and check that the fiberglass two hundred and fifty-gallon tank of JP-5 hasn't caught on fire.

Fire would turn our former flying machine into aluminum slag heap and make its value as a parts tree no more than zero. After the equipment had been made safe, it was time to see about getting the pilots removed from the aircraft.

My personal belief was that whichever pilot was responsible for causing this mess should be made to stay strapped into what's left of his seat. He should ride all the way back to MMAF on the end of a steel cable as cargo, slung beneath a CH-53.

Usually soon after a crash had occurred a squad of grunts would descend into the area for perimeter defense and to chase away all of the bad guys who were in the nearby bushes laughing out loud at our misfortune. The pilots, the radio encryption gear and most of the weapons would leave on the first CH-46 that had brought in the ground pounders. As usual the crew chief would stay with what remains of his aircraft if it had any salvage value at all. This was to make sure no one took any souvenirs other than photos.

When the area was declared safe and the bad guys had been chased away a safe enough distance, then and only then would one of the Sikorsky CH-53s from HMH-463 come out from hiding to remove the dead aircraft. A lifting strap was attached to the rotor mast and a drag chute was tied on to the tail of the now scrap helicopter so that it wouldn't twist in the wind on its way back to MMAF. After it was lifted back into the sky and on its way to its new home, the grunts

—

along with the remaining air crew would load up on the last CH-46 out of Dodge and return to base.

The dead aircraft was unceremoniously slung under the CH-53 and hauled back to the airfield like an unhappy fish in the claws of a fat hawk. The big Sikorsky would drop it into the bone yard at the south end of the field, near the sludge pond, where it could be observed by all the air crews during each landing.

This was kind of a silent reminder to everyone that flying around this part of the world was a dangerous business. While that was the plan, everyone who saw the wrecks always thought the same thing, "That could never happen to me".

In the world of helicopter repair, there were some situations where you could just remove the old broken part and replace it with something else that looked just the same. A quick acceptance test of the formally nonfunctioning system component and then off you would go to your next aviation

—

adventure. It was common that new parts often required extensive calibration to make them even function with the well-worn junk that was still on your helicopter.

New parts came from the factory with no wear in their moving joints as opposed to the existing component which could be accurately described as sloppy. Sometimes the condition of the part required us to use stainless steel safety wire or blade tape to bring unacceptable sloppiness into a tolerable floppiness. We learned early on that you were never going to get all the squeaks and wiggles out of these buggies.

To make this collection of old and new work together took time, experience and a lot of luck. When everything meshed after hours of work we would stand there watching with little smiles on our faces. In our squadron the crew chiefs were the only ones who cared about these rotating inanimate objects. We certainly knew that no one else ever had a single nice thing to say about the hours of devotion everyone put in to make our machines leap into the air again.

On the other hand, let one tiny little problem pop up or a single insignificant part fall off and both of your pilots would start flapping their lips, (over the radio no less) about the crew chief's lack of aptitude for mechanics and this obvious failing in aircraft safety.

In those days, helicopter pilots were the true chattering class of Naval Aviators.

Old worn out bearings in the rotor head caused what was called a beat. With a two bladed helicopter like the UH-1E there was always a certain degree of vertical shaking that was to be expected due to its design. When the shaking got

—

so bad that the pilots couldn't read the instruments then it was time for Mr. Fixit and his handy used parts bin. After many months of dealing with obstinate machinery I got to the point where I could troubleshoot most problems and fix them in one shot.

Late one afternoon I was approached by the flight line sergeant and asked to take over repairs on one of his problem children. It was plagued with a really bad beat that no one else could figure out. I went out, looked over the rotor system and pulled, pushed and twisted all of the push rods, their bearings and the main rotor hub.

Everything tested tight so I looked over the control rods between the pilot's cyclic controller and the hydraulic system. Everything looked good there also so we took the aircraft up for a test hop because sometimes you find that the problem is a part that only rattles in flight.

Up we go and the bird has a really bad case of the shakes, this one is the worst I have ever seen but I notice that it only occurs when the pilot wiggles the cyclic. While we are flying along I went to the back wall of the cabin and removed the large rear access panel. With the panel removed I could slide in under the transmission and look upward into the control tubes as we flew along. I immediately saw the problem.

I got on the intercom and told the pilot in a loud squeaky voice to land immediately. What I found was that one of the hydraulic actuators had broken loose from the firewall and was only being held in place with one bolt out of four. I reached up and pushed the actuator back into the firewall and held it there with my hand while he was flying. I told him to declare an emergency if he had to but get us down NOW! I said to make a minimum number of control inputs

—

and make sure that all of them are done very slowly. He was smart enough to do exactly what I said and got us on the ground before that last bolt snapped.

We set down on the airfield taxiway and shut down on the spot. If that part had separated from the firewall the aircraft would have been instantly uncontrollable and we would have crashed and died. I ended up with a hole in the palm of my hand from one of the control rod ends, along with a nice shot of hydraulic fluid under the skin.

No purple heart was awarded for that one either.

Most rules, regulations and assorted procedures were routinely ignored in our never ending battle to produce enough flying machines to make the daily flight schedule. Except for an unusual repair, no one ever consulted with the factory manual for procedures or even bolt torque values. We just tightened everything down till it was snug using our calibrated hands and then finished up the job with safety wire.

It was a truism in our world that .032 stainless steel safety wire cured most helicopter ills.

Starting power for our Hueys was provided for by a single Ni-cad battery the size of a medium size beer cooler. There was enough stored energy contained within this small box that it would   provide power for multiple starting attempts without a recharge. Given the size of our engine starter, that was an impressive achievement.

There were a couple of safety rules that we learned to follow the hard way. The first of the big rules was never wear a watch when you are repairing one of these aluminum birds. In the 70s watches either had leather bands or metal bands. Because a leather band would rot off of your wrist within a month, every watch on MMAF had a steel flex band to keep it close to its owner. This was an insignificant fact if you were a paper pusher or truck driver but a big no-no in the world of aviation repair.

Inside the outer shell of any helicopter is an unseen rat's nest of electrical wires, tubes, tiny useless components and steel cables. To repair a lot of this stuff we had to develop the skill to work without sight.

First, consult the big book both to see where this broken piece of junk is located and then how to get there without having to remove any more access panels. Now reach inside with one hand and try to locate the offending part by feel. Next work the same hand and assorted tools back into the hole and remove and replace the component. There was really nothing to it after all.

Anytime anyone was wearing a watch while doing this its nice shiny steel flex band would always become attached to an unseen bolt or another component and become one with the helicopter. The band would then break and your free government issued watch would quickly fall into an inaccessible dark region of the helicopter.

Now you had to tell the wizards in metal shop that you needed another exterior panel removed because of your broken watch. Yes, the watch which you were not supposed to be wearing. Oh, by the way. Be sure to bring an unopened bottle of the metal shop's favorite liquid refreshment to help with receiving a favorable reply to your request.

When your arm is inside the internals of the helicopter, the watch band will probably be in constant contact with the skin of the aircraft at multiple points. One afternoon a

—

mechanic's watchband came in contact with the main electrical feed line coming from the battery to the starter.

When he touched a non-insulated spot with this steel band it instantly turned cherry red due to the amount of electrical current ($I=E/R$) flowing from the starter wire to the grounded aircraft skin. ($R=0$). This would happen so fast that there would be smoke boiling out of the panel before the mechanic could even think about removing his arm.

Within seconds the steel flex link band would have become white hot liquid steel and welded itself together. The band then cooked into the skin of the mechanic's arm so it couldn't be pulled off, even though he tried.

There was never any water out on the flight line so the mechanic had to run into the hangar to extinguish his burning arm. If he was lucky the retention pins popped off the band and it along with the attached skin and cooked meat fell from his wrist. This would leave the guy hopping up and down with just a super large burn scar on his wrist and a grand war story to tell all the other worker bees.

We were also advised by those who had gone before to never wear a ring on your finger. Such a simple little thing to remember but the people who wear rings are sentimental fools when it comes to their little golden bands. It is the connection that provided them with memories of their past life. Take the ring off, put it in your pocket and you run the risk of losing it forever. "Better to keep it on your finger and just be very careful when you are working around the aircraft", each FNG would always say.

Working on any helicopter always means more than just standing next to a large aluminum box and turning a wrench. Every day you had to climb to the very top of the

—

rotor system to replace parts, adjust the blades or just inspect for problems before flying. After a short while everyone developed their own system for moving around on these oil coated shiny aluminum machines. Movement was always done with the primary objective of not falling off.

There were always daily inspections and pre-flight inspections which required all of the panels around the engine, transmission, tail rotor driveshaft, and gearboxes to be removed before flight. Oil samples and fuel samples were taken and sent off to be inspected somewhere in the dark corner of a large building in Da Nang.

When everything was tested, inspected, poked and prodded, all the covers went back on and locked down for flight. When the covers were back on most of us would use the steps to get half way down the side of the aircraft and then turn and jump to the ground.

Three or four feet of free flight always saved two extra steps.

Once you started the jump you could not stop and that was where the ring problem came into play. Because a helicopter is a relatively slow air creature its skin is attached to an interior structural frame by exposed rivets. As you slid down the side of the aircraft these rivets stuck up just enough to snag a ring.

Ninety-nine point nine percent of the time the ring would pop off the rivet with a minor tug and down you went. There was that point one percent where the rivet was too tall and the ring was caught as you jumped.

I watched one day as an HML-167 crew chief jumped down from his bird and this time the ring stayed attached to the

—

aircraft rivet. His finger slid through his ring like soft cooked meat through a circular golden knife.

If you have ever seen a cooked chicken leg with all of the meat stripped from it, then you know exactly what a ring can do to a finger. The ring with all of the skin, muscle and attached fingernail fell to the ground while the crewmember looked at the exposed bone in his finger in total disbelief.

That lasted about two seconds till the blood started spraying from the exposed veins above the ring and the pain signal hit his brain. Those of us on the flight line ran over and put a little tourniquet on what was left of his finger and waited for the MMAF ambulance to arrive.

They hauled him and all of his remaining fingers away. In those days there was no surgical replacement for missing parts and the unlucky crew chief was shipped back to the states with only four fingers on one hand and his golden circular meat slicer safely tucked away in his pocket.

It was a fact of life that every crew chief at MMAF got injured multiple times while racking up either flight hours or repair hours. They either got shot while out on a mission, hurt in a crash, or sliced and diced while working around high speed rotating helicopter parts.

To move a helicopter with landing skids we needed either a really strong diesel tractor, which the "DORF" (FORD spelled sideways), was not, or a set of removable wheels to make repositioning easier. Hook up the wheels, pump up their attached hydraulic jacks to lift the helicopter and we were ready to go.

Once we were done moving the bird we would gather up the wheels and find a place to hide them. The problem was

—

that they were too heavy to carry. The only other way to move them by hand was to squat down, grab their little pump handles, and do the duck walk all the way back to the hanger where they needed to be stored.

After being bent over for fifty yards everyone would get really tired and could think of nothing else except letting them go. One evening I made it all the way back into the hangar with my set of wheels when someone called out to me from one of the shops.

I turned right to look at the speaker while I kept walking bent over with my wheels following along. From the corner of my right eye I saw the tail skid of a helicopter and turned my head quickly forward to see where I was. At a fast walk my face impacted the sharp rear edge of the stabilizing fin on the right side of the helicopter.

Down I went.

I woke up to find that the impact with the trailing edge of the fin had knocked me out for the count. They told me that my legs went forward and my head had hit the concrete floor with the sound of a coconut falling off of a table. There was a cut on my face down to the bone from my left forehead, across my nose and onto my right cheek. With all the blood from the cut filling up my right eye socket everyone thought that I had sliced my eye open and my days in Vietnam were over.

The base ambulance arrived with much fanfare whereupon I was loaded up and carted off to sick bay. They kept me a full twenty-four hours checking for a lingering concussion and making sure that my brains had not been scrambled any more than normal.

—

Like the rat bite to my finger, this attack of the killer helicopter tail did not rise to the minimal injury level required for the award of a Purple Heart, but I was still trying.

On rare occasions, the war would loudly make its presence known at MMAF when the local Viet Cong decided they were done traveling elsewhere around the country causing chaos. We figured they checked their attack schedules and observed that we had gone long enough without someone attempting to blow up expensive military equipment inside the fence of MMAF. We would sometimes go months without a meaningful attack on our airfield, then the VC / NVA would get restless and so for a week it would become a nightly thing.

It was amazing to us that they were able to launch any type of attack at all considering that every weapon and each round of ammunition had to be hauled down the Ho Chi Minh Trail from North Vietnam. After they left the trail, all of their equipment and the people trained to use it, then had to hike almost seventy-five miles east across the mountains to reach MMAF on the South China Sea.

This was done for the most part by individual people using bicycles with heavy duty tires and simple packs on their backs. They only traveled at night because they would be spotted and killed if they tried to move supplies during the day. There were some trucks on the Ho Chi Minh Trail but they were limited to heavy loads that were difficult to disassemble. Thankfully these trucks were unable to drive across the mountains to pay us a visit.

A Russian 82mm mortar tube and base plate could be broken down into three or four parts, and each of the mortar rounds were packaged individually, but this was still a mighty heavy load. The big problem with a mortar tube was

–

you needed all of the parts to make it work at all. It was not one of those things where if you only had three out of four parts it would still kind of work. It took time to get all the tube parts together and then stockpile the ammunition.

The next problem was to find someone who knew how to use it effectively. Distance to the target is controlled by both the angle of the firing tube and the number of bags of propellant that were attached to the mortar shell. Right and left were controlled by a little crank next to the tube and the wind. It takes lots of rounds down the tube before someone is even marginally proficient in initial setup and firing.

The VC knew if the mortar rounds landed in the ocean or on top of the MMAF Officers Club, all the time and effort in getting the weapon system within range would have been wasted.

The other problem with a mortar attack was that it was not a fire and forget weapon. Even an experienced mortar man had to drop one or two rounds down the tube, then stick his head up to see where they landed. Correct the point of impact after the first rounds and then fire for effect with everything else you had left. At this time, if you were a smart Communist you would leave the tube where it was standing and get out of town as fast as your wild eyed water buffalo could carry you.

You did this because things were about to get very unfriendly in your neighborhood really quick.

MMAF was hit one time with a mortar attack in early 1971. The adventure started just after the sun was setting and the work day was over. Of course the NVA timed it for when all of the good shows were coming on the TV. By this time in the evening most of us were two or three drinks down the

—

road toward an acceptable level of intoxication and were in off duty mode.

We heard what sounded like a small explosion off in the distance but no one paid any attention to it because the Army demolition teams were always setting off charges, but usually never this late. A few seconds later we heard the next one and everyone figured out really quick what was happening.

Someone yelled, "Mortars" and in a second there was a mad rush out the door and toward the sandbag bunkers by those of us still sober enough to actually be worried. Some of the drunks just stood there with stupid looks on their faces wondering why everyone was running around and yelling.

The rounds kept hitting every five seconds or so and after about the fourth explosion we figured out that the bad guys had setup too far south of the base and didn't have the range to hit us on the north end. In an instant, everyone piled out of the bunker and climbed onto the metal roof of our hooch. Because we figured this was going to be a quality show everyone brought along their standard issue folding aluminum lawn chair for sitting and extra containers of beverages in case of thirst.

For some reason I remember that I was in possession of a large milk carton of cracked ice and real grape juice mixed with gin. We weren't the only dumb asses on the base doing this either. Everywhere you looked there were men with chairs and drinks climbing on to the roof of their hooch's trying for a grandstand view of the action.

If the NVA had been smart they would have dropped the first five rounds short and then when everyone was on the

—

roof, open up the range and catch everyone sitting around looking like fools.

Like the MIG fighter from the Chinese island, they never had enough imagination to pull it off.

There, off to the south, we could see the flash of the mortar tube when it launched a round and some seconds later the smoke and flying debris from the impact. I don't know who was responsible for setting up this attack but they had done a really bad job in planning.

The 82mm mortar launch site was way too far south and they didn't have the range to even hit the center of the base. The other problem they had was they were spending way too much time between rounds. It looked to us that their location had been spotted pretty quickly by the Cobra gunships which had launched after their third round had hit the base.

HML-367   AH-1G Cobras

—

The ability of HML-367 to launch that quickly had to be totally bad luck for the members of the mortar crew because it usually takes those guys twenty minutes to get anything in the air. The only thing we could figure was that a fully armed mission was either in the process of launching or they were just returning from medivac standby when the attack started.

In either case, up went the Cobras and down came their 2.75 inch rockets along with hundreds of rounds from their 7.62mm mini guns. All of the enlisted guys living in the MMAF ghetto had perched themselves on the top of their hooches and were chanting like it's a Friday night football game at the local high school.

The sounds of a hundred drunken voices yelling, "Hit em again, harder, harder", went out across the base.

Soon after the Cobras were on the scene there were secondary explosions and the bad guy's mortar rounds stopped falling onto the base. Everyone stayed on their roofs hoping for some more excitement in their hum drum lives, but the Cobras quickly put an end to all of that for this night.

We figured all the bad guys were dead, along with any local villagers and domesticated animals that were too stupid to leave after the first round had left the mortar tube. After this attack, the base commander increased ground patrols to the south of the field which made a couple of squads of riflemen happy because they didn't have to go way out into the wilderness to do their grunting.

A Russian 140 mm rocket could also be broken down into sections and transported by people with specially designed packs. The 122mm and 140mm rockets were a favorite long range weapon of the NVA because once it was fired there was nothing left behind to give away the bad guys location unlike the 82mm mortar tube. With the rockets you didn't need any fancy launchers or even a range finder for the weapon to be reasonably accurate.

Here is how simple they were. The local Viet Cong would obtain an incredibly accurate map of the base and the surrounding countryside thanks to the generosity of the United States Government. We printed them up by the thousands and handed out maps to anyone who asked. Using this map, the rocket launch director would figure both the distance and magnetic heading from the center of the base to the launch location.

Now using a stolen military compass, you draw a line in the sand pointing toward the center of the base. Dig a trench on top of the line just a little wider than the rocket fins with the far end a certain length and depth to give the rocket the proper trajectory and distance. The excess dirt would be hauled away that night and then they would cover the Russian 144 mm rocket in the ditch with sticks and palm fronds making them all but invisible from the air.

NVA rocket attacks always came between two and four am. Have they no decency? Everyone was tired from a tough day at the war and then it was rocket time. There was no way you could sleep through one of these events.

The rockets were less than one hundred feet in altitude when they passed overhead and their solid fuel motors were still burning with a hooch rattling roar. There were only a couple of seconds of rocket motor burn, but it sounded like it was coming through your roof. Next came an explosion that shook you and the foundation of your slum. Before you could even wake up there was a second rocket and then a third. By this time, you know the NVA has targeted your personal plywood dwelling.

You also wish that you and your slum mates had not been such smart asses and painted a giant red and white bull's eye on the hooch roof using leftover paint from the Christmas Ho Ho Hope project.

The morning's light revealed that while they sounded scary enough last night, the damage they produced on the base was less than expected. Because they had no internal guidance system most of the rounds hit open areas and unoccupied buildings. There were almost no injuries other than those caused by drunks falling out of their official Marine Corps racks.

On a side note one of the things that I learned that night was to never stuff your inflated one-man swimming raft under your rack for safekeeping. Being shaken out of a sound sleep by a communist rocket passing overhead, banging my head on the rack above me, and then falling on the floor is bad enough. In my dazed state I crawled around on the floor trying to get under my Marine steel rack for safety, but I was being pushed back by some unseen force while the rockets were impacting somewhere close.

This was very upsetting at the time and I never really forgave my raft for what it did to me that night. Putting it there kept our living area nice and tidy during the day but a fully inflated rubber raft makes it almost impossible to get under the rack during the occasional NVA rocket attack.

There were two things that were excellent trade items at MMAF which we got from the fixed wing base over at Da Nang in exchange for authentic war souvenirs. The first item was a pilot's oxygen mask, (in any condition) which was

—

used by the gun ship crew chiefs to protect their faces under the helmet visor when the gun ship pilots were shooting rockets at trees and small woodland creatures.

Little pieces of un-burnt propellant and molten metal would shoot out the back of the burning rocket motor and strike anything behind them. The person being struck would normally be the crew chief who had his head out the open door working his M-60 machine gun and looking for bad guys who were actually shooting back at us. Have the flight gear shop make up some helmet connecting snaps for the mask, leave part of the oxygen hose attached and you are cleared to stick your head out into the wind.

The white sand beach and blue waters of MMAF while looking north.

The other great item of value was the one-man survival raft that is found in the bottom of every fixed wing aircraft's ejection seat. These rafts like most other items in an ejection seat had a limited life span and as such were required to be replaced by the seat manufacturer, on a set schedule. There was never anything wrong with the raft's observed

—

performance in their new job on the beach but they were never good enough to fly as part of an ejection seat again.

Da Nang had no beach and there was nowhere else within one hundred miles that was safe for swimming due to marauding bad guys or fecal contamination in the water. Outside the MMAF east wire and within yards of my hooch was one of the finest white sand beaches in the world. The sand was made of ground up quartz crystals that were pure white. The beach extended for a good 50 yards past the east fence and crunched under your feet as you walked toward the water.

There were always small gentle waves from the South China Sea lapping at the shore line. Because there were no built up cities close by, the water was unpolluted and clear with a light green tint to it. This beach was absolutely perfect for our swimming and rafting pleasure.

The area was such a beautiful coast line that today there is a five-star resort sitting right on top of the sand where my hooch used to be.

*Go to **http://fusionmaiadanang.com/** to see the Fusion Maia Resort and what they say about the location.*

So forget the war, grab your shorts, a one-man raft and hit the beach. Float around in the shallows or ride the occasional large wave that came into the southern end. What? You say you don't have a one-man raft to float around on? I am here to tell you that there is nowhere else on base to buy your swimming accessories other than the HML-167 swim shop. We took cash and we were also willing to barter for a raft if you had quality war souvenirs of value.

There were only two things wrong with the airfield's white sand beach but neither one was a deal killer for us. The first was that the lagoon outside MMAF was the mating ground for all the sea snakes in that part of the world. We would fly over them during their mating season and they would all be together in a great ball of snakes twenty feet in diameter about a hundred feet from shore.

Sea snakes are actual air breathing snakes that only live in the water and are highly venomous. That being said, they appeared to be unconcerned about humans in the water and in all the time we were on the base we never heard of anyone being bit by a sea snake.

The second issue was with things in the water that came from the Hoi An River located about twenty miles to the south of MMAF. The Hoi An was a large river that had its headwaters in the mountain range to the west of Vietnam so it produced a fast moving large volume of fresh water.

The river pushed fresh water and all of the floating junk that it had picked up on its journey eastward, far out into the South China Sea. This water and its contents were picked up by the ocean currents and moved northward along the coast. Northward it went till it reached the shoreline of our base where some of the floating junk touched land again.

We figured it was the Hoi-An River that brought us a special present late one afternoon as we were walking into the hooch land shower to get our electro shock therapy for the day.

We noticed that everyone was standing around one of the outside corners of the building and sounding quite a bit more vocal than usual. Our group wandered over to look for ourselves and we got quite a surprise.

—

Next to the building was a full size king cobra snake in a full defensive posture standing with its head about four feet off of the sand and its hood fully open. That was one large bad ass snake. I was all ready to forgo my shower for the day when a jeep loaded with MP's pulled up, took one look at the snake and shot it full of .45 caliber holes. I don't know which was more dangerous to us, the cobra or the MP's who didn't think about where their .45 rounds would go after they passed through the snake and hit the concrete wall behind it.

While it was not as exciting as a two am rocket attack, the snake did give us something to talk about for a number of days. Everyone also became a lot more aware about where they were stepping around hooch land because, unlike a rattle snake, that thing didn't make much noise at all.

Because we were on the ocean, we had a special area of the beach where we tested our machine guns and all of the other firearms that had been in the shop for repair. We would load up the squadron jeep with the repaired firearms along with boxes of ammunition and then head down to the beach for target practice. Actually there weren't any legitimate targets floating out in the ocean except for the local fishermen who lived in the village at the south boundary of the base.

There was a set of rules between us and the fishermen that went kind of like this. You can take your little round bamboo fishing tubs directly out to sea and you wouldn't be bothered. If your bobbing little tub crosses over the southern boundary of our base, then you become a legitimate floating target.

We knew the absolute range of our M-60s and so did they but we were not philosophically opposed to shooting off fifty rounds at a forty-five-degree angle if we thought they were floating a little bit too close. This tended to keep the local VC from planning any kind of seaborne assault on our beach. You never know if they had toted a WWII surplus landing craft down the Ho Chi Minh Trail when we weren't looking.

Every couple of weeks we had big surprise for all the local fishermen far out to sea because it was Browning .50 cal. day at the range. Because of its size, the need for a mount plus the weight of all of the ammunition the CH-46 armories always brought out all of their big guns to the beach in a wagon train pulled by their DORF.

The guns were put on a heavy steel fixed mount and test fired out to sea. Five to ten round bursts from the big guns got the fishermen moving south in a real hurry. Every fifth round was a tracer and they were bright enough that you could watch them fly way out into the ocean.

Every time the 50's came out everyone wanted to play Sergeant Rock from the old comic books and hand fire one of the guns. I am here to tell you it cannot be done. The armory crew would load the gun with five rounds or so and then everyone would place their bets. The gun would go off and by the fourth round both the shooter and the gun would end up in the sand. The shooter would always have this look of surprise on his face but that didn't stop the next person from trying it.

Between our hooch and the MMAF beach was an open air pavilion with tables, chairs and a couple of weight benches. It was run by the MMAF Special Services who provided everything we needed for our leisure hours.

—

Special Services was kind of like the entertainment committee at a senior citizen's home. The only things they were allowed to do was G rated entertainment and of course that was no fun at all. We knew a couple of the local girls who would be willing to put on quite a show for no more than $20.00 US and two cartons of Salem cigarettes each but this was unacceptable to the brass.

The best thing that Special Services had to offer as official entertainment was movie night and they were all PG movies. They had some fairly new movies for us to watch but the only way they could show them was with a beat up 16 mm film projector. This machine never lasted through an entire movie without having the film jump the track or burn out the bulb. One evening we got to see the 1968 movie Bullit twice and then we started playing the chase scenes through the streets of San Francisco in reverse.

I always liked that movie.

The pavilion was also the place for squadron parties which were not always limited to squadron members because who could keep track of who was who. All parties consisted of beer, burgers, beans and more beer.

After the beer and burgers came the MMAF party games. Now these are not your standard state side party games but those specially designed to reach for the furthest limits of socially acceptable behavior in a Marine Helicopter Squadron and then go beyond.

I am talking about that all-time favorite party game known as, "chuck um up".

Here is how the game is played. First all of the players must be red level intoxicated or better than .25 blood alcohol so

—

they don't remember this event in their lives. Good thing no one was driving.

Next there were the rules:

First. Each contestant was given a pile of burgers, multiple cans of beer and an individual brown plastic salad bowl. The game started by eating at least three burgers and then quickly drinking lots of warm beer until the contestant thought he was ready.

Second. The contestant would barf up enough fresh beer and burgers into the salad bowl, filling it to the rim. If he didn't fill the bowl to the rim at first try he was allowed to continue to eat, drink and barf but during this time the first "installment" was getting cold.

An independent panel of judges would pronounce when the bowl was full and then the player could go on to the final part of the contest.

Third. To win the contest, the player was required to drink his full salad bowl and lick it clean. The first person to lick his bowl clean without re-barfing was declared the winner. After someone was declared the winner all players were allowed to throw up outside the pavilion without penalty.

This turned out to be the real man's standard of drinking games.

To say the least, we were really lacking in high end cultural entertainment at this facility.

—

Chapter 10

How to Push Start a Helicopter
Total U.S. killed as of February 1971 in the Vietnam War: 55,465

At the Marble Mountain Air Facility, life for all of us farmworkers was tolerable considering what year it was and where in the world we were located. Our base was a nice quiet corner of a world that had gone totally insane.

There were rare exceptions to our boring lives which involved rockets and mortars but for the most part the bad guys ignored us completely. We had a TV and radio station broadcasting daily from nearby Monkey Mountain. These stations provided us with all of the official government propaganda we could tolerate, along with reruns of old television shows to remind us of home.

At the end of a hard day of medivacs, resupplies and flying unappreciative generals around, we would come back to our little tin shack, grab a couple of beers, plop our worn out lawn chairs in front of our small black and white TV and watch reruns of, "Combat" and "I Love Lucy".

Official entertainment also included walking over to the enlisted club and drinking five cent beers till we passed out and had to be carried back to our slum. Unlike our brothers in the bush, we got all the food anyone cared to eat at the mess hall without having to open a steel can of balls and beans, warm it over an open fire and share it with an assortment of crawling or flying creatures.

All we were required to do was get up, have breakfast, fix the helicopters, eat lunch, fix the helicopters, drink beer and then go to bed. You didn't even have to fly if you didn't want to because only volunteers flew. Just say, "I don't want to fly today" and they took you off the flight schedule.

You could then spend the remainder of your day in the relative comfort of MMAF. Your work would all be done inside the security of a shaded steel hangar. Here you would fix broken helicopters and then return home to drink beer and watch TV inside your hooch. At HML-167 there was no shortage of worker bees waiting to take your place riding around in the back of a helicopter for a day.

How many grunts wished they had that kind of a good deal out in the bush? Oh sergeant, "I don't think I want to go on patrol today, could you take me off the list"? "Very good private, we would love to have you join us but if you don't feel like it then just stay here and polish the artillery while the rest of us go out hiking in the jungle for the day."

The problem with this was that everyday someone had to fly off into harm's way for resupply or to pick up wounded Marines. Fail to do either of these and the men in the bush would die. Because of the lack of a paved road system and the speed of infections and tropical diseases, most of our men wounded in battle would have died long before they could have been trucked back to an aid station.

In Vietnam if we were able to load the Marine inside our helicopter while he was still alive then he stood an incredible chance of survival. The end of war statistics showed that if our Marine was alive when we got him inside the cabin, only 9.9% died from the wounds they received. That's a pretty good record and one of the few things that all of us did over there that I am still very proud of.

When we flew our missions those numbers were not available to us but we knew that we made a difference in the lives of thousands of men out humping through the bush every day. There were times when we were called on to divert from one of our normal supply missions to pick up an

—

unknown status medivac. Landing sites were sometimes only a small clear cut red clay patch on a pathway through the jungle or some small rocky firebase on the top of a pile of rocks. The hilltop firebases were always the size of a gas station's parking lot with a sheer drop of five hundred feet on all sides.

Sometimes we would land and there were three marines that needed to go to 1st Med, not just one. What are you going to do, say "no, get out" because you only reserved space for one? We did what we had to do and we were always able to bring all of them out with us.

There were a few occasions when the load was just way too heavy for our little helicopter. On those occasions I would strap all of the injured men down onto the floor, get out and slam the door shut. I told the pilot I would wait here in the wilderness till the next taxi arrived to take me back to MMAF. Hopefully my transportation would be provided in time so that I might return back to the base and watch Combat on the TV instead of being an unwilling active participant in the real thing.

Standing in the mud and watching my bird fly away was not something I ever enjoyed doing. The beat of the rotors would slowly fade as the bird moved away down the mountain valley. Eventually even the high frequency whine of the engine was absorbed by the thick brush. It didn't take long until the realization set in that I was alone, standing on this exposed hilltop wearing my nifty green flight suit and plastic helmet.

The worst part of being left behind was the fact that I looked different than everyone else on the entire firebase. The most important rule out in the bush was, blend in and don't look different. No saluting of officers and no wearing of shiny badges of rank to make you stand out to the people walking around and watching you from out in the woods.

To any NVA sniper I was target number one as soon as I stepped out of the aircraft. I could be a visiting general and this flight suit was in reality, a general suit. What did they know? Every time I was a guest of the grunts I tried to find a very low place in-between rocks to sit. If I was required to move around in the open, I always borrowed someone's green camouflage jacket and steel helmet to wear.

When our aircraft first arrived at any outpost, unloading the boxes, supplies and ammunition was the first priority. When you have made space and lightened the load, then you can bring on the casualties. It was hard to make the grunts understand that we were always able to bring in a lot more cargo than we could takeoff with because gravity helps with the landing but works against the machine when it is time to return to the sky.

With only 1,100 horsepower, the Marine UH-1E was so underpowered it was very difficult to get back into the air after some of these landings. No matter, we never left anyone behind. On the mountain top firebases, we would launch off of the tiny landing area at full throttle and leap out into space without enough airspeed to hold altitude.

Gravity took us down toward the valley floor which allowed us to gain enough forward air speed and transitional lift so we could start climbing again. There is no amusement park ride in the world that can compare with a ride like that because there are no tracks to take you back up when you reach the bottom. It is also very important that the pilot doesn't snag a roll of concertina wire sitting at the edge of the base with your skids or you will never reach flying speed.

—

The aircraft would become one with the valley floor and this would be a bad thing.

Our faces were always hidden behind helmet visors and boom mikes so we got to pretended to be Mr. Aviation Professional when dealing with the grunts. There were no shields to cover any of the faces of my taxi's customers and I could see every emotion.

Fear of death, sharp throbbing pain from bullet or fragmentation wounds and broken bones. They displayed emotional shock and uncontrolled anxiety about what the next couple of hours of their unfulfilled teenage lives would hold.

Life or death was always presented unfiltered and in stark black and white reality to all of us who worked in the back seat.

Most of the time there were no niceties involved with loading the causalities. No chit chat or idle talk about the nature of his wounds, just slide the body inside, shut the door and launch. For all of my customers, life and death was sometimes measured in minutes and everyone knew it.

The casualties loaded on board were still covered in red clay and mud from where they fell. Their blood soaked uniforms were cut away and left on the stretcher while pressure bandages went right on top of the open wound without cleaning it first. The men loading the casualties learned never to take an extra second when loading because a helicopter sitting in an open field is a big expensive target. Take too long and it might not be able to leave with your buddy because of damage.

Usually four men carrying a litter would run over to us carrying their wounded friend who might still be bleeding

—

badly. They would always start screaming to go, just go and please help him. Grab a handful of pressure bandages from the corpsman being left behind and try to stop the bleeding as we lifted off.

If I was able to stop the first bleeder, I would turn him over on his side and look for other wounds. All I could do at this point was to try to stop the blood flow until the ride ended and the Marine was delivered to the team at 1st Med. No matter how badly he was hurt there was not a single thing more that I could do to improve his chances of survival.

In our world, especially for my injured passenger, speed was life.

I would look down at the man lying on the floor beside me. We both understood that my aircraft was the difference between their eventual return to a normal life back in the world or a slow, painful death in the jungle or on an inaccessible mountain top. They knew it and their buddies who carried their broken bodies over to our helicopters knew it also.

A lot of these men did a little extra or went a little further every day because they knew that if they ever had to look death in the face, the Marine Corps in general, and my helicopter in particular, would do whatever it took to get them out to safety when things went as bad as they could possibly go.

At the end of one of these days when the fuel tank is filled and the blades have stopped spinning, you just sit there on the metal deck of the helicopter and reflect on the day's activity. All of the wounded have been taken away to meet their fate behind the doors of 1st Med.

The spilled blood and dirt has been washed from the aircraft's worn aluminum deck leaving behind no trace about what happened today except in your memory.

Unlike the orange clay of the outposts and dried red blood from our wounded Marines, the vision of what was seen during those days will never be washed away.

Boredom will always get you to do things that a sane person would never even think of doing. It was boredom with my life hanging around the beach in Florida that caused me to join the Marines in 1968. In 1970 boredom caused me to ask to be transferred to Vietnam so I could get away from my daily dreary existence in Southern California.

Think about that one for one minute. There I was, 20 years old with no real responsibilities to speak of and in the best physical shape of my life. My base was on the coast between San Diego and Las Angeles during the beginning of the California sexual revolution. Love was free but instead of taking care of the needs of assorted young California ladies I directed my life's pathway toward something more exciting.

Looking back, I think someone put some kind of hallucinogen in my orange juice.

The truth was, it wasn't the North Vietnamese Army or even their little cousins, the Viet Cong that were the big killers at MMAF. The big killer without any doubt was boredom.

Parked next to our squadron in Vietnam was a squadron of flying toads know as CH-46's. These were ugly helicopters manufactured by the Vertol division of the Boeing Aircraft Corporation. This aircraft was designated as a medium lift helicopter as opposed to either the little pee pots that we rode around in or the jumbo flying elephants made by

—

Sikorsky that lived on the south end of the field. This squadron was HMM-364, and their call sign was, "Purple Foxes".

Like all of the helicopters in the Marine Corps inventory in Vietnam they looked wrinkled and worn out even though they were only a couple of years old. Their Marine Green paint soon faded from being parked outside in the harsh Vietnamese sunlight all year long.

No one ever took the time to protect their exterior from the elements and so they were blasted by the wind driven salty beach sand all year long. There were stains on the paint from hydraulic leaks or fuel spills, and their tails were black from the carbon exhaust of two General Electric gas turbine engines.

Look closely at any bright spot in the exterior dullness and you will find a recent patch job or two needed to repair damage done by either an AK-47 round or land mine fragmentation.

The only Plexiglas windows in any of these aircraft were forward of the crew door and only for the use of the pilots. Pick up a load of grunts and they were always getting excited about the littlest of things when they went for a helicopter ride. Every one of them had a bad habit of sticking their M-16s through the round cabin windows and shooting up the edges of the landing zones as they were in the process of being extracted from a firefight.

When the aircraft were new the squadron replaced the windows two or three times but finally everyone in the CH-46 squadrons just gave up and left all of the new windows in the hangar.

Unlike our Huey, this green bus had wheels with hydraulic brakes so it could roll around like an ugly three-wheel tricycle and stop where it wanted to without bumping into things. This meant that when they wanted to move their helicopter to a different location on the field they didn't have to lift the whole thing off the ground with jacks or pepper everyone within one hundred yards with a rotor blast of flying sand and dead bugs.

This is a very civilized thing for a helicopter to do.

There was also none of that leaping in and out of the cargo compartment stuff for these guys. In the back they had an

—

aluminum ramp that was hydraulically actuated so if you knew what you were doing you could just amble into the interior of the cargo compartment with style. The ramp like the rest of the decking inside the aircraft, had come from the factory with a very nice non-skid type of black paint.

Unfortunately, at this time in the lives of these aircraft, the anti-skid paint was just a forgotten memory and all that was left was a shiny aluminum surface which was always slick with a combination of jet fuel and hydraulic oil. If a crewman was not careful in how they ambled, they could be like many a new guy and slide right down the ramp and land on their butt in the dirt.

Well, so much for a graceful entrance.

The interior skin of the aircraft was mostly invisible due to a spaghetti-like mess of wires, aluminum control tubes and hydraulic oil lines running all along the top, from the front to the rear of the cabin. Sticking down through these assorted items was the rear transmission which was always leaking hot red dyed hydraulic oil on the deck and the rear ramp. Because this was a tandem rotor helicopter, the front transmission also leaked hot oil but it only dribbled oil on the pilots, so did anyone really care?

With their squadron being right next to ours they were always hanging around borrowing tools or using our DORF when theirs was broken. There always an open invitation from them to go for a ride in a real helicopter. So anytime boredom overcame common sense, we would do just that.

Check in with the pilots and have a seat in the back like the rest of the cargo. I started out with just a couple of test flights and then I got invited along on actual missions.

—

Nothing very exciting to the Purple Fox regulars, but to me it was something new, and anything was better than just sitting around drinking endless cans of beer and waiting for my return to the world date to arrive.

The first thing I noticed was how much more power this thing had. On a cold night we might be able to coax 1,100 horsepower from our single little Lycoming engine, even with my modifications. These bad boys next door had two General Electric gas turbines pumping out almost 3,000 combined horsepower to turn their rotors.

No falling off the mountaintop to gain airspeed with this ugly green toad.

Far worse than the oil leaks, or the fact that their metal shop fixed bullet holes with patches made from used beer cans, was the noise. In fact, the word noise does not begin to describe what it was like being inside a thin aluminum tube with two unshielded gas turbine engines on the outside and two internal transmissions that were turning that three thousand horsepower into a variable rotational motion.

The sound was so loud that it made your voice useless. If you yelled as loud as possible right next to some one's ear they might be able to hear a few screeches of what you said. Without sound suppressing microphones and padded earphones you could not communicate except by hand signals. We were told that originally there was a sound suppressing blanket attached inside the cabin to cover up this exposed mess and hold down the excess noise. We figured that it probably lasted as long as those little round Plexiglas windows.

While motoring along on our way to take care of a troop insertion at some far away swamp, the boss grunt was always given a piece of paper and a pencil. If the grunts had something important to say he had to write it out and it was then passed on to the crew chief. One of the first important lessons that I learned while riding around with the Purple Fox crew was, don't ever pay any attention to what the human cargo has to say.

After a while I found great wisdom in this statement.

Everyday someone on high found a new use for the Boeings; which I suppose sounded good on paper but presented more unexpected problems than they were worth. For example, the big thinkers in Washington decided it would be a wonderful idea if we bagged up all the rice in this part of Vietnam and took it to a safe location so the bad guys couldn't eat it for lunch.

Sounds like a good plan, let's use a multi-million-dollar flying machine, five crewmen and thousands of gallons of jet fuel to haul $1.00 bags of rice all over the place. Didn't our fearless leaders ever hear of a new invention called a truck? But then again we weren't big thinkers.

What do we know anyway? Obviously stealing their rice and flying away with tonight's dinner was an important part of winning over the hearts and minds of the Vietnamese people.

We would show up at the landing zone to find that the rice was already bagged up and ready to go. No one had any idea how much all this rice weighed so it's a balance between overloading the bird and making a single trip or having to come back to Big Stink Village for a second load. A line of local women with funny straw hats would load the rice into the helicopter till the crew chief says it's full and then off we would go.

The only problem was that these cheap burlap bags leaked rice from both ends and at the end of all the flights there was a thick layer of rice covering the cabin floor. What we found out later was that some of the rice had worked its way between the floor plates and fell into the bottom of the bird. There it sat for months until the rainy season started.

Because there were no windows in the back of the aircraft, the rain would just wash in during flight and then most of it would wash right out the back tailgate. That small amount between what came in and what went out was the amount that worked its way between the cracks of the deck and mixed with the dried blood and the rice down in the sump.

When the summer sun came out warming the aircraft, the rice would start to grow and the crew members now had the problem of mowing the cargo deck due to a field of rice stalks inside the aircraft. Everyone was just glad that the

—

generals didn't think to make us haul the water buffalos out of the area also. Who knows what would have started growing under the deck then?

The Marines would take their flying machines out every day and just beat the snot out of them in the course of doing their job, which was staying alive. After a while the helicopters started to lose that new showroom look. Because every other Marine aircraft on the base looked exactly the same, we really never noticed how trailer park trashy the entire Marble Mountain helicopter fleet looked.

There was one occasion when we were all brought back to reality.

For some unknown reason a single Navy version of our CH-46 flew in from a carrier that was beyond the horizon and landed at MMAF. Everyone figured the primary reason for the visit was so the pilots and crew could list this flight as a combat mission in Vietnam. They could then award themselves assorted ribbons and metals for bravery in the face of the enemy.

The enemy of course being the Marine Corps.

The Navy CH-46 set down at the North end of the base and by the time it had turned off the active runway at mid field, everyone had stopped working on their own aircraft. Crowds of Marines walked out of their hangars and stood around in little groups staring at this strange creature from beyond the horizon.

Their bird was painted Navy gray, complete with proper white lettering, numbers and official decals. It had all of its little windows installed and its gray paint had been waxed enough so that it reflected bright sunlight into the eyes of all of us who watched this spectacle. The Navy crew wearing

—

clean uniforms filled up their machine with our JP-5 at our fuel pits and then wiped away the spillage with nice clean rags. We looked at them, their uniforms and their helicopter like they were from a different planet.

Then without a "thank you very much for the fuel", they flew away, never to be seen again.

The most endearing virtue about any of the CH-46s was the sight of two .50 caliber Browning machine guns, one on each side of the cabin pointing in the direction where the bad guys might be located. The 7.62mm M-60 the Huey carried was ok for spraying an area to keep people's heads down but not known for serious destruction. We carried hundreds of 7.62mm rounds and could just keep shooting till the barrel started to melt and then bullets would fly in all directions. This happened more than once so we always carried half a dozen extra gun barrels for just such an occasion.

Port side .50 caliber machine gun

The .50 caliber Browning was an entirely different creature. There was no spray and keep their heads down shooting with this bad boy. The rules were to start shooting as soon as you entered into a hot zone and just aim at the tree line. The rounds out of this gun would shatter boulders and cut down trees along with anyone who was hiding behind them. If the bullets didn't hit them directly then the wood splinters and rock fragments would. Nobody from up north ever went toe to toe with a Browning .50 caliber machine gun and went back home to Hanoi to tell the tale.

Having an overabundance of spare time and a large quantity of items for trade allowed our little group the ability to acquire nonstandard equipment that would be of benefit to our squadron's mission. One day we came across an extra .50 caliber machine gun that had somehow fallen out of the military supply system. It soon became the property of our HML-167 flight line.

Now we tried to figure out a way to mount this beast to the Huey's thin cargo deck so we could have a kick ass gun for ourselves. Between the metal shop, flight line and the ordinance shop, we got Mr. Browning bolted down and ready for testing.

Not having a care in the world about the lives of the aircrew or one of the squadron aircraft, we took our newest creation into the sky over the South China Sea for a live fire test. Other than pushing the bird sideways a little bit and shaking the airframe so bad the engine gauges couldn't be read by the pilots, it seemed to work out ok.

Everyone was having a grand old time shooting the gun and whooping it up like we were at a high school pep rally. That was until we noticed that the recoil was causing the floor mounts to crack and disconnect the cargo deck from the airframe. Oops.

With great reluctance we stopped shooting our new toy which stopped the spread of the crack in the floor. That evening, with heavy hearts, we acknowledged that was one in country modification that was not going to have a positive outcome. We fixed the floor and removed all evidence of our well intentioned modification. We stayed with the M-60 machine gun and pretended it was ok but the problem was, we all had .50 caliber envy.

I got to play with the big guns during test hops out over the water but they never did let me man one during any of the real important missions in the CH-46. After a couple of missions, I was allowed to bring along my own M-60 to help out with the light work but that was as far as they trusted me.

CH-46 tail gunner or stinger waiting for mission to start

In the beginning I felt like I was like an extra bag of charcoal at someone's party. I was always kind of a pain in the ass during the planning stages but my little M-60 could be very useful in certain situations.

I was designated as the rear ramp gunner anytime they thought that someone might try to shoot at them as we lifted off from a hot LZ. First they took a gunner's belt, which is just an adjustable nylon strap about twenty feet long with a four-inch-wide waist belt attached to it and adjusted the length so you wouldn't fall out the back of the bird. Then we were all set to go. I would plant myself right on the seat by the ramp and as we lifted off, I would lay down on the ramp and look over the back edge for bad guys.

The pilots would pull full collective on the CH-46 to launch the aircraft out of the zone which caused the engines to go to full power and the back of the bird became blanketed in thick black engine exhaust. As the bird cleared the tree line the pilots would push the cyclic forward and the nose would drop down as we fought to gain both airspeed and altitude.

Sitting in the back of the bus, my job was to shoot anyone who hoped up from the bushes and shot at us or even looked like they are even thinking about shooting at us. Actually, if I saw any bad guys hop up I would shoot them and everything around them no matter what they were doing, the rest was just a legal disclaimer. Just their bad luck if they were just standing around on the corner, waiting for the bus when they got shot.

The US Navy and the US Marine Corps generally flew the same aircraft but they employed them in totally different missions. It was an unofficial standing order that the Navy would not accept delivery on any new aircraft until the Marines had been using it for a while and everyone swore

—

that the design (CH-46A) was still airworthy. Marine pilots tended to be a little harsh in the treatment of the engines and aluminum airframes.

A good case in point was watching a CH-46 get in and out of a hot landing zone. When it was flown by an experienced Marine pilot, this was a glorious thing to observe. Experienced Marine pilots had a number of in-country tricks, like the "button hook", that they used to get the most out of their aircraft.

Instead of a long straight in approach, an experienced 46 driver who had received his merit badge award for "hot zones" would come into the LZ low, as in under 100 feet and well over 100 knots. At the edge of the LZ the power comes off and the bird is brought into a steep high g turn causing both airspeed and altitude to bleed off, rapidly. Do it right and you will land right in the middle of the LZ with zero airspeed and zero rate of descent.

Do it wrong and you would end up ten feet above the LZ, out of airspeed and out of ideas. This would be known as a hard landing. In either case, you make it in to the medivac without getting additional holes in the side of the aircraft.

This, along with other accepted combat maneuvers were expressly forbidden by NATOPS. This was primarily because each one always exceeded assorted design limits for stress and reliability for the airframe. The problem was that when people are shooting at you with lots of big guns, no one really cares about placarded design limits or books written by people sitting behind large wooden desks back in Seattle, Washington.

The Boeing designers of the CH-46 had a justifiable reason to worry about the uncontrolled antics of the Marine pilots who were flying their aircraft.

It seems in 1967 a serious design issue was discovered with the airframe that led to the aft pylon and complete rear rotor system breaking away from the front part of the aircraft during flight. The Marine Corps lost six of the birds in quick succession, (killing almost everyone on board), before the entire fleet was grounded and an emergency fix was developed.

The fix involved the Marine Corps removing engines, gearboxes and the outer skin of each aircraft. Then at frame 410, brackets, braces and additional structural components were riveted and welded into place by Boeing technicians. Surprisingly the repairs worked and no more CH-46s broke in two and fell out of the sky, but its reputation as a crowd killer was hard to shake.

The name of "Boeing Body Bag" stuck around for a long time after this series of structural failures.

The Boeing CH-46 did have one trick up its gearbox that no other helicopter had. Because it had a tandem rotor design, it had totally different flight characteristics than a machine with a main rotor and a tail rotor. When the engineers created the CH-46 they blessed it with a magic system called, "hover aft", in an effort to somehow make up for its incredible ugliness.

With hover aft the CH-46 guys could just flip a switch and then the dual rotor system would change its flight dynamics. This allowed the aircraft to stay level while the rotor system tried to pull the aircraft backwards. This was the aviation version of using an automatic transmission on your car to

—

slow down. Instead of hitting the brakes, just shift your car into reverse and rev the engine. There was one little problem with the system. Boeing said it was only allowable for the pilots to use hover aft below 30 knots due to airframe limitations.

There was something in the memo about a weak aft pylon or something like that.

Marine pilots in-country didn't pay any attention whatsoever to that or any other directive from on high. Our CH-46s would come screaming into the LZ at 120 knots plus and pop on the old hover aft while pulling lots of power with the collective. It was like pushing the down button on an express elevator except you got a lot of airframe shaking, rotor popping and engine screaming to make your ride down into a hot zone under fire even more enjoyable.

The procedure might be way outside of the aircraft design limits, but down you went down like a fat rock in still water. Hit the ground hard and let the main landing gear struts take the punishment. The ramp was already in the process of coming down, so when the bird arrived close to its destination, they would start moving the grunts out the door or the wounded men, in. The pilot kept pulling some collective to keep the torque up, and never let the engines come off line.

Even as the last grunt was on his way down the ramp, the machine was already starting to lift off. They were back in the sky faster than you can say, "Last one home buys the beer". When the boys back in the old Boeing plant heard about this, they started squawking about, "airframe life" and not being, "structurally sound" along with other silly little things like that.

—

Soon official memos started flying. The Boeing technical representatives flapped their arms and wagged all of their fingers quite a lot but not one single pilot in any Marine squadron paid them any mind. The CH-46s were flown the same way as before, day in and day out.

No one could treat Boeing aircraft engineers like that so they took action the only way they knew how. They came out with an in-the-field aircraft modification kit that included a red warning decal and a hidden switch behind the instrument panel that was hooked up to the air speed indicator. This modification only allowed the hover aft system to work when the airspeed indicator on the instrument panel was below 30 knots. That way, the pilots would not be able to damage the bird and void the toad's warranty. This really pissed off the pilots because hover aft was something that actually worked, and unlike the engineers, the pilots were still getting shot at.

Life in a CH-46 squadron was not all turning and burning. There were a number of times when we would go out to a forward Army helicopter field, shut down and wait for our load of weary Marine riflemen to arrive by truck from wherever they had been off grunting. Inevitably the vehicle and its dusty cargo would always show up late for the advertised departure time.

Everyday our rifle toting cargo jumped down from the truck bed and straggled inside to take a window seat. The CH-46 then started up and away we would go off to take our customers home. This usually allowed us to be back in time to share in any boxes of goodies that someone in the hooch got from home.

There were some days that we felt like we were nothing but loadmasters on a noisy green dump truck.

—

At the end of one day we were parked at a forward Army base in the heat for over an hour with everything shut off and feeling very unappreciated. There was no shade anywhere except inside the aluminum can and nowhere cool to lie down except in the grass under aircraft's drippy fuel tanks. Nothing to do now but wait for our grunts to arrive so we can start up the bus and leave.

In their boredom, the pilots and the crew chief conspired together to come up with an ingenious plan to provide us with some quality entertainment. For twenty minutes they are standing around improvising a plan to pull this off. Not being a real member of their flight crew I was left out of this initial stage of their scheme.

Here's the background of what happens behind the scenes during a normal CH-46 start. When it is time to fire up the engines, the pilot opens an electric solenoid by flipping a switch in the cockpit. This allows pressurized hydraulic fluid to spin the starter of a little jet auxiliary power plant up in the tail. The sound of 3,000 psi hydraulic fluid hitting the starter is just like someone hitting a thick steel pipe with a very large sledge hammer.

After the initial bang, the little jet engine starts up which then provides electrical and rotational power to start both of the main engines. If you didn't know how the system functions it all seems like magic, and we could rest assured that the grunts didn't know anything about the aircraft's starting system.

The crew chief didn't tell me exactly what they are planning to do, but just said to play along. OK, I could do that. Anything is better than spending any more time here in Army land. We waited just a little bit longer and then the squeaky truck loaded with our passengers arrived.

—

These guys piled out looking like they have been fed poorly and abused by officers who knew what they were doing. They gathered into a dusty green line and schlepped inside the CH-46, set down their rifles, took off their packs and with pronounced weariness, let them drop onto the deck.

Act one: As they were all milling around inside the cabin, the crew chief comes out of the aircraft cockpit where he had been talking loudly to the pilots about some problem. He walked up to the grunt sergeant and took him outside to where I was standing.

Act two: The crew chief tells the boss grunt that there was a problem with the aircraft starting system. He was told that the aircraft's starting battery, (which there is none), has died and we needed all of his men outside to help in starting the bird.

Ok so far but I still haven't figured out what the game plan is. The sergeant was told that we needed to utilize an emergency start procedure involving the ground taxi interconnect that runs between the main gear and the starting motor.

The story told to them goes like this, "Because the starter motor could be used to power the main wheels for ground taxi, the main wheels could also be used in an emergency for starting the same little jet engine". In other words sergeant, "All of us are going to push-start this multi-million dollar helicopter so we can leave".

It is very hard to keep a straight face during all of this but the fact that all the grunts were really tired and still well armed helped a lot. The sergeant didn't believe one bit of the story but the crew chief showed him something in the main gear that convinced him. He yelled for his boys to

—

leave their junk inside the bird, get out here and gather round.

Act three: The exhausted grunts gathered in a circle around the air crew and their sergeant whereupon the bitching started. Not about the absurdity of push starting a helicopter, but why did they have to do it and not just let the aircrew do it. Who can argue with that kind of common sense? "Just push the stupid junk helicopter and we can get out of here", the sergeant yells at them.

The bitching stopped and they actually lined up behind the bird by the ramp support and at the rear of the fuel tanks over the main gear. The crew chief used a hand pump to raise the rear ramp off the ground, the pilot yelled out that he was ready and off we go.

The bird rolled forward till it reached about three miles an hour, (which is all the speed these guys have left in them), and the pilot begins his emergency starting sequence.

He mashed down and then quickly released both main gear brakes which caused the front end of the helicopter to dip down on the front landing gear strut. It looked and felt just like someone popped the clutch on a 62 Chevrolet. As soon as the nose gear bottomed out, the co-pilot flipped the hydraulic accumulator solenoid switch and with a loud bang, (kind of like the 62 Chevrolet clutch sounds like), the helicopter starting engine fired up.

Praise the almighty, it's an aircraft miracle!

The final act: With a loud cheer from the grunts I dropped to the ground in total exhaustion after doing more physical work in the last ten seconds than I have had to do all year at MMAF. They were patting themselves on the back while the

—

crew chief was shaking the hand of the grunt sergeant. Everyone climbed back inside the CH-46 while the main engines are starting up and took a seat.

I didn't say anything to anyone during the entire trip back to their base. No smiling and no chatter on the intercom in case one of the aircraft push starters heard what we were talking about. While we were flying along at three thousand feet was not a good time for them to find out what had just happened.

We landed at their base west of Da Nang and the squad picked up their sweat stained junk, exited from the cabin and walked off into the dust of another day. Thanks for the push guys. "We'll get the battery fixed for the next time", we promised as our voices were lost to the transmission whine.

It wasn't till we were leaving the ground that we all looked around and realized what we had done. Somewhere down there, there was an entire squad of grunts who were telling everyone they could find that they had just push-started a helicopter.

Of course, no one in their right minds would ever believe them, no matter how many witnesses they had, and so the fights would start and go on for weeks.

I never forgave myself for being a part of this awful deception. Perhaps never is somewhat of an overstatement, two days is probably a more accurate statement.

—

Chapter 11
PFC Raymond M. Clausen Jr.
Medal of Honor recipient

It is said that nobody ever goes out one morning with the intention of winning the Medal of Honor. When the president pins it on your chest, you become a "recipient."

Mike Clausen standing in the crew door of his bird

PFC Mike Clausen completed his first 13-month tour of duty in Vietnam while flying with HMM-364. Around September of 1969 he returned back to the States where he was assigned to HMM-261 at Marine Corps Air Station in New River, North Carolina. Being less than appreciative of stateside rules and regulation Mike lasted there for all of two months before he requested and received a quick transfer back to the war in Vietnam. In November of 1969 Mike Clausen returned to Marble Mountain and this time he was assigned to HMM-263.

Mike Clausen lived all of his days only to fly in his machine. Everyone who knew him could see that after 2,000 hours Mike and his 46 were more than just the sum total of man and machine.

Other members of HMM-263 stated that he tolerated the Marine Corps rules and bureaucracy only because they gave him his own 46 along with the pilots required to fly it. When Mike was in his helicopter he was the master of his rotary world and nobody could give him orders.

Well, actually they could give him orders, it's just that he wouldn't always obey them. Mike flew with an instinct that was developed after surviving over 1,990 missions in one of the most dangerous places on earth for helicopters and helicopter crewmen. If Mike felt an order was so wrong that it might endanger completing his mission he would not hesitate in telling the pilot, "No".

Whenever the bird was airborne he knew that it was his decisions that decided the fate of both the pilots and crew along with those on the ground who were praying for his arrival.

When Mike wasn't flying he was counting down the hours and the minutes till he could hear those engines start and feel his machine lift off again. Mike on the ground was just another lost soul wandering around the Marble Mountain

—

Air Facility but in the air his life was fulfilling and had meaning.

Mike's propensity for standing up to the officers and NCO's in his squadron was the only reason why he was a PFC Crew Chief after all those years. It was also the reason why he is remembered today.

On January 31, 1970 Mike's CH-46 named, "Blood Sweat & Tears" carried Marines from 3rd platoon, Alpha Company, 1st Battalion, 1st Marine Division from Hill 55 to an unnamed field west of Da Nang. On this day, 3rd platoon was being inserted as a blocking force to stop the movement of a large number of VC / NVA soldiers who were on the move.

It didn't take long before the men of 3rd platoon realized that they had moved into a live minefield. The sounds of explosions and the cries from men who were dying was all around them. The forward air controller and his radioman attempted to move to a safe location but tripped a mine that was between them.

Immediately men who were uninjured froze in place as the dirt, shrapnel and bone fragments from the last explosion fell around them.

PFC Clausen was overhead in his CH-46 watching as the men he had just dropped off were being cut to ribbons as each successive anti-personnel mine exploded. The CH-46 crew knew what had to be done and they also knew from previous experience what their risks were going to be if those men were to be extracted. Before starting down the crew removed their body armor and placed it under them on the helicopter deck in an effort to deflect shrapnel when they hit a mine.

—

Mike's machine came over the battlefield slowly at around 20 feet looking for a place to land. He leaned out of the crew door guiding his helicopter backwards into the only safe area in the entire minefield. With only inches to spare, PFC Clausen directed the pilot to set his main landing gear down in the two blast craters caused by the last explosions. While the mains were firmly on the ground Mike had the pilot keep the nose wheel elevated the entire time of the extraction.

Before the 46's ramp went down the aircraft pilot ordered that none of his crewmembers were to get off of the helicopter and assist anyone in the minefield. The pilot gave PFC Clausen a direct order which was heard by all of the crewmen, Stay in the aircraft", he was told. A normal Marine would have listened to the pilot, who was also the HMM-263 squadron commander and stayed on board.

PFC Mike Clausen was not a normal Marine.

Mike disobeyed his pilot and left the safety of his helicopter. He went off the back ramp and onto the ground which was littered with concealed anti-personnel mines. His travels that day took him far away from the safety of his helicopter as he helped the wounded men to move forward. Those Marines who were to seriously injured to walk were carried by Mike, back to his bird. While he was doing this he also led the way through the minefield for others who were uninjured but frozen in place.

By his example and leadership, he got them to follow in his actual footsteps and walk to safety.

After the closest group had been brought on board, PFC Clausen had the pilot lift the helicopter up so that he could move it to a second and then a third location of relative

—

safety. Mike went off the back of the CH-46 ramp and into that deadly mine field a total of six times before he finally had all of the living and dead on board.

On the sixth and final trip back to the helicopter Mike and another Marine were carrying the last seriously wounded man on a stretcher. As they reached the area of the port main gear another mine went off right next to them.

The mine blast knocked Mike off of his feet, killed the corpsman who was helping Mike with the injured Marine and damaged the helicopter. Mike got back up on his feet and assisted all of the remaining injured men into his helicopter.

Only then, when everyone else was on board, did he step back inside and tell his pilot to lift off and head to 1st Med.

Ignoring his own personal safety, he walked into the tall grass of that minefield six times and brought out all twenty Marines. In a number of interviews Mike Clausen has stated, "Each time he returned to his aircraft men would follow in his footsteps because they were under the mistaken belief that I knew where the mines were located".

On that day and in that place not a direct order from his pilot, not the sporadic AK-47 fire from the NVA hidden close in a tree line nor the ice cold fear of death by unseen mines could stop PFC Mike Clausen.

On that day and in that place PFC Clausen would not abandon his squad of Marines until they were all safe and on board his helicopter.

—

The following is taken directly from the Medal of Honor citation which was awarded to PFC Raymond M. Clausen Jr. at the White House by President Richard Nixon on June 15, 1971.

****

The President of the United States in the name of The Congress takes pleasure in presenting the MEDAL OF HONOR to

PRIVATE FIRST CLASS RAYMOND M. CLAUSEN, JR.
UNITED STATES MARINE CORPS

For service as set forth in the following CITATION:

> For conspicuous gallantry and intrepidity at the risk of his life above and beyond the call of duty while serving with Marine Medium Helicopter Squadron 263, Marine Aircraft Group 16, First Marine Aircraft Wing, during operations against enemy forces in the Republic of Vietnam on January 31, 1970. Participating in a helicopter rescue mission to extract elements of a platoon which had inadvertently entered a minefield while attacking enemy positions, Private First Class Clausen skillfully guided the helicopter pilot to a landing in an area cleared by one of several mine explosions. With eleven Marines wounded, one dead, and the remaining eight Marines holding their positions for fear of detonating other mines, Private First Class Clausen quickly leaped from the helicopter and, in the face of enemy fire, moved across the extremely hazardous, mine-

laden area to assist in carrying casualties to the waiting helicopter and in placing them aboard. Despite the ever-present threat of further mine explosions, he continued his valiant efforts, leaving the comparatively safe area of the helicopter on six separate occasions to carry out his rescue efforts. On one occasion while he was carrying one of the wounded, another mine detonated, killing a corpsman and wounding three other men. Only when he was certain that all Marines were safely aboard did he signal the pilot to lift the helicopter. By his courageous, determined and inspiring efforts in the face of the utmost danger, Private First Class Clausen upheld the highest traditions of the Marine Corps and of the United States Naval Service.

/S/ RICHARD M. NIXON

Chapter 12
The Da Nang Taxi Service
Total U.S. killed as of March 1971 in the Vietnam War: 55,894

By the time we had reached Vietnam in the summer of 1970 every early morning announcer on the armed forces radio network used the same opening for the first minute of his show. Every day started with the famous, "Good Morning Vietnam", which had been originated by Adrian Cronauer in 1965 when he was working the Armed Forces Radio Network morning show in Saigon.

It was actually a useful tool for us because in our neck of the woods all of the radio stations, meaning one, went off the air at 2200 hours. Because there was nothing but dead air and static till 0500 hours everyone on our base just left their radios on with the volume on high till we heard the blast of, Good Morning Vietnam.

This became something of an MMAF clock radio without a snooze alarm. After this joyful announcement, all of the AM radios across the base would spring into life and the Da Nang area propaganda machine went directly into high gear for the rest of the day.

In between assorted musical selections we got to listen to heroic stories of civic duty which involved winning of the hearts and minds of the Vietnamese people. The same geniuses who figured to outsmart the southbound NVA with the ever popular dawn air strike also came up with these multi-faceted plans.

This high level committee of Pentagon intelligentsia believed that the citizens of Vietnam would quickly rally to our side if we were seen to be nation builders instead of "foreign invaders of the week". Once this political enlightenment

—

274

came upon them the Washington planners knew that they would realize the error of their evil ways and embrace our vision of a new and improved colonialism. Think, "New France" without the image of dead Peugeots and Renaults rusting by the side of the road.

This futuristic vision of the United States improving their standard of living would cause the citizens to turn away from their old lives under communism. Winning the hearts and minds would cause everyone to march together toward a better life for themselves, their families and their nation.

These ideas made everyone want to stand up and sing the South Vietnamese National Anthem, that is, if anyone knew it.

These plans never did quite work out as expected in any of the local villages. But reality aside, these activities sure looked mighty impressive when presented in the form of three-inch-thick blue binders which were flown to Washington every week.

This was a time before military bureaucrats had turned a simple PowerPoint presentation into an art form. They still had to rely on the visual impact of bound pieces of paper to justify their existence. Reports always contained a plentitude of glowing first person reports by villagers whose lives had been turned around by our enlightened construction activity. Along with this written documentation came a stack of eight by ten glossy photographs which provided visual proof of each accomplishment.

Who can possibly deny mission success in the face of such overwhelming evidence?

The I Corps commander had been told by his boss in Washington that they were going to spend X amount of dollars every quarter on local reconstruction projects and that was that. While you couldn't count the number of hearts and minds that had been converted to our side, you could certainly count the number of dollars spent on this conversion effort.

Somewhere deep inside the great war machine known as the Pentagon sat a number of senior officers, along with their trusty staff, who worked night and day refining this proven formula. The U.S. military would contact the Vietnamese Army I Corps commander who would then contact the local province chief to obtain suitable locations for all of these new village enhancement projects.

The local province commanders had absolutely no concern about the welfare of any villagers but he was intensely focused in receiving cash kickbacks, long term residual funding, along with the outright theft of monies and building materials.

Using the knowledge passed down from past generations of bureaucrats, all of the local politicians conspired together to extract the greatest profit possible from the benign activities of the existing foreign devils.

To a man they didn't care whether the United States military was killing communists, saving souls for Jesus, or throwing live babies into a diesel powered paper shredder. Their only concerns were that at the end of the day they were not in any way held responsible for our activities and the money in their collective pockets increased substantially.

After the expected profit had been determined and the province commander felt it was in his best financial interest to continue, he and his associates did the equivalent of throwing darts against a map of their district to find a suitable location for this important civic activity.

Only then would the order go out to the Navy Seabees or the Army engineers to build a road, a bridge, a well, a school, or a whatever. No one anywhere along in the chain of command really cared what got built as long as the photos looked good and they got credit for the predetermined success of the project.

The official plan was for the U.S. military to bring in all the supplies and machinery necessary to complete the project. The village chief would then rally his local citizens together and they would then supply the labor. This would provide both nations with a joint success because everyone would be working together for the betterment of this new struggling nation.

The primary problem with this plan was that all of the young men in the local village were either killed in action or still fighting with the VC. Because of this, they were not available at the present time for ditch digging, road construction or nation building.

So, as usual, our side ended up paying for all the materials and doing all of the work. During the time of construction, all of the recipients of this largess stood around laughing at the construction crews behind their backs.

The reality of this situation was that none of the locals would ever help at all, unless they were paid union wages and even then they weren't much good. Their skill level never exceeded putting mud or bricks into a bamboo basket and then carrying it from one place to another. No one in any of these villages wanted any of this American junk, and

—

they certainly didn't want it reported back up the chain of command that they were helping the enemy for free.

What most people in Washington failed to comprehend was that Vietnam had been the victim of invasions from foreign armies many times in the past and they collectively knew from past experience, how to deal with the existing situation. They never got excited or demanded immediate results like our side was always famous for. Instead, they looked down the road twenty years and made plans based on what had happened in the past.

The Vietnamese nation as a whole realized that like those other invaders in history, the Americans would eventually grow tired of their country, declare victory, pack up their trash and go home.

Within a year of their construction, most of the building projects or agricultural equipment had collapsed from neglect, been blown up by the NVA or ceased functioning due to a lack of repair. Small moveable items with a commercial value would be removed from the village and sold in Da-Nang with the profits used to finance the local VC cadre.

In all of these villages, people had carried water from the nearby stream for thousands of years, and this was the normal way of doing things. The new well was nice, but no one knew how to fix the gasoline powered pump when it stopped working. In time every village would revert back to the natural ways of doing things.

No matter how the final story played out, the only thing that mattered to the United States was the activity that was going on right then. These stories of village construction projects were covered in print and on film by platoons of reporters

—

and news camera men. The local military newspaper that printed all this crapola was an eight page weekly known as the "SEA TIGER". It was packed with unlimited stories of atrocities done by the NVA and never ending military successes by the good guys.

After reading that publication I had no idea how anyone back in the states could ever think that we were losing this war.

After listening to the upbeat progress of our war on the radio while getting dressed, those of us with a normal day ahead would stager over to the mess hall. The trick in eating food at that hour was in trying to find something in the serving trough that didn't look or smell like week old road kill. Walking inside the mess hall from the early morning darkness into the harsh overhead fluorescent lighting caused the assorted breakfast dishes waiting for us in the food lines to take on a bluish white tint. This did not improve the visual impact of the food and reminded everyone of the movie, Breakfast at San Quentin.

First, check your steel tray and silverware in the bright light to make sure they had been cleaned properly. This ensured that only utensils without an oily residue or attached food particles would be acceptable, otherwise you may be the recipient of an intestinal surprise three or four hours later.

The normal safe foods were always dark dry toast, coffee with lots of sugar and an individual box of cereal if it was unopened and the expiration date was less than a year old. If you were adventurous there were always trays of cold pancakes, under cooked eggs and big sausages with tiny worms under the skin for your dining pleasure.

If our wakeup had been provided by the MMAF AM radio alarm service, it meant that today's schedule would not include dawn raids against unsuspecting iguanas or sitting around all day at the medivac alert bunker. Instead, cargo toting to lonely firebases, the Da Nang taxi service or maintenance test hops were in your future for the next twelve hours.

On this particular day, when I showed up at the office my assignment was to fix some of the non-flying junk parked at the end of our flight line. By mid-morning I was out at the very west end of our parking revetments sitting on top of one of the dead creatures trying to figure out how to fix this product of the Bell Aircraft Corporation without having it towed into the hangar. This was a day I wished they would let me wear one of those Vietnamese rice hats because it was really hot working in the sun and things were not going good with this machine.

Looking to the north with the HML-167 ramp farthest away

A pair of Sikorsky CH-53s taxied by just west of where I was working and they blew sand and little rocks everywhere. Now I was even more irritated than I was a couple of seconds ago and the morning was still young. It seemed strange that they would kick up so much dirt but they were past my aircraft now which meant they were someone else's problem. I put my head back down and went back to work. Suddenly I realized that the lead CH-53s was way too close to the east edge of the ramp!

On the north end of our parking area adjacent to the ramp where I was working there was a row of 12-inch-thick heavy concrete and steel shelters designed to protect the aircraft inside from incoming mortar fire. These shelters are about thirty feet tall and extend all the way out to where one of the CH-53s is taxiing now. For some reason the pilots did not realize they were off center and heading for the edge of the concrete shelters.

I had already started the jump from the top of my aircraft as both the sound of the impact and the shattered pieces of rotor blade reached my location. Chunks of concrete shards peppered the top of the revetment wall along with the windshield of the helicopter I was working on.

The only thing that saved me from being shredded by flying Sikorsky parts was the fact that I was already jumping off the top of my aircraft seconds before the impact happened. Other people were not so lucky. One Marine was killed when the lead weight on one of the CH-53 rotor ends broke off and flew away at near supersonic speed, striking him in the chest while he was walking near the accident site. He was almost cut in half by the impact and the blade tip that struck him was never found.

Within seconds of the impact the CH-53 pilot shut down both General Electric engines but shrapnel from the concrete wall and the broken rotors had smashed into the helicopter's right engine which broke its pressurized fuel lines. The heat

—

from the engine then started the broken fuel lines on fire. Black smoke began pouring out from both the exhaust pipe and fresh rips in the engine's aluminum cover.

I grabbed one of the twenty-pound dry chemical fire extinguishers, climbed up on the fuel tank directly below the burning engine and emptied the entire thing through one of the fresh holes in the engine cover. Once the fine gray powder dust from the extinguisher cleared I could see the fire was out. It was now time to leave before I was wrongly blamed for making another mess.

There were other injuries from the impact that ranged from minor to critical. The wounded CH-53 would need two new engines and an entire new rotor system, but it could have been a lot worse given all of the high speed trash that was flying around. Due to the location where I was working there was even a chance that I could have been injured and that would not have been a good thing. I went back into the shop and told them that they needed to tow that bird I was working on back into the hangar because it was just too dangerous to be working out on the flight line anymore.

We heard later that the co-pilot had actually been in control of the aircraft when it impacted the concrete structure, but even so, you knew who was going to be responsible for this very public disaster. This event was classified as a non-combat related aircraft accident which was a big black eye for HMH-463.

It was amazing to us to see how fast that CH-53 aircraft commander went from squadron pilot to assistant base mess officer.

The Da Nang taxi service involved using one of our UH-1Es to move high value passengers, cargo and paperwork

—

around the general vicinity of the big city during daylight hours. We would be sitting around drinking chocolate milkshakes when the call would come in from dispatch to pick up people at location A and take them to location B.

While this was a safe and uneventful way to spend the day, it failed to satisfy my primary reason for being in country and that was to obtain stick time. We always flew this mission with only one pilot because it was such a low profile operation that no one had even taken a shot at the taxi during all the years that we had the franchise.

Because of the almost 2 ½ foot stretch it took to get into our cargo compartment I had to ride in the back and make sure that all the Generals, Colonels and nurses got in without falling on their high valued faces. We would always get in extra trouble from on high if we had an incompetent General type person have an accident and scuff his shoes.

Day in and day out we would do the taxi thing and you never knew who your next passenger might be. We hauled lots of nurses who had to wear uniform skirts and this presented a real problem for them if they wished to maintain even a minimum amount of decorum. I solved part of this problem by pulling out my black steel toolbox, putting it on the ground and letting them use that as an aircraft step. It solved some of the problems but did not resolve them completely.

Most of the girls just hiked up their skirts, grabbed my arm and I pulled them inside our green aluminum taxi. Most got in the back with little problems and lots of laughing. One or two would slip and down they would go onto the aluminum deck and the uniform skirt would no longer perform the purpose for which it was designed. I found that this vision of exposed female anatomy came close to being an adequate replacement for any stick time that I may have missed during that day's aviating.

During our trips around town we would have to fly by the East end of the Da Nang airbase during flight operations. This allowed us to do that most favorite of activities known to any pilot. We got to fly as close to the ground as possible while also driving along as fast as the machine would go. In every other location on earth this is always a totally unacceptable official flying maneuver. Here it was not only allowed, it was required.

Sometimes you just had to love this place.

The reason for this rule has to do with the location and positioning of the two main Da Nang airfield runways. It seems that the Da Nang airbase was located close to the center of the city and the east end of its concrete runway almost made it to the beach at Da Nang Bay. Due to the winds which always came from the ocean, most of the fixed wing aircraft took off on the longest concrete runway which pointed toward the sea. Because they were heavily loaded or just under powered, they sometimes struggled to be more than five hundred feet in altitude when they passed over the beach.

This beach was the official corridor for all helicopter traffic going north or south and we were required to be at or below one hundred feet when passing to the East of the Da Nang airfield. Down we would go to the point where we were flying at or below the rooftops of the houses in the city, and so close to the beach we almost put one of our skids in the sand. On occasion you would notice muzzle flashes caused by the local citizens shooting at us from an alley way or house window, but we were expressly forbidden to shoot back into the city.

—

Well, what they didn't know wouldn't hurt them one little bit. There were two reasons why we carried AK's and M-16s. First we could fire back without the pilots hearing the sound of payback. Just lean out the door and empty an AK magazine of thirty rounds into the city towards the general direction of the flashes. Not that we could actually hit anything with one of those pop guns but at least we got a feeling of personal satisfaction from the recoil.

If we shot one of the door guns, it would shake the entire airframe with its rattling around. Then the pilots couldn't pretend that we weren't redecorating the interior of a few of the local residences with 7.62mm rounds. Second, if we actually managed to hit someone of any importance with the AK and they complained, the logical defense was that they were shot by the local NVA, not by us.

In all of the indoctrination lectures everyone went to before setting foot in country the instructors emphasized the fact that the lineage of Vietnam and its people went back for thousands of years. We needed to understand the rich culture and heritage that they possessed before we could understand them as a people.

We were also told not to judge them by western standards. That was the classroom and this was the real world. Here in the real world, the rich culture of the Vietnamese people boiled down to that daily event that I and hundreds of other crewmembers witnessed every time we flew over the beach.

Every morning at dawn, hundreds of citizens from the city of Da Nang would go down to the beach on the shoreline of the Bay, squat down and crap right on the sand like a pack of dogs. We would be cleared by the tower to pass under the runway approach and there would be men, women,

—

boys and girls all over the beach up to the water line in the squatting position.

Two thousand years ago the Roman Empire found that sanitation was an essential part of civilization and required it in all their settlements. Yet here we are in this place in 1970 flying over "shit beach", which was populated by hundreds of squatting citizens who had inherited this rich Vietnamese heritage and culture.

This was the time when we got down really low and tried to see how many of them we could knock over with our rotor blast. Either that or come up behind them when they are squatting with their backs to us and give them such a scare that they were able to complete their beach activity in record time.

Later in the day after Da Nang's citizens had left to do other things like work as a cook or waiter in one of the many fine dining establishments in the city, all that was left were brown lumps all over the white sand beach. The lumps just waited for the tide to come in and wash everything out to sea.

This country was very nasty on just so many levels.

The only problem we ever had with the Da Nang taxi service franchise was with a single landing zone on the west side of the city which was open to the entire civilian population. On some days it was not even guarded by individuals from the local South Vietnamese Army and yes it was pretty bad when we actually looked forward to that miserable level of security.

Traffic could enter through an always open gate which was wide enough for two small trucks at the same time. The

—

roadway was a steel mat surface which went about twenty feet past the gate till it reached the landing zone. The LZ itself was a square, about thirty feet on each side with three rows of Concertina razor wire around the entire exterior starting at the gate. Outside of the Concertina wire were many acres of planted green rice fields complete with official Vietnamese worker bees and a small collection of black Asian water buffalos munching on the greenery.

In the spring time, all of the kids (and probably their parents too) would make kites for flying in the annual breeze that came up every year and blew steady for a week or two. The winds were strong and consistently blowing from the same direction for the entire time they lasted. This made for perfect kite flying weather in Da Nang.

This was quite the sight to see from on high as we flew from one location to another. Over Da Nang there must have been thousands of kites, each one was a different color and individual in both size and shape. Box kites, dragon kites, tiger kites and hundreds of other designs, all done by hand and flying a couple hundred feet above the streets of the city. Leading up to each kite was a long strong cord that attached it to its proud owner.

As the day progressed we found our aircraft was having a real problem with the flying kites during the approach into the little square LZ on the west side of Da Nang. These kites were directly in our flight path and high enough that we couldn't make a safe approach to landing. We tried zooming over the tops of the kites as we went to land but when we returned later that day we found they were even higher than before.

This time the pilot decided to teach those street roaches a little lesson so he dropped down into the mass of kites with

—

287

the Huey. The blades cut a path through the kites and when I looked behind us all I saw were airfoils crumpling to the ground in shredded pieces. The main blades went right through the paper and cord and did no damage to our machine. We felt sorry about the kites but shame on them for not moving them after we buzzed them the first time.

There is a war on you know.

The next day I had the same pilot and we were still employed by the same helicopter taxi service. We went to two or three new locations around town and did our pick up and drop off thing with no mechanical or passenger problems to speak of. About noon time, dispatch sent us out to pick up one individual and transport him to the west Da Nang LZ. We picked him up and after turning on final approach we found that the damaged kites had been either repaired or replaced and our final approach was full of kites again. No problem for us because we had the answer to this flying paper problem right at hand.

Down we went into the kites like a weed whacker through dry grass and then we popped out directly over our LZ. We landed and I opened the door to a sound that I had never heard before. The rotor system now had a high pitched whistle and I couldn't see the tubes or the rotor mast anymore. I told the pilot to shut the aircraft down so that I could take a look and see what's wrong, now.

When I climbed up onto the roof of the helicopter I could see right away what our problem was. When we flew through all the kites some of the string had become entangled in the rotors and just needed to be pulled away. As I started to pull, the cord wouldn't break and actually got tighter around the mast the harder I pulled. It was then that I saw what our little kite flyers had done to us.

—

After the first day of kite destruction, the little bastards had used nylon fishing line and thin steel wire instead of standard cord for their kite string. This didn't damage anything on the helicopter but it took me almost half an hour with wire cutters to untangle that mess. During the time I was working to untangle the kite wires you could hear laughter and people yelling at us from the interior of the nearby slum. The paper toy flying season ended soon after the nylon line episode so we didn't have to escalate our level of violence against the kite flyers in order to show them who the real air boss was.

In addition to every other problem we were required to put up with, there was now a small group of raggedy neighborhood brats living in the slum near this L.Z. They were becoming a constant source of irritation to our helicopter operations by their actions.

This pack of motherless children figured that grabbing onto the skids of our helicopters as we were lifting off was going to be the closest thing to an aircraft ride they were ever going to get in their lifetime. Every aircrew hated to look up and see these kids break from cover and run toward their helicopter like a pack of rats. The greatest worry we had was of a possible unseen fragmentation grenade in the pocket of one of those little roaches.

It was well documented that children had been known to toss frags inside US helicopters as they were lifting off. For this action the kids would be awarded the VC equivalent of an Eagle Scout badge. Any survivors from this aircraft disaster would spend many days trying to explain to the NATOPS board exactly how they allowed this to happen.

Even without any explosives, there was the unexpected change in weight and center of gravity that occurred when one or more of the kids would grab the back of the skids and hang on as we started to lift off. Because of their unauthorized behavior I had to listen to lots of bitching from the aircraft's front boardroom every time something like this happened.

My first attempt to drive off this mob of little vandals was a complete and total disaster that almost cost the squadron (meaning of course the guy who signed for the aircraft), a wrecked ship. We had been putting up with this total disrespect of our rules and regulations for almost a week. Finally, after listening to an unusually long and colorful complaint from the aircraft driver, I decided to do something to resolve the issue.

Later that same day we again landed at the west zone and dropped off our passenger. I watched as he walked into the road and out of sight. While we were waiting for the next mission to be dispatched I spotted a group of kids hiding behind the entrance gate wall. Springing into action I prepared my equipment for their anticipated attack.

As the helicopter started to lift off a pack of these children jumped out and ran right past the uncaring local Vietnamese Army guards. When they were about thirty feet from our aircraft I released the spoon from a CS riot gas grenade and dropped the burning can about ten feet in front of them.

At first they didn't pay any attention to the can because every Vietnamese kid knows what a regular smoke grenade looks like. In about two seconds that grey chemical burning gas cloud filled the air around them and they quickly found out that this wasn't just colored smoke.

—

The problem with this CS gas idea was in the length of its reach, not with its effects. The great thing was that the kids had forgotten all about the helicopter and were now just running around in large circles trying to make the pain in their eyes go away. The Vietnamese gate guards also paid a high price for failing to secure the LZ as the cloud expanded to cover them while they were at their posts. While this secondary result was not quite as satisfying as watching the kids scream in pain, it was ok.

What I had not taken into consideration was that my helicopter was nothing more than a very large fan that flew through the sky by displacing great quantities of air downward. Very simply it used its rotors to push air down, sideways and then suck it back up into the top of the rotor system. Now it sucked up air which was loaded with CS gas and spread it everywhere.

Within a second the gas was all through the aircraft cabin and my pilot for the day got a big snoot full. I am here to tell you that you cannot fly a helicopter, blow your nose and clear your eyes at the same time. I jumped into the co-pilots seat and flew the bird until he got his runny nose and teary eyes under control.

After that little adventure we should have changed his call sign to "Dribbles".

Unlike the enlisted guys who spent many weeks of quality time at Parris Island, it seems the officers missed out on a lot of the standard fun training that we received. In particular, they were never exposed to CS gas and I am able to report that its effect came as a real shock to "Dribbles". What a little sissy he turned out to be. I flew all of the way over for the next pickup with both of the rear doors locked open to remove any remaining molecules of the CS gas. We thought

—

that we had all of the residuals of CS removed from the cabin but our next passenger disagreed.

We both came to the same conclusion that this was not one of my better ideas and should not be repeated, especially if we planned to have one of those General type people on board later in the day. The dirt children living in the slum realized that the CS gas attack had been unsuccessful and so they continued with their daily physical assault on my helicopter.

In the olden days before the internet and the ability to buy everything on line, the paper Sears catalog was the greatest treasure known to deployed service men everywhere. If you didn't mind waiting three weeks (like you had a choice), and you had the cash available to pay for shipping, you could obtain a lot of very useful items either for yourself or they could be shipped home as a gift.

One of the best tools that one of the HMM-364 crew chiefs had purchased months ago was a *Daisy Air Gun* along with dozens of cardboard tubes filled with copper BB's. The men of HMM-364 always used this weapon to go on hunting expeditions for wild base rats at dusk.

Because he was familiar with the problem we were having with our little slum creatures, he gave me the gun to use along with a sock full of BB's for my shooting enjoyment. I could hardly go to sleep that night thinking of the pain I was going to inflict on those two legged slum roaches' tomorrow.

Our next day had progressed along to the point where we had completed two trips into the west L.Z. without any sign of the children. They seem to have a better intelligence network than our guys did. I was starting to believe that I might have to return the BB gun with no additional notches

—

on the stock.   When we launched from the zone after completing the second hop I noticed that one of the water buffalos had wandered over to the edge of the Concertina wire on the outside of the LZ.

There was now a small child of about six or eight years of age lying on its back and holding onto a small stick.   The child's job was to guide this great horned beast around the field by smacking it with the stick and pulling on a single rope tied to its nose ring.   This allowed it to eat in the proper areas and spread its fertilizer across the mud of the rice paddy evenly.

A tiny child on the back of a giant water buffalo was a very normal sight in this part of the world.   To us all of these rice paddy beasts appeared to be gentler than standard Holstein dairy cows back in the states.

Third mission of the day at the west LZ and the slum kids have returned.   VC indoctrination school had probably let out for the day so the children were directed to harass Americans either for homework or extra credit.   As we set down on the mat I could see them in their standard hiding place behind the gate wall where the guard would normally stand.

Today the guards weren't there and the kids were having an especially good time planning our daily ration of harassment.   It may have just been my imagination but there seemed to be more of them today than normal.

Our unsuspecting passenger got out without falling to the ground and walked away and into one of the local office buildings.   We sat there for a minute while the pilot got his next set of instructions and I prepared my weapon for battle. The rotor blades bit into the air and changed their pitch

—

which was a signal for all of the slum creatures to make a break for our skids.

I pulled out my trusty *Daisy pump action BB gun* and opened fire. I shot the first couple of kids in the upper body because they had no shirts on so it hurt them a lot more. When they started getting hit and saw the rifle they thought it was a real weapon and turned and ran with a look of true panic on their round little faces. (Being that it was a plastic Daisy air rifle it was easily confused with our standard M-16). I kept shooting into center mass as the slum rats beat a hasty retreat and scored additional points.

This was a great day for our side because the enemy was now in a complete rout.

All were in a rout that is except for one kid. He was a little older and slightly bigger so he wasn't afraid of the *Daisy*. I saw him break from the crowd and run towards the aircraft. I hit him twice in the chest and while it slowed him down a little it didn't stop his forward progress. When he got within ten feet he took a BB right between the eyes and that did stop him.

We were at about three feet in altitude and just starting to climb so I figured it was time to claim victory and put the weapon down. When I looked up the kid had recovered and quickly covered the distance between where I had shot him and my helicopter. As I watched in disbelief he jumped up and grabbed the top of the skid with both hands.

If I had some bug spray, I would have got him in his smiling upturned little mouth but I didn't so there he hung for a second or two. As he looked down for a place to land I stepped onto his boney little fingers with my flight boots and pressed his hands against the top of the skid, hard. My

—

weight locked his fingers onto the non-slip coating so he couldn't pull away as we started to climb.

I waited until we were a little above ten feet and passing over the Concertina wire surrounding the LZ before I released him. In that instant we both found out that he couldn't fly. Helicopter kid missed all of the concertina wire and fell right into the deep black muck and water of the rice paddy.

While his forward motion did cause him to pass over the stacked rolls of razor wire his flailing arms did not miss the water buffalo. From out of the sky he fell and smacked the mighty beast right in the face as he landed with a big splash of black goo and green rice stalks directly in front of its nose.

Vietnamese water buffalos were docile creatures that had existed for many generations without any flailing creature attacking them by diving out of the sky.

Initially shocked and bewildered, the water buffalo's instinct for survival took over and he was now in full attack mode. Immediately the little kid who had been sleeping on the back of the beast was airborne and flying rearward in a high arc. It appeared to me that he was going to land safely in the rice paddy mud quite a distance behind the creature. The kid who had smacked the beast on the nose now became the center of this berserk buffalo's attention.

Helicopter kid jumped up and was trying to run away through the black glue like muck while the buffalo did its best to stomp him using its front hooves and impale him with its horns. Seeing fifteen hundred pounds of enraged death behind him the kid quickly figured out that he was not going to be able to outrun this bovine on open ground.

—

In an instant he turned hard left and jumped headfirst into the rolls of triple Concertina wire.

This was his only logical way to escape the rampaging beast and save his worthless life.

As we flew off into the sunset I saw all of the locals who were working in the rice paddy running over to the location of the great flying kid adventure. I knew they didn't see exactly what had happened because they always work with their heads down and never look up for anything.

Now they did not look at all happy because it appeared to them the kid must have climbed over the wire and done something to the water buffalo to cause this great disturbance. Lucky for all involved this was my last day on the Da Nang taxi service for a long time.

Chapter 13

The Marble Mountain Sludge Pond
Total U.S. killed as of April 1971 in the Vietnam War: 56,187

A degree of understanding about the Marble Mountain Air Facility (MMAF) is needed before I go any further. Gaul may have been divided into three parts but our world only had two, the Marine side where the real men lived and the other side, also known as the Army side.

Almost every night there was a low level war going on between the different Marine squadrons on the base, usually involving large quantities of alcoholic beverages, fist fights and CS gas grenades. It was not uncommon to have a gas attack during the night, wake up in the morning with your gas mask on and not remember when you put it on. It was amazing to us that no one ever died from a clogged gas mask filter when they were sleeping. When everyone grew bored of fighting each other, the Marine squadrons would unite and attack the Army side for some imagined or improvised affront.

The Marines held the beach on the East side of the base while the Army set up camp on the West side. There they were closer to the main gate and could make it into the local village quicker. The base runway divided the two groups and became a nightly obstacle that we were required to cross when sprinting onto the Army's side of the base to steal helicopter parts.

The Army guys never really wanted to play soldier, so we usually just stole boxes of their junk and went home with their implicit approval. The Army had lots of boxes filled with their Huey parts that fit our UH-1Es just fine and also lots of Plexiglas sheets that we used for replacement windows in our hooches.

Due to the distances involved and the lack of a satisfactory victory over the Army, these cross runway missions were rare, except when we needed parts. We learned that our nighttime incursions into the land of the enemy usually resulted in a series of memos and harsh letters being transmitted between the two commands but nothing of any consequence ever came of it.

We justified our actions because we figured that the Army squadrons always had more parts on hand than they ever needed and the Marine supply system really sucked. Removing helicopter parts from the care and control of the Army wasn't much of a challenge because as soon as it got dark, their squadrons shut down the operational part of their war and everyone went home for the night.

The Army guards who were left behind to keep their junk from being stolen were always sitting around one of the far bunkers smoking dope and listening to music from a tape deck. To compensate for the Marines always stealing their stuff, the Army underground supply system would routinely charge us outrageous prices for our orders of dope and booze which they managed to smuggle onto Marble Mountain from someplace unknown. We figured that they were buying it in wholesale lots from an Air Force businessmen in Da Nang.

The Army side of the base had a single Huey squadron which had more helicopters than the entire inventory of the USMC. On some days there were herds of Army helicopters arriving and departing at all hours of the day which disrupted the natural flow of work on our side of the base. Their side had one little squadron which we thought was interesting and so we took some time to go over and talk to their aircrew and pilots about the aircraft.

—

This squadron was comprised of nothing but de Havilland Beavers which were made in Canada and used primarily as a bush plane in the civilian world. The plane looked like an oversized Cessna with a tail wheel and a huge radial engine for power. Until we got to MMAF we didn't think that there was a single radial engine in use anywhere in the US military at that point in time. We were told that the engines were newly manufactured but their design was left over from WWII. Hard for us to believe but there they were in all their oil dripping glory.

We had all sorts of aircraft flying into MMAF, but when the beavers would go to take off, we would stop what we were doing and watch. First they would line up on the runway centerline and push the throttle forward which sometimes produced a series of small backfires. Then the smoke would come out of the exhaust as all of the accumulated engine oil was removed by the increase in temperature and rpm's.

If there was a strong wind coming out of the north the Beaver would go about two hundred yards down the runway and start climbing up and away. By the time the Beaver was halfway down the runway the aircraft would make their turn to the west and be gone. One of the pilots told us that the plane took off at 80 knots, cruised at 80 knots and landed at 80 knots. They never did tell us exactly where they cruised to, what they did or where they went but we notice that when they came back there was a lot of mud on the wheels and sides of the planes.

Their squadron motto was, "Low, Slow but Reliable". Well I guess if you are flying an 80 knot aircraft in the same war with 1.5 Mach McDonald Douglass Phantoms you have to have something to brag about. That squadron was not going to be the home for any retired fighter pilots from the Air Force with that kind of attitude.

—

One of the serious problems we faced was that the Marines were not allowed off base except if their job required it or they possessed a special pass. That meant no trips to the local village for an evening's entertainment of tea drinking and poetry reading with any of the local bang-bang girls.

This problem was solved by either bribing the guys manning the perimeter fence and climbing through a specially prepared hole in the wire or obtaining a forged pass. Some of those guys manning a Remington typewriter may not have been worth anything in the helicopter repair business but they sure knew how to procure official looking documents for a very reasonable price.

The form of payment that was requested by the local fence girls was always in the form of Salem cigarettes not the military play money we were required to carry. Most of the standard services that they provided carried a price of two cartons, and did those girls ever love those menthol cigarettes. As with any fine establishment, extras are always extra and all prices were to be negotiated before services commenced.

Stories of the locals hiding razor blades inside of their anatomy to cut lust crazed military men were found to be untrue. We found out later that this story was a malevolent fairy-tale propagated by the base medical personnel in an attempt to hold down the rate of VD among the enlisted men. We soon learned that the Vietnamese people had been in the human service industry for a long time, and knew how to treat foreign devils properly so as to extract the maximum profit from them before they were forced to exit their county.

Intentional physical injury to a long time Salem cigarette paying customer was not good for business.

—

The locals learned early on that with a regular frequency, the military brass would require all the U.S. troops to turn in the ugly funny money they had in their pockets to be replaced with a new and improved version of military play money.

Two days after the date of the trade in, all of the old money was declared without value. This would really piss off a lot of people trying to make a living from the military out in the villages. This was done with limited success in an effort to disrupt the local black markets, and to also make our lives more complicated. The primary result of this disruption of the monetary exchange system was to produce a very efficient barter economy involving stolen U.S. supplies and equipment.

During my time in Vietnam all was not flying, fixing and drinking. The base I was on, like every other one over there, had the need for certain utilitarian functions. These were required to keep the troops clean, fed, and marginally intoxicated at night. This required that all of us enlisted guys spend a couple of weeks away from our normal duties and be assigned to doing real manual labor somewhere on the base.

Some of the guys got disgusting mess duty, (peeling potatoes, washing dishes and stacking an endless stream of cans in hot little buildings), some guys got general repair duty, (painting, filling sandbags, killing rats and building little wooden things) and some of us got to do other jobs, special jobs.

I didn't have a regular work assignment like everyone else, I was special. One day I got to be the armed guard for the liberty truck going into Da-Nang. Special jobs require special equipment or so we were told by our masters. I was ready for my new assignment with my own AK-47 and one of the Vietnamese straw hats that had been left over from last week's trading session.

I argued that it was camouflage in case we were attacked on our journey but the higher ups just weren't going to buy that one. So from some dusty corner of the base they dig up an entire wardrobe of clothing and accessories that is required by the official rule book for the liberty truck guard to wear.

I was required to go full grunt, without the heavy pack of course. My new uniform consisted of a metal helmet, flack vest, and a cloth bandoleer full of twenty round magazines for my shooting iron, which ended up being my own recently issued M-16. At least this provided me with the look of a real Marine if not the motivation.

While my backpack didn't have enough equipment for a three-day hike in the woods, I had stuffed in enough tools to survive the day in case things went downhill in the transportation business. My supplies included a nice Army .45 Colt-1911 and two extra magazines plus two fragmentation grenades and one white phosphorous grenade which was light gray with a yellow stripe so it could be readily identified.

I now had the equipment necessary to protect the truck and its passengers. Actually, my plan was to at least create enough confusion during the enemy's attack on the truck that I could escape in the white phosphorous smoke.

The Da Nang special pulled up at the pickup point inside MMAF and we took on our first load of happy passengers for the day. It took about half an hour to drive all the way to the big stinky city. Here we waited around for a little while until we got a load for the return trip, then off we went again.

—

There were so many military trucks on the two lane road to Da Nang that we looked like green salmon swimming upstream to spawn. When there was a problem on the road, all the traffic stopped and we could almost walk down the road on the tops of all the vehicles knowing that our feet wouldn't hit the pavement. Everyone always believed that there was safety in the large number of ugly green trucks.

Tell that to the salmon who always die at the end of their journey

.

After three or four trips into town this drive has turned into a real boring activity. There were hours of sitting on a wooden bench in the hot uncovered bed of the truck accompanied by much horn honking and watch checking to see if the day is going to end soon.

Late afternoon we were returning to MMAF from Da Nang on our last run. We had three marines in the back of the truck along with about 1,000 pounds of assorted cargo destined for the supply group at MMAF. As we were driving back on the main road, I saw that one of the Marines in the back of the truck was riding along leaning against the seat back with both of his arms stretched out on top of the wooden seatbacks.

From somewhere back behind us came a 90cc Honda motorcycle which passed the truck directly behind us and moved into the twenty feet of empty space between our two moving vehicles. The motorcycle, with two male teenagers on board, waited until there was a break in the opposite direction traffic and started to pass our truck.

As the motorcycle went by, it slowed next to the Marine with his hand outside the truck body. This allowed the motorcycle passenger to reach up and pull the man's watch off his wrist by breaking the retention pins.

—

A lot of things happened at once after that. An oncoming truck was either dozing off or saw what had just happened, because he swerved out of his lane and tried to hit the two thieves. That size truck would have turned them into red road paste.

The motorcycle driver saw the truck come at him just in time to avoid being hit. The Honda driver quickly hit his brakes and dove in behind our truck, somehow without falling over or losing his passenger. As he did this the passenger held up the watch in one hand, pointed and laughed at us.

This was not one of the smarter things he ever did in his short little life.

The oncoming traffic was so heavy the motorcycle couldn't pass us and the truck behind us had moved closer to cut off any other route of escape. We were doing thirty miles an hour and we had the thieves trapped inside a moving metal box.

The driver and all of the passengers, especially the guy who lost his watch, were yelling at me to shoot the little VC bastards before they could get away. I said I had a better idea, because once you shoot a civilian / VC bastard, many hours will be spent in the boss's office filling out forms and telling the same untruth over and over again to bored people sitting in front of a typewriter.

The tailgate of the truck had been down for the entire trip because some of the cargo that we had loaded wouldn't let it close properly. This wound up being a good thing for us. I grabbed a pair of wire cutters from the truck's tool box and climbed over the boxes of cargo till I was at the last items to be loaded on the truck.

These items on the rear of the truck were big three foot in diameter rolls of Concertina brand razor wire that were held together with thin steel bands. I reached over and before our little friends on the motorcycle could figure out what was happening I snipped the retention bands and together three of us kicked some of the rolled razor wire off the back end of the truck.

The rolls took one small bounce before the wire opened up like a giant Slinky of death and the motorcycle bandits drove straight into it. The wire wrapped around them and their bike which instantly shut down the rotation of their front wheel.

Razor wire after it had been stretched out

This motorcycle, now wrapped up in razor wire (and with them still on board) did a forward summersault and crashed to the pavement. Well, not exactly to the pavement because there were a couple of layers of razor wire between them and the black asphalt roadway below.

The truck behind them tried to stop in time but the driver was laughing so hard that the front of his truck drove over the motorcycle, thieves, and wire combination, compressing everything until it hit his front drive axle.

We were lucky because after all of the vehicles had stopped moving we found that his truck had not been damaged. The driver was able to back away revealing a fresh razor wire / VC sandwich on the road below. Leaving everything all tangled together, six of us put on gloves and removed this entangled mess from the roadway. We pulled and tugged until it was out of the way and into a ditch by the side of the road. We were able to accomplish this activity without any of us getting as much as a scratch from the galvanized razor wire.

This was turning out to be our lucky day.

The owner of the stolen watch dug into the pockets of the very unhappy motorcycle passenger and found his watch along with two others. He removed the undamaged watches, stepped on the two thieves and walked back to our truck.

Using assorted tools, we smashed the fuel tank, engine and gearbox of the motorcycle after we sliced up his tires with a trusty K-Bar knife. Everyone got back in their individual trucks and drove off leaving the two thieves to figure their own way out of the wire.

They both were still alive and quite vocal about their situation as we drove away, even after all of that. We figured that they would soon be up and about and resuming

—

their life of crime after a short recovery at the local VC hospital.

As for the missing wire, we just scratched it off of the list and put some initials next to the correction. When we got back to the base we offloaded the passengers and took our cargo over to the MMAF supply clerks. We explained that some items couldn't be found at the warehouse but they would be on the next shipment. Because the Marine supply system was such a disaster, this type of thing was routine and no one ever questioned us about it. I could now see how some supply sergeants were getting rich over here and it wasn't by selling Concertina wire.

After my truck guarding day was over, I got to spend other days overseeing a chain gang of Vietnamese mama sans who had been assigned to fill up and stack sandbags all day long. This was one of those jobs that made you wish you were sitting in a hot airless office being overwhelmed by stacks of papers that had to be typed on your manual machine before the end of the business day.

First thing in the morning you would go over to the base mama san desk at the operations office. This is always located in the back of a green metal building where I picked up my squad of Vietnamese worker bees. Each group always came complete with one mama san who was designated as the leader because she could speak a few words of something that might be some form of English.

Either that or she was good enough with sign language that you could marginally communicate. After leadership assignment, I slowly marched this rice straw hat wearing, betel nut chewing, foreign language jabbering group over to their assigned location for the day's activities. You have to be extra careful because along with betel nut chewing comes

—

betel nut juice spitting, and that stuff was a special kind of nasty.

I would have to explain or point out what the job entails and then find myself a nice place in the shade to rest. Once the mission was understood, they were like a bunch of little machines that would work and jabber between themselves until lunch. They all ate the same disgusting thing for lunch that looked like pickled fish and smelled like rotten eggs.

Soon everyone would go back to working, yacking and betel nut chewing till the end of their work day. I think the entire population was born to be bureaucrats because they never worked hard or even very efficiently but slowly the job got done or the clock ran out.

Ding goes the work bell and then we all marched back to the starting point.

The second day of MMAF chain gang guard duty started out like the first. Find out where the worksite was, pick up my charges and march them off into base history for another day. We arrived at the location which that day, was in officer's country at the north end of the base.

I saw the stack of unfilled sandbags before me and without a word, I pointed out the job that needed to be done to the worker bees. They gathered around and started filling and stacking sandbags without me having to say anything else, which was great.

About an hour into the job the team leader came up to me, opened her mouth and in perfect standard US quality English asked me a question about the job. I don't even remember what she said I was so amazed.

I looked at her like she was from the Andromeda galaxy and said, "What", and she repeated the question. I gave her the answer and she turned to the other workers and said something to them in Vietnamese. She turned to walk away but I couldn't let her get away that easy.

This girl told me that she had been sent to California in the early 60's at the start of a foreign student exchange sort of thing. She had spent eight years going through middle school and then regular high school in Southern California. For some reason, after graduation she was not allowed to remain in California even though she wanted to stay. The US Government forced her to return to Vietnam where now, after all that expense and education, she worked on our base filling sandbags.

We must have talked for half an hour and then she said she needed to get back to work with the rest of the crew. I never saw her again working on any of the sandbag crews during the time I was employed as an overseer.

Looking back on this encounter I realize the power of a common language to instantly transform a "foreigner" into a relatable person with common values.

I told some of my co-workers in HML-167 about this English speaking Vietnamese person and they all came to the same conclusion. There was no doubt that she had been shanghaied by the bastard base officers to work in their secret topless strip club and massage parlor.

There were some days I got to work with the MP's at the front gate inspecting the Vietnamese operated trash trucks as they entered or left the base. My job was to make sure they were not stealing anything with any residual value to the military. Stealing little things was both expected and allowed, but you would not believe what they tried to haul out the gate disguised as garbage.

The biggest problem we had with their incessant stealing was that for them, this was the only reason they came on base. Even though we paid them quite a bit for trash pickup, their days were always spent trying to find valuable items to load up and haul through the gates for sale in downtown Da Nang. We quickly came to the realization that once they found something they could steal; this was the end of their garbage loading day. They would immediately load the found item up onto their truck and drive off the base conveniently forgetting to pick up the trash on their assigned route.

We worked out a compromise with the trash toting locals. If they could find something inexpensive to steal that had no military value we would look the other way, but the trash

—

310

had to go. That meant that desks and racks were ok but no aircraft parts or ammunition. Also the stolen stuff had to be on the bottom of the base trash so that we got some actual value out of their theft.

Laugh all you want to about the system but it worked pretty good for both sides. On more than one occasion I have had the trash drivers walk up to me with a box containing linked 40mm grenade rounds or loaded M-16 magazines and turn them in. The ammunition that they turned in probably saved the lives of some Marine out in the field. We also figured that once the war was over we were going to leave everything where it was and the local people were going to strip the base down to the beach sand anyway.

They were given a gold star for the day and were always allowed to steal something expensive when they turned in ammunition.

There was no running water in Marble Mountain as most people today understand it. We had running water in the mess hall, the hangars and at the communal showers but we did not have flush toilets anywhere else on the base. At least there were none that we knew about.

What we had instead of a toilet was a basic item known to military people everywhere as a four holer. This is a plywood shack with one door, screens instead of windows and four holes cut into sheets of ¾ inch plywood for your sitting pleasure.

There were many of these facilities scattered all around the entire base. They all were painted a disgusting green color and each came complete with a multitude of Vietnamese flies which were not painted any color. Because there was no running water at these facilities, an individual's personal

–

production was deposited via gravity into a holding drum directly under each hole.

This steel receptacle contained about six inches of JP-5 jet fuel to hold down the smell and keep the unpainted flies under control. These human deposits sat, floating in the jet fuel, all day long, cooking in the heat and humidity until it was time for their collection.

Four Holes for your Sitting Pleasure

Once a day, this material was picked up by a select group of local Vietnamese contractors. These sanitation specialists all had their own large trucks, large for Vietnam anyway; and four workers who were assigned to each truck.

We were told that all of the workers and the contractors had been screened to ensure that they were not VC operatives sent in to spy on the secret military activities of the base, (ha). It was our personal belief that the local VC administration would punish non-performing members of their cadres with assignment to this job until they improved their attitudes.

A month of this duty and they would be ready to charge the base outer perimeter wire for the glory of old Ho Chi Min.

The product of each individual four holer was transferred by hand to a multitude of open fifty-five-gallon steel drums sitting on the back of these collection trucks. During the day when these barrels became full of semi-solid material they were transported by these sanitation workers to the sludge pond located at the South end of the base.

Once there, the truck would back up to the edge of this place of incredible nastiness with its tailgate hanging over the edge. These workers would now pour the contents of the barrels from the back of the truck into the pond with much splashing of semi-solid material and obscene yelling in Vietnamese.

The sludge pond where this soup was poured was just a hole dug out of plain old beach sand with dimensions of about thirty feet square and downward to an unknown depth. It was located between the end of the runway and the chain link perimeter fence.

This sludge pond material, consisting of human waste, paper products and JP-5, was poured into the pond by the locals for months until it was finally full. Full meant that the sand under and around the pond was so saturated with JP-5 and assorted pathogens that it would not absorb any more liquids and the solids had filled the hole up to the brim.

To understand the pond, you had to understand the times that we were living in back then. There was no such thing as an Environmental Protection Agency. Anyway it was only

Vietnam so who cared about a little sludge pond? I mean we were spraying Agent Orange by the truckload every day over the jungle, the villages, and our own troops so what's the big deal about a little bit of semi-liquid nastiness cooking in the day's heat.

It was now time for me, Lance Corporal of the week to spring into action. I got called into the MMAF Executive Officer's cave and was asked if I would burn the sludge pond as a favor for him. Not wanting to turn down such a generous offer and also having visions of getting to burn something up with the blessing of those on high, I said, "Yes Sir".

The rules were; there were no rules. It was a sludge pond. Have fun.

As any good pyromaniac knows, while there may be no rules, a good, memorable fire requires planning and accelerant, lots of accelerant. I talked to a couple of the guys who had gone before me in the sludge business and learned some of the tricks of the trade. The most important information that I received was that JP-5 was real hard to light off without a booster and don't ever get downwind after ignition, in fact don't get downwind at any time.

See, good planning is going to pay off.

Early in the evening of the big day it was time to prepare for my big event at the sludge pond. It was just starting to get dark and normal activity inside the base was beginning to slow down.

Another important bit of advice I was given from those who had gone before was, never have a fire during the day, all anyone ever gets to see is just black smoke. At least at night there are dancing yellow and red flames shooting high into the night sky that will light up the smoke column and provide entertainment for the huddled masses.

To get everything ready for this night's activities, I had one of the mobile aircraft refueling trucks back up to the sludge pond with his leftover jet fuel from the day's aviation events. The refueling truck looks like a large version of a home fuel oil delivery truck except it is painted the same disgusting green color as everything else on base and it has an engine driven pump that can transfer a 100 gallons of JP-5 a minute from a 1 ½ inch nozzle. That is like shooting water from a fire hose.

We unreeled about twenty feet of hose and fired that bad boy up. The driver got his machine pumping and I sprayed till we had a deep layer of fresh jet fuel over the entire pond along with the edges of the pond, my boots and part of the road.

We shut down the pump and as we were reeling up the tanker hose the driver figured out what we were planning to do tonight at the pond. He mumbled something, jumped into his truck and took off down the road and out of sight just as fast as his ugly green truck would take him. As the fuel truck was making his escape, one of the other guys, (fellow partner in crime), arrived in our jeep with two metal 5 gallon cans of gasoline. JP-5 doesn't evaporate quickly and the ground was so saturated that it was not going anywhere for a little while.

We sat there by the side of the pond waiting until the stars came into alignment and everything was ready for the big show. At the correct time we unscrewed the tops off the gasoline cans and poured their contents onto the sludge. We then punched holes into their sides and tossed them out into the center of the pond. When the cans hit the sludge the

—

remaining gasoline flowed out and stayed on the surface because gasoline is lighter than kerosene and those steel cans were lighter than the sludge.

My fearless crew of sludge associates realized that things were going to get ugly in a hurry so they took the jeep down the road a good distance and waited for me to complete my ignition mission. I stood there, close to the side of the pond smelling the fermenting fragrance with a Zippo lighter in one hand and a new, never been used roll of toilet paper in the other. We had nothing but the best for this job.

Remember timing is everything so I waited.

Straight ahead, about ¾ of a mile out on final approach for landing onto the runway behind me was a CH-46. Now was the time. The Zippo lighter worked, as they always did and the toilet paper caught on fire, like it always does. I gave this paper roll my best throw and this burning paper torch went up in a tall flaming arc and landed right into the middle of the sludge pond. Before it hit the sludge I had turned and started running away as fast as I could through the deep sand.

Not everything works out exactly as planned but this event was not bad. When they say that gasoline vapors are like so many sticks of dynamite they are not kidding. I only got about twenty yards down the road before the vapors lit and the blast wall knocked me down like one of our hangar doors had fallen on me.

The concussion wasn't as bad as I had thought it was going to be but I heard later that it did rattle quite a few windows on the base. Luckily not all of the gasoline had turned into vapors so I didn't get the full effect. After the initial blast, the transition of the gasoline from liquid to vapors was

—

happening at a rather rapid rate and the JP-5 was also starting to vaporize and ignite. I got up and continued running along the road toward the waiting jeep.

Upon arrival at the jeep I turned and looked back and it was then that I observed a group of base perimeter guards also running in our direction. Those guys had been manning the fence and bunkers closest to the sludge pond at the time of ignition.

Somehow in all my planning I had forgotten to tell them what we were doing to their pond that night. To a man they expressed to me their displeasure with both the size of the explosion and the closeness of the flames to their now very toasty bunkers. The guards closest to the sludge pond were forced to abandon ship for the night and wait till the flames died down before they could return to their little sand bag homes. I hope none of that sludge pond smoke got in their outpost and added a new flavor to their coffee making utensils.

The CH-46 that had been on final approach tried to miss the black oily sludge smoke column rising rapidly from the burning pond but was only partially successful. I bet that stuff smelled nasty. Being a true warrior the pilot continued his turn out of the smoke and landed at the other end of the runway.

I wouldn't be surprised if he logged one tenth of an hour of actual instrument time for that turn in the sludge pond smoke.

There was a side note about the interaction between the CH-46 and the tower when the sludge pond lit up. The aircraft controllers in the tower had cleared the CH-46 to land and then, because there was no other aircraft on the runway they

—

turned their vision away from the south end of the field for just a second.

While they were concentrating on doing something else, the shock wave from the sludge pond ignition rattled the windows of their tower, which caused them to look up in panic. When they looked back to the south all they saw was a ball of yellow flames and black smoke right where the CH-46 was going to be passing over at about that time. The air traffic controllers got all excited and thought that another Boeing had crashed on final approach. Fearing the worst, they reached down and hit the alarm button for the crash crew.

Things in tower land went downhill from there till the they got a nasty call from the CH-46 about the sludge fire. Because crashed aircraft rarely call and complain, they were stunned into silence until they saw the aircraft flying northbound over the beach and finally figured out what had happened.

By the time I reached my associates waiting for me down the road, the fire was really burning with enthusiasm. Even at our distant location you could feel the heat from the boiling sludge pond and things were really popping, so to speak.

The entire pit was a massive red and orange fuel fed fire with flaming paper products climbing high into the night sky along with impressive columns of thick black smoke. In addition to the heat and smoke there were also low frequency thumping sounds that we could feel through our boots. These mini quakes were coming from deep underground where pockets of air and methane were lighting off.

—

I have to admit that this was a fire of the highest quality and I will guarantee you that many a gallon of human sludge and JP-5 went up in the form of black oily smoke that night.

We looked down the runway as one of the airfield crash crew trucks drove over and parked at our location. They gave us a firsthand account about all of the excitement we provided for the boys up in the tower. The driver said that crash crew had been briefed earlier about the burn and their job was to sit by the fire until it went out later that night.

For those of you who are unfamiliar with crash crew, they are like a real fire department except they drive funny looking specialized Oshkosh fire trucks which were designed for putting out aircraft fires and not useful for very much else.

Sometimes our war against the Army forced us to be creative in how we attacked them and this was one of those occasions. No banzai charge across the runway for me. What was sweetest about this adventure was I could accomplish my assigned mission with a look of complete innocence, (remember LAX) and total deniability.

Remember that we were on the beach side and they were inland and at night the difference in temperature between the land and the ocean would always cause a gentle breeze to blow inland from the water, all night long. That was the primary thing that I was waiting for before I lit my little sludge world up.

Tonight the gentle sea breeze floating eastward contained large black sooty particles of partially burnt sludge combined with the smell of burning human waste and poorly combusted hydrocarbons.

—

This smoke and ash cloud settled over the Army side of the base like a 1960's Los Angeles smog on a summer's night. I bet there was many a person on that side of the base who went to sleep wearing their gas mask, and it was not because of CS gas.

Teach them a thing or two about overcharging us.

Chapter 14

They Looked Like Flaming Beer Cans
Total U.S. killed as of May1971 in the Vietnam War: 56,389

Innovation and progress were not unknown concepts to those of us surviving in this foreign land while we worked hard keeping America safe from the spread of evil Communism. Even as the war was winding down and more and more units being disbanded, the military continued to come up with new but always creative ways to try and kill us before our departure time arrived.

With an announced timetable for withdrawal, overpaid government contractors rapidly cobbled together their latest and greatest miracle weapons, aka; junk, for evaluation. These untired designs were quickly loaded on large Air Force transports and flown across the big pond for examination and assessment in their personal war zone testing ground.

This testing was done so the engineers and their assorted flunkies could see how their new and improved product worked in a location where people would be disrespectful to it. There was also the benefit that the contractors didn't have to actually pay anyone to conduct this live testing. The official term for what they did to us was called, "Combat Evaluation". Good examples of this were the CH-46A and the Marine rifleman's favorite weapon, the M-16A-1.

The latest example of military progress in 1971 was the new AH-1J Bell twin engine Cobra attack helicopter. It sure looked great parked out on the flight line with its fresh green paint job shining in the sunlight. The clear Plexiglas canopy was so new it didn't even have any stress cracks in it.   This new Cobra had twin engines which gave it 1,800 horsepower, a 3 barrel 20mm Gatling gun in the nose and 4 hard points on its little green stub wings for rocket pods.

This flying machine was death on a stick.

Every one of the pilots of HML-367 wanted to be the first to be checked out and be assigned to fly this NVA killing machine. So, with all the pilots lined up like kids at the neighborhood ice cream truck, they assigned this Super Cobra to every mission they could and flew the snot out of it. They took this thing out and stressed it way beyond what it was supposed to do.

Even though they had this great twin-pac super 1,800 horsepower engine, it seems they had saved design and testing hours by keeping the same transmission and rotor system from the older single engine, AH-1G model.

The engineers solved this minor issue regarding unproven reliability by putting a red power restriction label above the torque meter so that everyone would know where the design limits were and not to exceed them. This would unquestionably keep the old parts safe while the new stuff was being, "combat evaluated".

Remember the story of the Boeing CH-46A and the placarded restrictions regarding hover aft? It seemed that engineers were the same no matter which company they worked for. They designed a machine that would perform way beyond its allowable limitations, but they put it out into the real world anyway. They covered their engineer butts by placing a decal above the torque meter and expected combat pilots to actually pay attention.

Silly engineers, decals are for stateside.

—

It didn't matter what you were flying because when you were being shot at by people with no appreciation for your equipment or your mission, no one took the time to read the little decals above the transmission torque meter.

The end result was that the boys of HML-367 went and twisted the new engine to full power and maybe even a little more, which went way over the gearbox and rotor system torque limitations. Well what do you know? They started getting cracks in the steel rotor head from the center of the hub all the way out to where the blades were attached.

Oops, your fancy new flying machine is grounded.

This equipment failure put the Generals located in the war planning room kind of in a bind because they had just shipped most of the old single engine Cobras off to Japan for rebuild. No old Cobras left around and now the new ones seem to be as dead as tuna in a can.

What to do? Simple said the generals, turn the old beat up and underpowered UH-1E's back into gunships and run them until our wonder birds have been repaired and are ready for additional combat evaluation.

Early the next morning our fearless leader gathered all of us together in the hangar and explained that we were returning to a more gunship orientated squadron. He stated that this was because of certain mechanical issues involving new equipment at an unnamed squadron down the road.

Spontaneous loud laughter along with an assortment of uncalled for crude remarks directed toward HML-367 broke out from inside the ranks of the enlisted men listening to this announcement. The HML-167 officers stifled their personal comments with a very noticeable effort. After this cheerful

—

323

news, we picked five of the best performing slugs in our fleet, took the doors off and turned them back into gunships. We had our final time in the sun for about a month till we were once again turned from armed mean fighting machines back into small green flying pickup trucks.

It took that month until the boys at Bell Helicopter came up with a more robust design for rotor hubs that would fit on their wonder bird. We figured that they always had a stronger design in the works but now they had to take the time to do proper testing on the rotating parts.

After a while, the Bell engineering staff finally solved the problem of the cracking hubs and shipped over the new and improved replacement parts for HML-367 to install. The broken parts were replaced, the tarps came off and the new Cobras went out and did their duty. Everyone felt that this lack of testing on the original hubs back in the states could have led to the catastrophic loss of both the aircraft and crew but no one was surprised that it happened.

The boys in HML-367 were a little humbler about their new killing machine after this episode, at least for a while.

With all the geniuses in the Pentagon and thousands of highly paid thinkers in private industry, it took the work of half a dozen enlisted men in-country to come up with one of the better ideas for making life miserable for the NVA.

The primary problem we had from day one was that the VC / NVA guys owned the night. When the sun went down the Americans abandoned the countryside to the bad guys and went back into the safety of their fortified bases till morning.

The NVA would then come out of their hidey holes and either steal or destroy all of the work that the Americans had done during the day. Public executions, physical destruction and psychological intimidation put the fear of Ho Chi Min into the local villagers. This was how war had been fought in this country since the French colonials came over and introduced rubber plantations to the everlasting gratitude of the local population.

This ability to control the night, along with lousy French battle planning was the reason that the Vietnamese were able to throw that group of trespassers out of their country back in 1954.

This reality was thrust upon them when the French lost the battle at Dien Bien Phu. At that time, they were forced to drop their weapons, (which they were quite good at) and straggle off into the sunset. As a condition of surrender the NVA made the French take their rusty and unreliable Renaults and Peugeots with them.

What our squadron guys came up with was a way to take back the night.

It was a crude invention even for those days. It had none of the polished mounting brackets or encased wire bundles like those inventions that came from the factory, but unlike them this thing worked like a charm.

The trick was to accomplish two objectives without a lot of heavy equipment so it could be toted around in one of our underpowered Huey's. The first objective was to find the bad guys in the dark and the second was to light them up so the gunships could hit them before they could hide.

The inventors took a full size spotlight that was normally mounted on the gun barrel of an M-60 main battle tank and then bolted a medium range starlight scope on top of it.

—

This combination was attached to a swivel mount that allowed the light to hang over the side of the helicopter. This placement allowed the operator to look straight down without any hardware restriction. Looking through the starlight scope on a moon lit night was like looking at an old 6-inch green screen computer monitor through a single eyepiece.

Not enjoyable in the least but it worked as advertised. The starlight scope allowed us to see people walking through the jungle with enough definition that you could count bodies and see what type of weapons they were carrying.

1st generation starlight scope mounted on top of a tank spotlight

If the night was super dark with no moonlight, then we would use the tank spotlight in infrared mode. It lit up the countryside with a light which was beyond the ability of the human eye to see but it turned night into day for those of us working the starlight scope. For us it was just like magic because the black jungle below was projected on the screen as green daylight with people being brighter than the background.

326

From day one the NVA had been taught that to us, they were invisible at night. They were told that the only thing that could give away their location was if they shot at us and we saw their muzzle blast.

The result of their training caused them to completely ignore the sounds of our helicopters even while we circled overhead. We could stay overhead and watch as they walked through the woods without a care in the world, actually following them all the way to their next job site.

The bad guys never knew what was happening to them until it was too late.

The way it worked was like this. Our light bird and two gunships would sit on the ground and wait until one of the forward outposts called in and said they had movement out in the bushes near their location. We would launch and fly out to the outpost that called in the movement. The light bird would be given a direction and distance from the base where the bad guys were located and we would slowly fly out in that direction. The two gunships would circle above the light bird while it motored out to find where the action was.

Once we found the NVA, we would watch them long enough to make sure that they were not just some local villagers wandering around at 2:00 am checking on their rice crop. If we saw they were carrying packs and weapons, we would contact the gunships above us and tell them we had a target.

The Cobras would get set up by using the upward shining little lights we had installed on the top of the light bird and wait. We would give them a countdown from ten. At three they would start their runs and at 0 we would flip on the white spotlight.

At that point a couple of things happened all at once. The NVA would go from total darkness to being instantly be bathed in an intense white light. The next thing that would happen is they would always look up, directly into the spot light which would totally blind them. Once they figured they had been discovered, out would come the AK-47s and they would start shooting at our spotlight. During the few seconds they had left, all of their attention would be on our aircraft and they would never notice the gunships coming in from the other side.

In less than three seconds they went from hardworking Communists fighting for Uncle Ho into a kind of a red and green NVA paste splattered along the trail. This flying starlight scope was magic because it worked each and every time we took it out.

As long as the outposts could hear the bad guys, we could always find them and remove their will to fight. Tactically it was a resounding success that would have been a real game changer if it had been invented back in 1968. Since the war was over now, it was too little, too late.

As with all good things it did have some drawbacks. The first problem was that you needed two operators to work the starlight scope / spotlight combination. The first operator used the starlight scope to find the bad guys and get everything set up for the gunships. When he turned on the visible spotlight, the white light made him totally blind for a good two minutes.

The procedure we worked out called for the second operator to be standing over his shoulder waiting for the switchover.

—

When the visible light came on he took control of the spot light and picked a point on the ground for reference. Now we just concentrated the light on that spot until the bad guys started shooting at our aircraft. Once they started shooting we could adjust the beam and blind everyone on the ground right before the gunships turned them into moist worm food.

There was something about the green starlight scope image that ruined the operator's ability to see in normal light. When the visible light came on, the starlight scope operator had to roll towards the middle of the cabin and just hang on until he regained his sight.

When we first started doing this stuff, there were no manuals or procedures to guide us. On the first night of using the starlight scope the blindness had not been anticipated. I am here to tell you it was a total shock. When the visible light came on I yelled for the left gunner to come over and take control of the device because for some reason I couldn't see anything.

We got lucky and the light stayed where it needed to be during the time it took him to make it over to my side of the aircraft. The first time this happened I was sitting in the darkness and was really hoping that this blindness thing would be temporary; but back then, who knew. Next to that business with the crazy Korean general, this was the scariest aviation thing I have ever had to do in the war.

There was one other problem that showed up during the time that we were doing this light bird thing. When the young Communists were walking down the trail with all of their friends from up north and looked directly into our flying tank spotlight, they were completely blinded and unable to aim at anything with their AK-47s.

—

The same did not hold true for anyone on the ground with a large caliber anti-aircraft weapon who was able to see the reverse side of the light bird. In that case our aircraft was illuminated like a backlit neon sign for all to see.

During one nighttime hunt, an NVA crew manning a Russian 12.7mm gun did not waste any time before they shot off 20 rounds from a 100 round can while we were looking in the other direction.

The only thing that saved us from an untimely end that evening was one of our Cobra gunships was circling almost directly overhead of the 12.7mm when it opened up. He saw the first of the purple tracer rounds on their way towards our ship and figured out what was happening right away.

The Cobra turned its nose gun on the NVA position and before the gun crew could change targets, they were treated to a shower of high explosive rounds from the Cobra's 20mm Gatling gun. These high velocity bullets passing through their bodies caused them to lose all interest in the activities of our light bird.

I have two reflections brought about by being the intended recipient of fire from the Russian 12.7mm, (.511 caliber) machine gun. The first is that there was no doubt who was shooting at you. Unlike the US military, the bad guys had tracers of many different colors.

They always had lots of white, blue and purple tracers while the only color our side used was orange. On most nights it seemed like the purple tracers were their favorite with white coming in second. It was not uncommon for the locals to shoot off a can of one hundred rounds up into the sky even though you were over a mile away.

–

Given the distance that ammunition had to come on someone's back, it seemed pretty wasteful to us.

The second image that will always stay with me is that when a 12.7mm tracer is heading directly towards you on a dark night, it looks like someone is shooting a purple flaming beer can directly at a little spot right on the tip of your nose. Your first thought when you see one coming at you in anger, was that this thing can cut my Huey bird in half and I was standing in the way of them accomplishing their mission.

The author standing with a captured 12.7 mm gun.

These flaming beer cans of death looked mighty big and scary every night we had to deal with them.

Each day the aircrews would go to the flight line with the expectation of a continuation of yesterday's events but that was never the way things worked out. The war's wheel of fortune would always spin unseen and outside of anyone's control. It was our luck that it usually stopped on something unpleasant and our lives would be forever changed. Forces that we had no knowledge of were engaged in battle beyond our visible horizon and these events would always alter our life, sometimes forever.

Our helicopters and crews would be requested at a remote location for a few days to bring in standby air support in case things did not go as planned for one of our ground units. This was not a serious adventure involving a significant number of troops and equipment because if that were the case they would have sent the Cobras.

We were all given a few hours to gather up what we would need to live in some semblance of comfort and then off we would go, flying away for our next adventure in jungle land. Most of these day trips involved flying to the north which meant passing by the Da Nang Air Base. This gave us the opportunity to drop in to the Air Force side to pick up a little refreshment before flying off for fame and glory.

The Air Force side had a combination general merchandise store and cafeteria with one of its access doors right on the edge of the flight line. We would call the Da Nang tower and tell them we need to land on the Air Force side and in between the landings of real aircraft they would shuffle us onto the taxiway. Now the Air Force side had one thing in that store that was not available anywhere else in this part of

-

the world. They had a chocolate soft ice cream machine and thirty-six ounce to-go cups.

To us this was frozen chocolate and sugar heaven.

We would land the gunships, fully armed and ready to go on their flight line directly outside the cafeteria door. We made sure that the rockets were pointed towards an open area between their buildings and not across the base to the Marine Corps side. I mean it's one thing to accidently blow up an Air Force hangar or one of their F-4's but it is quite another to damage any Marine Corps aircraft.

The crew chief on the other aircraft and I would run inside the snack bar while our aircraft sat outside with their rotors turning at idle speed waiting for our return. We each would fill four 36 ounce cups to the brim with frozen chocolate goodness, pay the clerk twenty cents for each one and head back out to our waiting crews. This purchase might not be the most important mission of the day as far as the Marine Corps was concerned, but we knew it would be the tastiest.

One pilot would fly while the other stuck his face in the milkshake then they would trade off the flying duties so that this frozen ice cream was eaten before it turned to liquid due to the Vietnam sun. There really wasn't much danger of that because those chocolate flavored delights were always gone by the time we had left the controlled airspace north of Da Nang.

We would then gather up the empty Styrofoam cups and flip them out the door so that they will become one with the jungle environment. Our way of saying, thank you South Vietnam. Thank you for the gratitude you have shown us for the lives and treasure we have squandered in an effort to

—

save your nasty little country from your Communist brothers to the North.

The Army had a number of remote bases far away from civilization that we used for these multi-day events. One of our CH-53 cargo helicopters would bring in our supplies which were carried underneath their aircraft in a cargo net. The load would usually be delivered about three feet above its desired location and always purposely dropped into place with a large thud. We would live with broken boxes and dented cans for the entire time we were there thanks to that thud. If the dumpster drivers were from HMH-463, then we would always provide their hooches with a 2:00 am surprise consisting of multiple CS gas canisters when we got back to MMAF.

Just our way of saying thanks.

Rockets and cans of machine gun ammunition were also transported to the base for our use and enjoyment. That stuff usually came by Army truck and was always waiting for us upon our arrival. It may have been in place for use by the Army and we just did a little paperwork swap to handle the ownership issue. It also may have been that we just stole it like we normally did with the Army stuff we found lying around. Who knew and who cared. We had it and it was our intention to put it to good use by making the lives of the bad guys miserable.

While we were sitting around with nothing to do which would improve the war effort, we were sometimes assigned to help the Army play war. It seems they had a couple of infiltration routes off to the west that they wanted to close down and they had a new toy to do just that. When the stateside engineers were not making a better Cobra or improving the M-16, they turned their thoughts to

—

individual death and destruction. Well that was our business, so let's see what they had come up with now.

What they had designed was a new type of plastic land mine that we could drop from the air. These came sealed in metal boxes with a plastic inner liner. The mines were stacked inside the plastic liner which also contained some kind of liquid chemical which kept the mines inert. We were told that as long as they stayed wet they were harmless. Allow them to dry out for about an hour or so and they could be set off by the least amount of pressure, anywhere on the mine. They were small enough and had the color of a dark brown camouflage so that they would be difficult to see in the mud, especially at night.

They loaded a couple of boxes of these things on my aircraft and off we went. The Army guy went along for the ride and showed us the trails leading along the base of a mountain range where the bad guys traveled at night. He said that even though they were in the bushes watching us as we flew around, they never fired at any helicopter, even during the daytime. Everyone figured they were planning something special and didn't want to give away their strength.

The process of seeding the area with mines was quite simple. My gunner would open up a box and hand me the wet mines as we flew right down the middle of the trail, slow and low. I would look over the side of the Huey and toss mines like little square Frisbees onto the cleared sections of the path. We spent an hour or so doing this and must have tossed out 100 or more of the sneaky little boogers. After this grueling day of mine tossing we returned to the base for the rest of the day to celebrate our success and listen for muted explosions.

—

Like everything else over there we never did find out if they worked or not but at least we never had to do that again.

This short time we spent away from the confines of the MMAF chain link fence allowed us to wander around in the local villages which always sprung up close to these outposts. Some of the Army guys who were stationed there took us around and showed us the sights.

Not much to look at, I mean if you have seen one mud hut with an attached water buffalo you have seen them all.

He told us that the trick to knowing if it was safe to be wandering around in the village during the day was to watch the kids. As long as they would come up to you and ask for money and try to steal things out of your pockets than everything was ok and the local VC were far away. The day you had to be careful was when you went to town and the kids were nowhere to be seen. That meant that the bad guys were hiding in the bushes watching what was going on.

We would hang around the outpost till our latest mission was completed, then we would aviate to a new location and continue to sit around there. Most of the time there was nothing to do because the local bad guy commanders would learn about our missions long before we ever did. Once they found out we were going to be doing the old search and destroy in their back yard the bad guys would have to decide if it was to their advantage to fight or fade away into the jungle.

Ninety-nine percent of the time they would retreat from the area we were planning to explore after they had provided our troops with the finest in booby traps and land mines. This was so our guys would have something to do during their hikes through the countryside.

The NVA would also leave all of their fighters who were too sick or injured to evacuate as their rear guard defensive unit. They knew they were dead anyway so they strapped their co-workers into trees or hid them in camouflaged holes waiting to fight our troops when they walked near them.

If they were too sick to hold up an AK-47 then the NVA would booby trap their body with pressure mines or hidden hand grenades. Some of their larger and more valuable equipment couldn't be moved quickly so it would be well hidden in a location where it was rarely, if ever found.

It took a while, but soon everyone from the Marine Corps figured that this latest adventure was going to be a total waste of time and lives. We loaded up our grunts, stole as much of the Army's equipment as we could get away with, and back to Marble we flew.

After we returned back to MMAF, the typewriters would start clicking and soon another successful Marine Corps adventure / deployment would go down in the record books for all eternity.

West of MMAF, past the swamps and over the misty mountains, was a place known to all Americans as the Ho Chi Minh Trail. The Vietnamese who built it always called it the Truong Son Road because its beginnings were through a mountain range of the same name.

Starting outside Hanoi, the trail worked its way southwest for a distance of about eight hundred miles. It stayed along the Vietnam / Laos border till it entered into Cambodia where it turned eastward with a thousand fingers to reach the southern battlefields in Vietnam.

—

The Ho Chi Minh Trail was not a single path through the wilderness like its name would imply. In actuality it was a maze of individual trails crisscrossing through the underbrush with hidden locations for supply dumps and river crossings that never showed above the water. Everything was designed to be invisible from the air.

A small portion of the trail consisted of a hard packed road that was suitable for heavy truck traffic and that was always on the list for nightly bombing. When the U.S. developed the ability to pick up vehicle engine heat signatures from the air, life as a truck driver on the trail became very short with a predictable violent end.

One of the quirks about the Russian weapons and explosives that were carried in these trucks and used by the NVA was that they were a lot more unstable than the stuff we worked with.

All branches of the U.S. military used a common plastic explosive known as C-4. It packed a large amount of energy and was great for blowing things up. On the other hand, it was so stable that a small chunk could be broken off and lit with a match and it would just burn. This heat source could actually be used for cooking if nothing else was available. It smelled horrible but no one ever got hurt. With the Russian brand of plastic explosives, you took your life in your hands if you ever tried that.

If the truck drivers on the Ho Chi Minh trail ever bunched up and one of their convoy was hit, the concussion would travel down the line and pop each truck like it was part of a string of firecrackers. The results were normally the same if you found a column of porters hauling explosives in their oversize backpacks while walking single file along the trail. Get one and you got them all.

—

These were really tough transportation jobs, as government employment goes.

For the majority of the way south an almost invisible network of small trails existed only wide enough for one person and a cargo bicycle. These bicycles were loaded with up to three hundred pounds of supplies and moved by human power. In places where the triple layer jungle canopy was not enough to hide the activity below, the local trail workers would string netting from tree to tree and cover the holes with greenery.

They were also good at providing decoys for our aircraft as well as hiding the good stuff from sight. They would pick a site close to a known river crossing and paint logs and old hunks of metal to look like a truck park or ammunition dump. Then at night they would light the smallest fire near the edge of it as if there were men camping nearby.

The bombers would call for basketball flares, and when they looked down they could see what appeared to be stacked ammunition. Then the rest of the evening would be spent dropping dozens of bombs into the jungle while the real supplies sat under cover miles away.

Those guys were mighty sneaky.

It was estimated that over two million men either worked on the trail during the time it was in existence or traveled over its surface on their way south. Just a small fraction of the men who walked south on the trail ever made the return trip home.

Before leaving their base around Hanoi to go and fight, a number of the soldiers purchased a tattoo that read, *"Born in the North to die in the South"*.

—

A lot of them never even made it to South Vietnam before they were killed. If our Air Force didn't drop a bomb on their truck rest areas or ammo dumps, they might be the recipient the red rope of death from a "Spooky" AC-47 gunship.

Their soldiers could also die from natural causes on the trail. This included the diseases of malaria or dysentery, or from floods, landslides and bridge collapses. Snakes and spiders could bite you, tigers could eat you or you could just die from exhaustion.

Untold thousands were buried in unmarked graves by the side of the trail for its entire length. Even so the NVA never stopped moving south to fight for the unification of their county in what they called the "American War".

After over ten years of fighting, looking at maps and planning strategies, the generals in the Pentagon decided to kill two Communists with one stone. Their primary plan was to take a large force of South Vietnamese soldiers and air lift them into a location where they could attack and then block the Ho Chi Minh trail in Laos.

This action would provide the Army of the South with a public big time win against the Army of the North. This would also put South Vietnam in a terrific position of strength when the U.S. forces soon declared victory and pulled out of the war. Shutting down the trail would also dry up the men and materials needed for the north to produce any offensive action in South Vietnam for years to come.

The first phase of the operation involved returning to the Marine base at Khe Sanh and reopening Route 9 from there to the Laos border. As usual, everything started late which

—

allowed everyone to take the official timetable and toss it out the window.

The base took longer to open up because of some left over unexploded ordinance and just plain old thick red mud everywhere. Route 9 was in such bad shape that only tracked vehicles and light jeeps could make it through the mud and use it for transportation. Equipment that was supposed to travel overland by truck now had to go by air and this expanding disaster just went on and on and on.

When the South Vietnamese Army finally entered into Laos the NVA was waiting for them because their spies had given them months of advance warning. The bad guys had long range artillery already set up to hit the few jungle clearings that were available for aircraft to land in. They also had our favorite gun, the 12.7mm, sitting up in the mountains overlooking the landing zones so they could shoot holes in any of the approaching or departing helicopters.

This was one time I was quite happy this was a 100% ARVN/US Army operation.

Our squadron was required by higher ups to send a couple of Hueys up north in support of this disaster and so off we went. There were enough inter-service rivalries so that we were not invited to participate in any of the aviation activities inside Laos itself. That was ok with us as we were quite content to lounge around the general vicinity of Khe Sanh, being little green flying go-fur's for the grand decision makers.

What we saw and the stories we were told by the pilots who were actually involved in this adventure confirmed that our decision to stay in the rear with the gear was a good one. It seems that the military intelligence had highly

–

underestimated the strength of the NVA in that section of Laos. Besides the usual ant like hordes of people that the northern army always brought to a battle, this time they had tanks and other armored vehicles which they used quite effectively to overrun some of the South's newly acquired outposts.

This caused an actual panic amongst the ranks of the South Vietnamese soldiers who absolutely refused to participate in any additional adventures in Laos.

When the ARVIN brass found out they couldn't attack any farther west, they just shut down the entire operation without any warning and decided to go home. One day they are in attack mode and the next day they told everyone, never mind, we're leaving now. This tactical retreat maneuver was carried out with even less skill and organization than the original attack adventure.

The South Vietnamese troops who were still fighting in Laos learned through the rumor mill that all of their leaders had left them to the tender mercies of the NVA and had gone back to Saigon. They rightfully figured that they were now dead meat. They immediately threw away all of their equipment and jumped into any vehicle they could find in an attempt to get out before they were killed.

What do you call 5,000 South Vietnamese troops hanging from the skids of helicopters?

That was our orderly retreat from Laos.

After watching this mess unfold in front of our very eyes we figured that the bad guys would be knocking on our door pretty soon. As usual the NVA was smart enough to leave well enough alone and did not try to expand their successful operation. They had accomplished their primary mission which was simply to prove to the world that the South Vietnamese military was totally incompetent and the "American War" was lost.

Even we knew that at this point.

After all of the troops from South Vietnam had been thrown out, the NVA troops went back to fixing the trail and moving equipment southward. At the same time our side went back to the typewriters and pounded out long articles about how the action in Laos was a brilliant victory for the US and South Vietnamese Armies. In the end it seemed as though both sides got what they wanted.

In the world where we were living, black was white, white was black and reality was not required.

At this time in the war about 56,389 members of the U.S. military had died in service to a very unappreciative nation. There was a short list of locations in Vietnam where our dead were prepared for transport back home. The Air Force side of the Da Nang air base was the only location in the northern part of the country where the remains were shipped from. C-130's and C-141's would fly in from Okinawa with supplies for the war and on their return trip they would be loaded with stacks of those dull gray aluminum coffins that everyone has seen.

During some of our down time on the Da Nang air base we were assigned to park near the area where the bodies were being loaded onto waiting Air Force transports for their final flight home. It is one thing to look at pictures and realize what was going on, it was quite another to see the event in person.

The primary thing that I still remember to this day from witnessing that activity was that our war dead were never given even the most basic level of respect. I witnessed that there was not any thought given to the bodies of our fallen service men who were being loaded onto military aircraft for their final journey home.

We sat in stunned silence, watching the parade of dead military men in unmarked aluminum shipping cans. We figured it was just a function of the times we were living in and the sheer volume of bodies passing through Da Nang that had turned Marine and Army heroes into just silent cargo. The men working at the mortuary services were just plain overwhelmed by the volume of dead.

The silver caskets containing the bodies of our fellow warriors were placed onto a standard military aluminum aircraft pallet till its surface was full. Three metal caskets comprised the first layer.

Then because of an unyielding requirement to properly utilize the carrying capacity of each aircraft, another layer or two of gray metal boxes were placed on top of the first so that the aircraft could carry its maximum load of "cargo".

—

The bodies were stacked onto the pallet and then strapped down tightly with used and dirty nylon cargo straps. This pallet load of heroes would be transported out to the waiting aircraft by a large forklift and then slid into place. People will say that this never happened and that everyone was accorded a minimum of respect.

I am here to tell you that like most of the BS coming from our fearless leaders, this was not true.

Maybe in those days the numbers were too great to provide for the individual flag draped coffins and level of respect that we demand today. I am sure that the mortuary service was underfunded and they did the best they could. Looking back, we knew that a hero's' final journey should have been handled in a much better way than how the military did it.

Only stateside military units and caring individuals provided appropriate ceremonies of honor when our fallen warriors arrived back home to the United States.

By 1971, the citizens of our nation were ashamed of the military and of the work we were doing in their name. The military had only done the job that was thrust upon them by the Congress and President of these United States.

Even though they were responsible for prolonging the war in Vietnam, I never remember hearing stories of US Senators or Congressmen getting spit on or being called baby killers by their constituents, when they returned home from Washington D.C.

In Vietnam the US military ended up doing all of the work and all of the dying, yet they were still the ones who received all of the blame.

—

Chapter 15

We've Been This Way Before

It's usually never a good thing when all of the officers in our squadron receive an invitation by the base commander to attend a "special" meeting at his second home. The rumor mill was in high gear before the first silver bar lieutenant was loaded onto a rented truck for the short trip down the road to the MMAF Marine Officer's Club.

Everyone knows a sergeant who works for a major who is close friends with the base commander. This sergeant knows for a fact that the meeting is about this or about that and has passed this secret information into the ears of a select member of our squadron. We never believed any of this talk because we had been fed so much crapola during our time in country that we could smell stinky propaganda when it was floating through the air.

The HML-167 Helicopter Crew Chief's Protective Association was determined to cut right through this fog of war. As a group, we wandered over to the only squadron officer left in the hangar and demanded answers. This lieutenant was not allowed to go along with the real HML-167 officers because he had just arrived in town and was the official squadron Lieutenant FNG.

Junior officers, just like junior worker bees, always get left behind when there were significant issues that needed to be resolved
.

His supervisory function on this day consisted of maintaining discipline while the real officers were away and also to look important. Now on most days he was lucky to find the proper squadron hangar in the darkness, today

—

though, he had to pretend that he actually knew what was going on.

As part of this act he listened intently to all of our venting. He took even took notes about the lack of accurate information about our squadron's status. He also did this with a look of deep concern on his face, which we all thought was a nice touch. His statement to us was given with a complete understanding about "our situation", "but he had direct orders that he was not allowed to divulge any information to the enlisted men".

The truth was that no one told him anything either but he couldn't say that to the peasants.

So we sat around, complained loudly to each other and impatiently waited. Without being told, we knew it had to be something really important. It seems that they were in such a hurry to zoom off to their meeting with the Colonel they had forgotten to give us some kind of pretend job to do before they all hauled ass.

Either we had lost the war and it was time to go home, or they were packing up the entire squadron and moving it to another location in Vietnam. We all figured this was so that the Army could take over our side of the base. Those slimy Army bastards coveted our beach.

Officially losing the war and going home would not be such a bad deal. On the other hand, it was universally understood that moving never wound up being a good thing to those being transferred. I was understood that Marine Corps organizations were never shifted up the food chain when it came to prime base locations.

—

Everyone always thought of this resort as being just a rundown green painted slum on the beach by the South China Sea but at least it was our rundown beach slum. There were a lot worse locations to be stationed in Vietnam because I had already seen most of them.

After about two hours of sitting around we heard the sound of the squadron trucks moving up the hangar road with the CO's jeep in the lead. This was a good thing because if we had done something really stupid, or at least gotten caught, our CO and his jeep would be on the way to the 1st Marine Division General's palace on the hill overlooking the city of Da Nang.

About this time, he would have been explaining his lack of leadership to an unsympathetic Lieutenant General's ear instead of leading the HML-167 truck parade back to its bleached steel home.

The trucks pulled up and all of the officers piled out with big smiles on their faces. They didn't have to say anything because we knew it was all over. We still didn't know who had won or what the score was but at this point in our lives none of us actually cared. For us the war was over.

The time had come for us to declare victory, pack up all our rotary wing equipment and go home.

A loud call from on high went out and directed us to assemble in an official formation in front of the squadron hangar. We looked around to some of our junior fearless leaders for direction about this squadron formation standing stuff. We didn't know if anyone had any idea how to pull this off, because in all the time I had been there no one had ever attempted to get the troops to produce an official squadron formation.

—

348

In true Marine aviation fashion, everyone kind of milled around with different leaders loudly giving conflicting orders until one of the Majors figured this formation thing was a total waste of time. The order was changed and now they told everyone to just stand in front of one of the helicopters. This we could do without any additional direction.

The HML-167 Commanding Officer slowly climbed up on top of the helicopter and latched onto the rotor hub before he told us what we already had guessed. The war for us was over, and we were to pack up the squadron in an efficient military manner and prepare to transport it home.

How we were to return the squadron back to the other side of the world no one had a clue, but at this point, no one cared either. After our fearless leader's inspiring speech, we gave one big cheer, turned around and walked away.

Everyone, including the officers, left the hangar and continued walking all the way back to their green slums and started a party that would continue for the rest of the day. It was ten-o-clock in the morning and it was time to start punching holes in the tops of cold steel beer cans because we were going home.

No more "short timer's calendars" or worries about dying on that last mission. We were done and home safe, unless we got squished by a runaway Army truck or the local NVA decided they needed to rocket the base, one last time.

Our original plan, which went through every enlisted man's mind at the same time, was to drink all the alcohol we could find and then set the entire squadron, including hangars, aircraft and hooches on fire.

The next morning after the fire, when we woke up we could just leave without any of that packing up stuff. First we would throw the machine guns and all the ammunition we could carry into the back of the trucks. Next we would just leave the entire place, including melted aircraft, for the locals to scrap while we sat at Da Nang drinking chocolate milkshakes and telling tales of great aviation adventures. Finally, after we had rested for a while, a nice Air Force flying bus would arrive to take everyone home.

We were informed later that our fearless leader did not think highly of our plans.

Early the next day we found that the squadron big boss along with a select group of organizational weasels had come up with an actual plan of action. This allowed the squadron pencil pushers to type out an activity list for every shop to accomplish before departure. That was the way we found out what we needed to do to shut down operations and transfer our half of the base over to the Army.

Each one of the helicopters had to have all external equipment removed and the doors and broken windows replaced. Each aircraft had to be made flyable so that it could at least make it the twenty miles over to the Da Nang airfield. Once it arrived there it was to be stuffed into a large plastic bag, put on a large gray boat and shipped to Japan for a total rebuild at the Kawasaki aircraft factory.

This was no problem at all for most of the fleet, except for the two hangar queens that only moved when a strong wind blew across the airfield, and then only when we forgot to close the barn doors.

We tried to get the CH-53 squadron down the road to tote them to Da Nang as an external load under the cover of

—

darkness. If they had done that for us, then we could pretend that the aircraft flew in overnight. The answer from the prima donnas at HMH-463 was a big fat NO! What a time to develop a slavish devotion to the USMC rule book.

Normally these guys could be bribed to do all kinds of things, but not now with the chance of actual freedom staring at them less than a month away. They weren't taking any chances and now we were in deep and serious helicopter parts trouble.

Times being what they were, our C.O. decided to light a fire under the ever popular Marine Aviation Supply group commander's ass. This was the person who had been responsible for these hangar queens in the first place and we planned to dump this entire non-flying aluminum mess in his lap. With sufficient arm twisting and large quantities of liquid refreshment a deal was reached and the parts were in hand within a week.

At least that was the story we were told, but the truth was a little more interesting. It seemed that a certain I Corps Marine General had become sufficiently annoyed with the supply section that he took a personal interest in our dilemma.

We found out, through unnamed sources, that the General told the supply group commanding officer that the parts would arrive on time or he and his entire happy supply group would have to stay at MMAF until the aircraft parts arrived. Then once the parts arrived, they would have to figure out how to install them, test the aircraft and then fly the birds across twenty miles of swamp to the Da Nang airfield.

—

It was said that a look of total fear came onto the face of the supply guy and his hands started shaking. Fear of actual work will do that.

The consensus among all of us worker bees was that we should have done this to the supply people / jerks a year ago.

Things were changing fast in slum land. The grounds surrounding our tin subdivision looked like the world's largest yard sale with dozens of slightly used refrigerators, bicycles and folding lawn chairs lined up by the roadway. Attached to each was a price so low that even today I am ashamed to reveal what things were sold for.

As time went on, individual sales stopped being the norm and we ended up selling everything to the Army guys by the truck load for unheard of bargain prices. It even reached a point where everyone pulled out their surplus AK-47s and other weapons that could not be sent back to the states by mail and sold them to the local Army officers on the other side of the base for somewhat reasonable compensation.

Reasonable but certainly not the top dollars we could get from the Air Force C-130 / C-141 pilots in Da Nang for the same item.

Even though HML-167 had been retired as an effective fighting unit, the men were kept working for weeks shutting down and packing up individual shops. Without any advance notice and in no particular order, groups of our fellow worker bees started receiving orders for deployment back to the states.

The ordinance shop went out the door as a group within a single day once the aircraft had all their weapons removed. One night they packed up all of our shooting irons and then they were history. The rest of the shops were thinned out by what seemed to be total random selection. Orders would

352

come in, goodbyes were said, and then people you had worked with for a year were just gone.

Wander around between our little galvanized tin housing units and you would find that some of the hooches were cold and empty while others only had one or two people living in them. Toward the end, a few of the boxes still had inhabitants but most of the others were just dark, lifeless plywood sheds. Even though people still lived in hooch land the smoke, lights and music we had come to expect had become nothing more than a faded memory.

Stereo equipment was boxed up and mailed home or like the refrigerators, bicycles and lawn chairs, sold to the Army for next to nothing. After the initial excitement wore off, we sat around and watched as our little plywood world contracted and died.

Once again we had no control over major events that were happening right before our eyes.

During the last days, a couple of the remaining crew chiefs and I were responsible for the final flight of each aircraft. We learned to pre-flight them very carefully because you never knew what parts had been used to make the remainder of these UH-1E dumpsters flyable. When the crew chief and the lucky pilot (always an FNG), were satisfied with the aircraft's mechanical condition, they would depart MMAF for the last time and 20 minutes later, arrive at Da Nang for a final shutdown.

After the aircraft paperwork was turned in and properly signed for, everyone would sit around and wait for transportation back to MMAF. Sometimes the ride back ended up being in the bed of an Army truck but usually someone at our home base directed one of the remaining airworthy CH-46's to stop by and pick us up.

One day after the last of the aircraft had been delivered to Da Nang, my orders came through. On that day I was like one of the classes I took a lifetime ago in Bishop Barry High School. I was history. It was my time to pack up all of my semi-legal items, pick up my orders, and get on the next military truck to the Da Nang Air Base.

As with any good game, the military kept score in the form of medals and other awards. I ended up with a highly coveted set of combat air crew wings with three stars and thirty-two strike flight awards. A strike flight award is basically an air medal that was given for every twenty combat mission that you flew inside of Vietnam.

Never did get a purple heart for that Vietnamese communist rat bite though.

All of us waved goodbye to the base as we were driven through the main gate for one last time. No one stationed at the gate looked up or even paid any attention to our final departure. It was obvious we were the only ones who cared even a little bit that we were leaving.

All of us on the truck carefully watched the locals standing by the side of the road who were mumbling in Vietnamese about the retreating foreign invaders. Little did they know of the pleasures they were going to receive from their brothers up north within a couple of years.

The drive to Da Nang was special only because it was the last time I would ever have to make it. I looked over the side rails of the truck and saw the same road side venders, mud huts and grazing water buffalo as that first time when I

–

was heading south along this road almost a year earlier. We all felt that this was a land of eternal stagnation.

Through the city and around the corners we drove till we were stopped at the entrance gate to the airbase. The gate guard gave us a quick look over and we were passed onward. Our truck made its way over to the departure area where we were unceremoniously dropped off.

Slowly we made our way across the parking lot lugging our gear and entered the ever present dimly lit Quonset hut for final processing. Our orders were inspected and additional documents were added. Our names were cross checked against the paperwork that we carried, our military ID cards and the departure list.

They didn't want anyone trying to sneak out too early you know.

We soon noticed that this processing was quite different than the normal military operation we were used to. The clerks were quite pleasant and had everything correct. We were soon transferred to an air conditioned empty hangar where there were nice chairs to sit on, music to listen to and something cold to drink while we waited for our flight.

I have had worse treatment at the Atlanta International Airport on a quiet Monday.

It almost seemed as though they were going out of their way being nice to us for our last hours in country. We all questioned what was going on and the best we could figure out was that during all of the years the Marines had been doing this, things did not always go smoothly in departure land.

More than once they probably ran into some actual bush crazy grunt who had been on the front lines killing people at close range less than 24 hours before he arrived inside their departure terminal. On a normal day it didn't take much to set one of those guys off and the stress of this final departure was not normal.

Within seconds of either meeting a bored clerk or suffering an attack of Post-Traumatic Stress Disorder he would have pulled a hidden KA-BAR knife out of his boot. Then, without a sound he would have tried to kill one or two of the clerks who had been annoying him. Even if he didn't try to kill the clerk, jamming the razor sharp knife blade into the typewriter rollers would go a long way toward getting their attention mighty quickly.

At this point in the war no one understood PTSD or what it was doing to the troops. Also for the most part, no one cared. The general consensus of the medical community at that time was that the men had done their duty and survived it, so they would be ok. Give everyone a combat action ribbon and thirty days of leave before their next assignment and they would be just fine. Let someone else deal with their physical and sociological problems twenty years later down the road.

Within two hours of arriving at Da Nang, we were loaded into the Freedom Bird and with no ceremony of any sort; sent on our way home. With much black smoke and noise the aircraft lifted off from the concrete runway and when the wheels were up and locked our seated group of refugees was over beautiful Da Nang Bay heading eastward. Next stop Okinawa.

After dreaming about this flight for almost a year it wound up being anti-climactic if I am to be honest about it.

—

Most of us would spend three days in Okinawa getting all sorts of additional medical tests, lots of yummy Marine Corps chow to eat, and pages of additional forms to fill out. You have to love the sound of a typewriter running at full throttle when you look down and see your leave papers in the rollers. The best thing about Okinawa was going to bed and knowing that no one was going to be waking you up at 0400 hours to prepare for a dawn mission.

The most productive time I spent in Okinawa was at the Marine PX where I bought new sets of underwear, uniforms and boots to replace the ripped and mildew stained set I was wearing when I first arrived. The last set of Vietnam issued uniforms that I owned, complete with JP-5, Agent Orange and DDT insecticide residue went into a base dumpster.

Incorrectly, I figured I was free of that stuff forever.

Very little of the time that we spent on Marine Corps Base Smedley D. Butler was constructive either to our mental or physical long term health. Our favorite pastime was to go to the PX to purchase Playboy magazines, assorted candy bars, and lots of Cokes. We spent the remainder of the day putting these items to good use. The guys who had been on the front lines would buy cokes, candy bars and potato chips by the box and bring them back to their hut, close the door, and pass them around till they couldn't eat anymore.

Some of us would walk over to the eight foot galvanized chain link fence that separated us from the Japanese citizens who lived on the island and watch a totally foreign world that existed just yards away. In the three days I was there we were never allowed outside the fence to walk in this land of strange people.

—

We were told that early on in the war it was common for returning Marines to be allowed into town for some rest and relaxation. This stopped after numerous bloody riots instigated by drunken Marines with improvised weapons.

It didn't look good for the Corps to have someone live through thirteen months of Vietnam only to die in the mud behind a seedy bar in Okinawa. In addition to this there also was a sharp statistical rise in cases of antibiotic resistant VD infecting the local population of bar girls.

For some reason our access to the city was cut off.

This left the library, the PX and the base enlisted club for our evening's entertainment. As to be expected the returning troops flooded into the E Club and tried to drink it dry. Large scale fights were a nightly occurrence (even with a detachment of MPs on site) and stabbings were not uncommon.

I declined to participate in the E Club night life because after all my adventures flying around in country, I had no desire to wind up in the Okinawa sick bay with metal poisoning. There was no way I was going to do one little thing which might delay my departure from this green cage.

Three days came and went and one morning, as if by magic, my name appeared on the bulletin board outside our Quonset hut. Be lined up at such and such a location at such and such a time for transportation back to the real world.

Yes…

The trip back to Hawaii was as long and boring as the trip out but for some reason no one really cared. For most of the trip we sat in silence, marveling at the fact that we had

—

actually made it out of that place alive. None of us realized on that day what the long term effects would be to our minds or what the chemicals that were sprayed over us almost daily, would do to our bodies.

Unlike WWII there was no month long boat ride across the Pacific which allowed those combat veterans time to unwind after the war. Unlike them, we were stuck on a 550 mile per hour flying cattle car.

Some of the men would be walking up the steps to their home within seven days of personally killing NVA soldiers, close up with a knife, rifle shot or fragmentation grenade.

Half an hour out from landing in Hawaii, everyone was handed a US Customs declaration form to fill out. We were told that we needed to fill this out if we were bringing any items back into the US from our overseas vacation. These people have got to be kidding. Mine, like most of the rest went into the center isle to be trampled on by wandering souls. All of us had just about reached the breaking point with filling out forms and putting up with meaningless regulations.

We landed and once again it was a dark and quiet night in paradise. No idea what time it was and I made no effort to find out either. Oh goodie, another line to stand in.

This time there were a number of desks at the head of each line with a clerk type person in a different type of blue uniform stamping papers. You know you can't do anything if you don't have a paper to stamp. So after a while the Marine in front of me reached this fat guy in his nice blue uniform. He looked up at him and said, "Where's your official declaration documentation"? The Marine told him,

---

359

"I have nothing to declare except for myself and the paper has been thrown away".

Mr. Blue uniform doesn't like that answer one little bit and proceeded to loudly berate my buddy in line because he doesn't have the proper documentation required by this department for entry back into the United States.

At this point in our lives we were not in a good mood at all. After spending a year in Vietnam getting shot at while flying around in aluminum death traps we are mighty grumpy. Does this guy think any of us going to take his crap because we don't have the proper official form? Together we loudly proceeded to explain to him, using words we thought he could understand, what all of us thought of him, his job and all of his little forms.

A semblance of order was restored when the head form filling-out supervisor observed the naked hostility of the sea of green uniforms surrounding him and his men. He quickly made a leadership decision. He grabbed a blank official form from a stack on fat boy's desk, wrote a name on it, checked the box that said nothing to declare and gave it an official stamp.

It was time to walk on because we were now cleared to cross the Rubicon.

That afternoon we left Hawaii for our final leap across the Pacific. I landed at my favorite airport, LAX without any further incidents. No, I didn't see Mr. Leonard and I had no plans to waste any of my precious time looking for him. I was tired of airports; I was tired of airport managers but most of all I was tired of sitting in cramped aircraft. Eastern Airlines found a nice seat for me, nonstop from LAX to Atlanta where I was transferred almost immediately to my

—

final flight into Tampa. The aircraft landed late in the evening and I was again greeted by nothing.

Welcome home from the war in Vietnam, O great aviation warrior.

Well, kind of a welcome home. In those days' no one in Tampa was rude to uniformed service men as opposed to the actions of the citizens in the City of San Francisco. There were a couple of military guys that got off at the same time that I did and no one noticed them either.

I was to find out later that not being noticed was the best we could ever hope for in 1971. All of us were to learn that not talking about where we had been and what we had done was going to be the best course of action in the United States at that time.

The first order of business when I got home was to change out of my uniform and into civilian camouflage as quickly as possible. A big floppy hat hid the lack of hair and my normal bad attitude hid everything else.

The next day I found out that some of my friends were having a birthday party that evening. I decided to show up and see what had been going on for the last year. I arrived, early as usual, and spent the first hour or so finding out who was still around and who had moved on. Lots of good gossip to catch up on, you know.

About 9:00 or so, a couple of the people walked up to me and started asking me about where I had been for the last year and what I had seen. When I reminded them that I had spent the last year in Vietnam flying around in helicopter gunships they wanted to hear all about it.

—

They turned the record player off and kind of gathered around while I got warmed up. Never one to pass up an opportunity to flap my lips, I proceeded to tell them about life and death in a Marine Light Helicopter Squadron 167 while it was in Vietnam.

My helicopter stories started out with standard resupply missions to mountain top firebases. I then progressed to tales of flying the Korean General around to go shopping at Da Nang and the kites flying over Da Nang. As the evening went on, the stories got a little more in depth about what life over there was really like.

Towards the end, I explained what it was like to reach deep inside a jagged wound with my dirty fingers in an attempt to stop a Marine from bleeding to death. Then I told them about the sight of gray brain matter and blood pulsing from a fresh bullet hole in someone's head. In a whisper I spoke to them about having a young Marine look up at you and die in your arms as you prayed your aircraft would make it to 1st Med before his life ended.

They learned from me about the smell of burning jet fuel from a wrecked helicopter. The sight of dead NVA lined up for a body count next to the LZ after a battle inside the wire of a mountain top firebase. I finished up with my recent adventure about flying in the light bird and reflected on the last seconds of life for the men and women we intercepted on the trails.

In an offhanded manner I kind of laughed and said that when they were hit with machine gun fire they became a running string of human firecrackers. I may have told them that a direct hit with one of our 2.75 rockets would turn them into dripping red plant food, but I can't remember.

—

Forgetful of my surroundings, I drifted into silence lost in my memories. When I looked up the entire room of 30 people was dead silent. There was this look on their faces like I had just arrived from Mars. No one said anything to me for the rest of the night and I left soon thereafter. It seems that I was a tad bit more graphic that evening than what they had been routinely exposed to on the sanitized nightly news.

I learned quite a bit that night about how the reality that I had observed conflicted with the reality everyone else believed they knew.

All of us had known that the war was lost soon after the first day of being in country. You could see it in the hopelessness of the enlisted men and you could read about it in the fake dispatches that were sent out by our military. On April 30, 1975 Saigon fell and now our generation was responsible for the first true military defeat in US history since the Civil War.

It took years but the truth finally set in. We were an embarrassment to the citizens of this nation that had sent us to fight in what would be the first of many political wars. This national disgust extended even into the halls of some of the major veterans' organizations.

During the 1970's a Vietnam Veteran who went to join one of the major veterans' organization was often met with open hostility from the entrenched WWII and Korean War members. Men who served in Vietnam were told that while they met the posted requirements for membership, they were not welcome and should find another place to hang out. Look around today and see which veterans' organizations are dying for lack of new blood and you will know which ones didn't want us back then.

—

I saw a bumper sticker one day and realized that these guys got it right. It kind of summed up the post-Vietnam experience for most of us in one sentence.

"Never Again Will One Generation of Veterans Abandon Another"

Today the return of America's veterans from our current wars is celebrated with hometown parades, family parties and thirty second news clips showing everyone's joy at these great reunions.

Good for them, they deserve every bit of it.

It's strange but even today; these public displays of pride with flags waving, people cheering and cameras recording is as distant and foreign an experience to me as that nation of Vietnam was to a lost 20-year-old kid back in 1970.

Today's homecoming celebrations make most Vietnam Veterans feel like stepchildren who were sent away to boarding school for a year only to find that their parents had moved away without telling them during their absence.

—

To this day an entire generation of Vietnam Veterans are still treated like homeless outsiders looking through the glass of a locked door at the next generation's Christmas morning. We can see the illuminated tree, hear the voices and almost touch the display of presents but all of us know there will never be anything inside of America's house for us.

Made in the USA
Middletown, DE
12 January 2017